Personal Construct Perspectives on Forensic Psychology

Personal Construct Perspectives on Forensic Psychology provides a new approach to the three main areas of application of forensic psychology: rehabilitation of offenders; work with the police; and research and consultation on legal issues and processes. It challenges the mainstream approach to viewing offenders, emphasizes responsibility for life choices, and eschews the biomedical view of people.

Experienced practising psychologists, who work with offenders in the community and institutions, share their perspectives and illustrate their discussion with case studies and personal research. Reviewing relevant literature in many substantive areas including violent, sexual, and mentally disordered offenders, working with police stress, and treating offenders in prison, these outstanding authors deliver a strong argument from a personal construct perspective.

In an area of increasing interest, *Personal Construct Perspectives on Forensic Psychology* provides a solid background for further growth. Forensic practitioners, theorists and researchers, social workers, nurses and probation officers – all those who work with criminal offenders or the criminal justice system will benefit from this book's many insights and clinical tips.

Personal Construct Perspectives on Forensic Psychology

Edited by James Horley

Brunner-Routledge
Taylor & Francis Group

HOVE AND NEW YORK

First published 2003 by Brunner-Routledge
27 Church Road, Hove, East Sussex, BN3 2FA

Simultaneously published in the USA and Canada
by Brunner-Routledge
29 West 35th Street, New York, NY 10001

Brunner-Routledge is an imprint of the Taylor & Francis Group

© 2003 selection and editorial matter, James Horley; individual chapters,
the contributors

Typeset in Times by Mayhew Typesetting, Rhayader, Powys
Printed and bound in Great Britain by TJ International, Padstow, Cornwall
Paperback cover design by Louise Page

British Library Cataloguing in Publication Data
A catalogue record for this book is available from the British Library

Library of Congress Cataloging-in-Publication Data
Personal construct perspectives on forensic psychology / edited by James
Horley.
    p. cm.
    ISBN 1-58391-224-X (pbk.: alk. paper) – ISBN 1-58391-223-1 (hbk.:
alk. paper)
1. Psychology, Forensic. 2. Personal construct theory. I. Horley,
James, 1954–

RA1148 .P466 2003
614'.1–dc21

                                                    2002153103

ISBN 1-58391-223-1 (hbk)
ISBN 1-58391-224-X (pbk)

Contents

List of contributors

Jack Adams-Webber is Professor of Psychology at Brock University in St. Catherines, Ontario. With over 30 years of contributions to personal construct theory, he is the author of numerous articles and books, including *Personal construct theory: Concepts and applications* (1979, New York: Wiley).

Jody Bennett is a graduate in psychology of Augustana University College in Camrose, Alberta. Her research interests include domestic violence and forensic assessment. She provides counselling services in a women's shelter, and she does volunteer work with offenders through a local probation office.

Anthony Eccles completed a doctorate at Queen's University in Kingston, Ontario. He runs a community-based clinic for sexual offenders that provides services to probation and parole, the courts, and child welfare agencies. In addition, he is the Director of the Frontenac Institution Sexual Offender Programme. His research interests include denial and minimization among sexual offenders and phallometric assessment methodology.

James Horley, who holds a Ph.D. from Queen's University in Kingston, Ontario, is the author of numerous journal and book articles, many concerned with the assessment and treatment of sexual offenders. He is Associate Professor of Psychology at Augustana University College in Camrose, Alberta. Prior to his present position, he worked in a variety of forensic settings, including maximum-secure prisons and a forensic hospital. He continues to provide psychological services to offenders in a community-based setting.

Julia C. Houston is a Consultant Clinical and Forensic Psychologist with the Forensic Mental Health Services, Shaftesbury Clinic, Springfield Hospital, Tooting, London. She has extensive experience in the clinical assessment and treatment of offenders, particularly those described as 'mentally disordered'. She is the author of the 1998 book, *Making sense with offenders: Personal constructs, therapy, and change* (New York: Wiley).

William Walker has a Ph.D. from Queen's University in Kingston, Ontario. He has experience in both community and institutional corrections. Currently he is Director of the Sexual Offender Programme for Pittsburgh Institution, a federal correctional institution in south-eastern Ontario. His research interests include the treatment of persistent denial among sexual offenders and patterns in sexual aggression.

David A. Winter is Professor of Clinical Psychology and Director of the Doctorate in Clinical Psychology at the University of Hertfordshire. He is also Head of Clinical Psychology Services and Coordinator of Research for the Barnet Sector of Barnet, Enfield, and Haringey Mental Health Trust in the National Health Service. He is the author of *Personal construct psychology in clinical practice: Theory, research, and applications* (1992, London: Routledge), and of some 80 further publications, primarily on the clinical applications of personal construct theory and on psychotherapy research. He is a Fellow of the British Psychology Society and has served as Chair of the Society's Psychotherapy Section as well as in various positions within the UK Council for Psychotherapy.

Preface: Constructive alternativism and personal responsibility

Jack Adams-Webber

George Kelly (1955) developed a constructivist model of 'person-as-scientist' within the framework of which a host of psychological issues have been reformulated. Although it evolved originally in the idiographic context of his own clinical experience, and is classified widely as a personality theory (e.g., Pervin & John, 2001), this model has provided the theoretical ground for novel hypotheses in many areas of inquiry, including cognition, psycholinguistics, life-span development, psychopathology and education, among others. Its extraordinary deployability and scope is evidenced further by an expanding range of applications in such disparate fields as artificial intelligence, cultural anthropology, psychiatry, experimental aesthetics, nursing, management, marketing, analysis of political debates, and literary criticism, to cite a few examples. As James Horley points out in his introductory chapter, the various contributors to this particular volume review a rapidly growing body of research that has extended the range of convenience of Kelly's model into the relatively new area of forensic psychology.

Kelly (1955) based the central assumptions of his model on a single epistemological premise, his principle of "constructive alternativism". It asserts that 'reality' does not reveal itself to us directly, but rather it is subject to as many alternative ways of interpreting it as we ourselves can invent. Hence, we have the rich diversity of human experience. Moreover, according to Kelly (1955), our current representations of events are anticipatory in function. In order to predict our future experience, each of us develops a "personal construct system" and attempts to accommodate it to the unknown structure of reality. This system affords the underlying ground of coherence and unity in the ongoing experience of each individual.

Although any particular sequence of events lends itself to a variety of different interpretations, some ways of construing it probably will prove more useful in the future for anticipating similar events. As events do not directly reveal their meanings to us, it must be the anticipatory constructions ('hypotheses') which we impose on them that endow them with whatever significance they may have in relation to our own behaviour. Thus, Kelly's constructive alternativism carries definite implications in terms of how human behaviour relates to both internal and external 'stimulus' input. He explicitly argues that "one does not learn certain things from the nature of stimuli which play upon him, but only what his (or her) cognitive framework permits him (or her) to see in the stimuli" (Kelly, 1955, p. 75). In short, people have the capacity to represent events, not merely respond to them. It follows that each individual is personally responsible for choosing what specific constructions of events will inform his or her actions.

In formulating this model, Kelly (1955) eschewed any distinction between 'behavioural scientists' and the 'subjects' of their inquiries. He claimed that all persons, in their "scientist-like-aspects", seek to understand their experience and anticipate future events. In short, Kelly applied his constructivist model of scientific activity to the explanation of all human behaviour. Each individual not only constructs his or her own hypotheses for anticipating events, but also evaluates and possibly revises them in the light of the results of behavioural experiments based on these hypotheses. Thus, as Horley (see Chapter 1) notes, "Kelly viewed all behaviour as experimental".

Kelly (1970, p. 12) posited also that each individual's personal construct system is organized hierarchically "by arranging implicative relationships, as in Boolean algebra, so that he [or she] can infer that one construction follows from another" (cf. Ford & Adams-Webber, 1994). Thus, whenever we confront a choice about what course of action to undertake in a particular situation, the potential outcomes of each alternative will be anticipated in terms of relations of implication among our personal constructs. Kelly's *choice corollary* (1970, p. 15) asserts specifically that "a person chooses for himself [or herself] that alternative in a dichotomized construct through which he [or she] anticipates the greater possibility for the elaboration of his [or her] system". This proposition clearly implies that in every case the alternative construction of self which seems to provide the better opportunity to enhance one's overall capacity to anticipate the future will be selected, even when that alternative may have been associated with negative consequences in the past.

At times, one's construction of self will be selected in such a way as to pull one's construct system together into a more coherent pattern (a "definitive choice"). That is, a particular construction of self may represent an attempt to further consolidate the current structure of one's system by minimizing inconsistencies in terms of implicative relationships between constructs. At other times, one may choose that alternative construction of self which seems to afford more scope for extending the range of convenience of one's construct system into new areas of potential experience (an "extensive choice"). Whatever the direction of choice, the perceived outcomes will be evaluated in terms of our network of hierarchically organized constructs (Winter, 1992).

Consider the following relatively simple hypothetical example of an "elaborative choice" as defined by Kelly (1955). Suppose that in Sally's construct system the dichotomous distinction 'polite–rude' entails the distinction 'kind–mean'. She may typically behave in a manner which she regards as 'polite' because this seems consistent with her hypothesis that she is a 'kind' person, thereby supporting the current logical structure of her system. On the other hand, it might occur to her that it could be 'kinder' in the long run to be 'rude' when an acquaintance whom she finds especially boring continues to phone her daily. Therefore, she may be prepared to entertain the hypothesis that under some circumstances it could make sense to be 'rude' in order to be 'kind', thereby extending the potential range of convenience of her construct system in order to accommodate a novel experiment. On the other hand, it would make no sense in terms of the current structure of her system to be 'mean' to someone in order to be 'polite'.

From a Kellian perspective, an individual could enact the role of a 'criminal', because it seems more personally meaningful in terms of its predictive implications within the context of his or her own construct system than does any perceived alternative. For instance, an adult male who construes himself as attracted sexually to adolescent boys may find that he is able to effectively predict how others will respond to his sexual activities only when he plays the role of 'pervert'. Thus, he may experience relatively less anxiety when 'molesting' adolescent boys than if he were to attempt to initiate sexual encounters with consenting adults. The world of adult sexuality, as he construes it, may contain many unknown hazards and the prospect of a vastly reduced capacity to anticipate the outcomes of his behavioural experiments.

Furthermore, he may have developed a specific subsystem of constructs ('schema') with his sexual experience as its focus of convenience. Whenever he enacts the 'deviant' sexual role that he has elaborated for himself within the context of this 'specialized' subsystem, he does not experience much anxiety because he usually 'knows' what to expect, including some potential outcomes that he evaluates negatively and would prefer to avoid. If the range of convenience of this 'problematic' subsystem is limited to the sphere of sexual activity with adolescent boys, it also could remain functionally isolated ('dissociated') from the rest of his personal construct system. Consequently, when he enacts the role of 'pervert', his actions have relatively few implications throughout his construct system as an operational whole. Possibly, the only source of significant psychological conflict in his life may be his difficulty in integrating his sexual experience with the rest of his self-concept. On the other hand, as he has little or no sexual experience with adults, he has no basis for predicting how they might respond to expressions of sexual interest on his part.

Skene (1973) reports a case history (recently summarized by Adams-Webber, 2001) involving a 19-year-old man who had been remanded in custody for treatment at a psychiatric hospital following his second appearance in court charged with sexual acts with adolescent boys. A sample of his personal constructs was elicited during a clinical interview, after which he completed a repertory grid (Kelly, 1955; Adams-Webber, 1996) in which he successively rank-ordered photographs of 8 adult strangers (4 women and 4 men) on these constructs. The results were interpreted by Skene as follows:

> He had some confusion in his sexual roles. He did not differentiate homosexual from heterosexual feelings and he identified with neither. Homosexuality did not therefore exclude being attracted to the opposite sex. Nonetheless, he saw some differences in the two sexual roles; homosexuality implied being quite manly and happy-go-lucky, but getting one into trouble.
>
> (Skene, 1973, p. 291)

This client participated in a "fixed-role" experiment (Kelly, 1955; Adams-Webber, 2001) in which he played the part of a hypothetical "John Jones", depicted in a brief role sketch prepared by Skene as a "jolly, very happy-go-lucky chap", who is both talkative and a good listener, unusually casual in conversation, and always agrees openly with others. He is interested in current affairs, and is a good sportsman who organizes games with other patients, and enjoys dancing. It is important to note that in designing this fixed role prescription, Skene made no attempt to focus on the client's 'criminal' behaviour.

The client enacted the part of "John Jones" for 6 weeks during which he met with Skene 12 times. He also kept a diary in which he recorded his daily experiences. According to Skene (1973), the client encountered few problems with the role. He participated actively in the functions of the hospital social centre, as well as those of several sports clubs. He also learned to dance. Moreover, he started to "go steady" with a woman of about his own age, and he claimed that he had "demonstrated his affection for her".

At the end of 6 weeks, the client was advised that he could discontinue his enactment of the part of "John Jones", and he was encouraged to adopt any role that he found comfortable. Skene reports that the client "continued as happy-go-lucky, interested in sports and entertaining, but apart from this, abandoned the John Jones character". Following further psychological testing, he was discharged from the hospital. Skene interprets his second set of test results as indicating that there "was still the association between heterosexuality and homosexuality . . . but the patient wished, and was able to relate better to the opposite sex" (1973, p. 291).

A follow-up evaluation after 5 months revealed that the client had found a job, had a circle of male friends of his own age, and had joined a sports club. His girlfriend (it turned out that she was married but separated) had become reconciled with her husband and had stopped dating the client. Nonetheless, he was "contemplating courting another girl". His final test results, according to Skene, indicated that "he currently construed himself as like people who were attracted to the opposite sex in the usual way". At the time of this final assessment, there had been no further reports of sexual activities with adolescent boys. Skene concluded that there had been a general increase in social competence and a decrease in anxiety about his sexuality.

This case history illustrates several important theoretical implications of Kelly's model. First, 'treatment' is viewed as essentially an experimental project in which the clients serve as the 'principal investigators' and their own behaviour serves as the 'independent variable'. Each individual client, with the help of the therapist, designs specific experiments, carries them out independently and then evaluates their outcomes. Thus, the therapist functions more or less as a 'research supervisor' (cf. Bannister & Fransella, 1971). At the end of the project, the client is encouraged to take full responsibility for appraising the results in whatever way makes the most sense to him.

Second, the primary objective of 'treatment' is to afford ample opportunity for clients to improve their accuracy in anticipating the responses of others to their behavioural experiments. They should be invited to assume the stance of a 'personal scientist' with the capacity to represent and predict events, not merely respond to them. The role of the 'therapist' is to provide methodological assistance in designing specific experiments in order to test the clients' own hypotheses about what kind of persons they are, and revising these hypotheses in the light of new evidence. In short, the function of the so-called 'therapist' is helping their clients to experiment thoughtfully with their own behaviour on the basis of their personal constructions of events, not to represent 'reality' to them. All clients are seen as 'personal scientists' engaged in open-ended programmes of inquiry in which they continue to pose new questions through their behaviour and evaluate the implications of the results in the contexts of their own personal construct systems.

Third, it is crucial to encourage clients to entertain alternative hypothetical constructions of themselves and test them in their own experiments. This requires that therapists develop a working understanding of the idiosyncratic meanings of those personal constructs upon which clients probably will rely in interpreting the results of their experiments. For example, if an individual currently construes herself as 'aggressive', the only alternative from her own perspective might be 'passive', which in her construct system implies being both 'weak' and 'vulnerable'. A therapist might suggest that she try out a new distinction in evaluating her behaviour which may not have occurred to her before, for example, 'prudent' versus 'rash'. At first, she could find it difficult to fit this 'novel' construct into the current structure of her system with respect to its specific predictive implications; however, she can begin to elaborate its meaning by trying to anticipate what might happen if she were to be more 'prudent' in experimenting with her social environment. That is, by using this hypothetical construction of self to develop one or more new predictions and then testing them, she may be able to eventually integrate the new construct into her self-construct.

The key to this strategy lies in the fact that the new construction of herself is easily seen as only a hypothesis that may or may not prove useful in the future. Its utility can be evaluated in terms of the results of experiments in which the client's own behaviour is the only independent variable. She may discover that she can predict and control the consequences of her conduct significantly more accurately when she acts in a manner that she considers to be 'prudent'. She may continue to construe herself as 'aggressive', but now she discriminates behaviour that is 'aggressive' and 'prudent' and also 'effective' from that which is 'aggressive', but 'rash' and 'futile'.

The self-concept which this client has developed and elaborated over a period of many years is also only a set of interrelated hypotheses. On the other hand, her past experience represents the outcomes of repeatedly basing her behaviour on these specific hypotheses. Thus, she may not easily envision any substantial alternatives to remaining her current self. In short, clients may not readily grasp the implication of Kelly's constructive alternativism that all of their self-ascribed virtues and faults are only hypothetical interpretations of events that are subject to possible revision or even eventual replacement by more useful alternatives.

It follows that therapists should constantly emphasize that their clients' self-concepts are essentially hypothetical in nature and consistently encourage them to experiment as thoughtfully as possible and carefully observe what happens when they behave in certain ways. Therapists should also admit candidly that they do not know what sort of persons their clients should become eventually. This is something that will gradually unfold as they continue to undertake new experiments. Thus, therapists always should insist that their clients assume personal responsibility for deciding what hypothetical constructions of themselves to test further.

In conclusion, Kelly's fundamental epistemological premise that all events lend themselves to interpretation in terms of a variety of different constructs implies that there is an opportunity for each individual to develop his or her own unique system of personal constructs for representing his or her current experience and anticipating the future. It does not follow, however, that all constructs are equally useful for interpreting a given event. It is likely that some constructs will prove more useful than others for predicting similar events in the future.

Individuals typically derive hypotheses about themselves on the basis of the hierarchically organized relations of implication among their constructs. They can test those hypotheses experimentally by using them to structure their own behaviour and evaluating the results. Our self-concepts are constituted and regulated entirely by such hypotheses. According to Kelly, we all are 'personal scientists' engaged in open-ended programmes of experimentation in which our own behaviour is the only independent variable. Our hypothetical self-concepts can be continually re-evaluated and revised in the light of the results of our behavioural experiments.

In the framework of Kelly's model, 'offenders' are not a distinct class of persons, nor is 'criminal' behaviour different in principle from other forms of experimentation (cf. Houston, 1998). It follows that the 'treatment of offenders' does not require our resorting to any specialized procedures, but rather, it also can be viewed as an investigative project designed to elucidate problems in the clients' lives as they personally experience them. These clients also should be encouraged to assume the role of 'principal investigator'. That is, they should assume personal responsibility for deciding what hypotheses about themselves to test and what experiments to conduct, and eventually for evaluating the outcomes in terms of whatever constructs seem most useful to them for anticipating the future.

References

Adams-Webber, J. (1996). Repertory grid technique. In R. Corsini & A. J. Auerbach (Eds.), *Encyclopedia of psychology* (pp. 782–783). New York: John Wiley & Sons.

Adams-Webber, J. (2001). Fixed role therapy. In R. Corsini (Ed.), *Handbook of innovative therapy* (pp. 255–262). New York: John Wiley & Sons.

Bannister, D., & Fransella, F. (1971). *Inquiring man*. Baltimore: Penguin.

Ford, K. M., & Adams-Webber, J. (1994). Knowledge acquisition and constructivist epistemology. In R. R. Hoffman (Ed.), *The psychology of expertise* (pp. 121–136). Mahwah, NJ: Lawrence Erlbaum Associates Inc.

Houston, J. (1998). *Making sense with offenders*. New York: Wiley.

Kelly, G. A. (1955). *The psychology of personal constructs*. New York: Norton.

Kelly, G. A. (1970). A brief introduction to personal construct theory. In D. Bannister (Ed.), *Perspectives in personal construct theory* (pp. 1–29). London: Academic Press.

Pervin, L. A., & John, O. P. (2001). *Personality: Theory and research*. New York: John Wiley & Sons.

Skene, R. A. (1973). Construct shift in the treatment of a case of homosexuality. *British Journal of Medical Psychology*, *46*, 287–292.

Winter, D. A. (1992). *Personal construct psychology in clinical practice*. London: Routledge.

Chapter 1

Forensic psychology and personal construct theory

James Horley

The past two or three decades have witnessed a surge in exploration of the relevance of psychological theory and research to
matters pertaining to various justice systems, especially criminal
justice. Much of this effort has been confined to the assessment and
treatment of criminal offenders, but there has been recent interest
in such issues as the psychological profiling of criminals and juror
selection. These topics, and many more, form the basis of what has
come to be known as forensic psychology (see Brigham, 1999).

In the English language, the term 'forensis', or forensic, originally described public debate or discussion, derived from its Greek
root 'pertaining to the forum' where debate was conducted in
ancient Greece and Rome. Over the past 200 years, however, it
came to refer more narrowly to debate or dispute in courts of law.
Forensic psychology, now the subdiscipline of psychology concerned with applications of psychological principles and research to
the law and offenders, can be traced to at least the late nineteenth
century (Bartol & Bartol, 1999) when psychologists began to apply
their findings to legal, usually criminal, cases. One of the earliest
books in this field was written by Munsterberg (1908) of Harvard
University. Munsterberg presented a number of areas of potential
psychological relevance to the public. He argued, for example, that
eyewitness testimony is often unreliable, a point well taken in light
of much recent research. While Munsterberg's project saw little
success during his lifetime, in part because of opposition from
lawyers and other legal professionals (see Wigmore, 1909), he at
least planted a seed that would bear fruit in years to come. This
was especially true at Harvard, which became a centre for legal and
criminal psychology. A number of Munsterberg's students – such
as Marston, who not only invented the character 'Wonder Woman'

but developed a 'lie detector test' (Marston, 1917, 1921) – emerged as pioneers and leaders in what was to become forensic psychology.

Work applying psychological findings and ideas to legal and criminal fields flourished from the 1930s to the present. Contemporary forensic psychology has branched into three main areas: rehabilitation of offenders, consultation of various forms with the police, and research and consultation on legal issues and processes (Hess, 1999). The rehabilitation of offenders, including both psychological assessment and psychotherapeutic services, has grown dramatically over the past half century, especially in Western Europe and Canada. Work with the police, dating back to the 1910s (Terman, 1917), has included assisting law enforcement with the consequences of dealing with offenders (e.g., coping with stress), police selection, line-up procedures, and more recently with the psychological profiling of offenders. The psychological research applied to the law, both criminal and civil, has addressed such issues as jury selection and eyewitness reliability and testimony.

If we examine the most significant area, at least in terms of the most extensive literature, of forensic psychology, the assessment and treatment of offenders, we find a rather curious situation. Much of the clinical work with offenders to date has been informed, either explicitly or implicitly, by biomedical perspectives. Included here would be personality type-trait approaches (e.g., Eysenck, 1977; McCreary, 1975) that emphasize biological, inborn, and enduring characteristics that lead to criminal behaviour. The dominance of biomedical models is curious for a number of reasons. First, it leads to the paradoxical and disturbing situation of finding individuals criminally responsible for their actions, yet their actions are not really under their control (i.e., due to, say, their inherent neuroticism). To be fair, however, the same criticism can be made of learning theories, at least insofar as they remove personal responsibility from the individual and shift it to the social and/or physical environments. Second, perhaps a more serious concern from a rehabilitative perspective, is the lack of hope for change that results from a 'diagnosis' of pedophilia or antisocial personality disorder, although there is possibly the faint hope of the 'pill' to cure the presumed disease entity. Another concern about the dominance of biomedical models is 'symptom management'. Rather than address underlying reasons for offensive acts, we are often content, perhaps because of the ease and power of modern psychiatric medication, to contain the aggressive or abusive expressions of offenders. Finally, the dominance of the biomedical models has meant that alternative perspectives have not been considered seriously. Even when other approaches are presented, they are often compromised by attempts to reconcile with the biomedical perspectives and, thus, they fail to outline and to document the actual and potential richness of alternative perspectives. Obviously biomedical considerations, such as neurological injury/disease and biochemical imbalances, should be examined in specific cases of offensive behaviour, but different theories provide important clinical perspectives in the assessment and treatment of the majority of offenders.

What account or explanation of offending behaviour are we to employ should we reject the biomedical model and analytic units such as types and traits? This we may well do on their own 'scientific' grounds (e.g., the data of offensive behaviour do not fit the theories because we have no disease entities underlying many or most psychiatric disorders relevant to offending). Learning or strict behavioural theories, while undoubtedly accounting for some mechanisms that underlie some offending behaviour (e.g., Laws & Marshall, 1990), appear limited in terms of their abilities to describe and to explain a variety of offensive acts. Many forensic clinicians have championed a cognitive-behavioural alternative (e.g., Marshall, 1999; Marshall & Barbaree, 1990), in large part due to their established efficacy in the treatment of offenders (for a review, see Andrews & Bonta, 1998). The problem with such a generic term, however, is that it can run the gamut of rationalistic theories (e.g., Ellis, 1962) to constructivistic (e.g., Kelly, 1955), and it can even include some social learning theories (e.g., Bandura, 1986).

Even constructivism or constructionism is a broad camp, and detailed discussions of etymology or epistemology are beyond the scope of this book (but see Stam, 1990; Warren, 1998). What all constructivistic theories emphasize is personal meaning, language, and experience. The world view, or life philosophy, of the individual is not just relevant but central to constructivism – how the client construes his or her own world must be understood before a means of successful intervention, in the form of altering the client's perspective, is achievable. The constructivistic theory that has been used and promoted by a number of forensic clinicians (e.g., Horley, 2000; Houston, 1998; Needs, 1988) is personal construct theory (PCT). Since its development by Kelly (1955), PCT has offered a unified psychological theory, personality assessment techniques, and clinical interventions to psychologists in various areas of practice (see Neimeyer, 1985, for the development of PCT). The relatively voluminous literature generated by PCT attests to the fecundity of the theory (for literature reviews, see Adams-Webber, 1979; Bonarius, 1965; Fransella & Bannister, 1977; Winter, 1992). Some of us believe that it is time to extend PCT, in a systematic and formal fashion, into forensic psychology.

Experience, labelling, and offending

In general terms, how might a PCT-based account of offending appear? Needs (1988) has noted that while Kelly (1955) had nothing to say directly about offending and forensic issues, his theory can be applied to the field both broadly and narrowly.

One obvious limitation, already implied above, of the biomedical models to understanding criminal behaviour is exclusion of human agency. Agency, autonomy, and choice appear crucial to an adequate explanation of individual social behaviour to many observers (e.g., Weeks, 1995). Individual humans tend to be viewed medically as dependent upon or determined by biology, either genetic/neurological anomalies or biochemical/endocrinological imbalances. Freedom to choose a course of action, based on personal experience, even if the act might be interpreted by the vast majority of observers as 'negative' or 'undesirable', is not possible or at least not a significant consideration according to biomedical or learning perspectives on offenders. PCT, on the other hand, emphasizes experience and choice. According to Kelly (1955), a person chooses for him or herself that alternative in a dichotomized construct through which he or she anticipates the greater possibility for extension and/or definition of his/her construct system. What Kelly is concerned with here, and more generally with his theory, are the psychological reasons for particular acts. Call it motivation if you will, although Kelly chose not to use such a term. The importance of asking and examining responses to motivational questions, especially for offenders (e.g., Scully & Marolla, 1984; Taylor, 1972), has been accepted by many investigators in various disciplines but examined by relatively few.

"Extending a construct system" is one main reason for selecting one act or behaviour, and Kelly (1970) viewed all behaviour as experimental, or a tentative trial to observe whether an outcome was acceptable or not. Having sex with a young boy or killing a rival gang member could allow an individual, as normatively unappealing or repulsive as it may seem, to experience power or status through self-understanding as 'attractive' or 'tough'. The extension to an individual's construct system – really, one's self-concept – does not require any degree of social acceptability, although social demands undoubtedly shape an individual's likely construal of an act before, during, and after the experience. Definition, for Kelly and PCT, refers to more explicit and clear self-definition. The act of murder or rape could lead to a more refined sense of self. Whether the self-referent includes a 'negative' label such as 'killer', 'pervert', or 'loser', or whether it would lead to a 'positive' label such as 'predator', 'strong man', or 'someone no one messes with' probably is a function of the actor's thinking at the time and the immediate social feedback that they receive.

One problem issue that arises concerns the question of limits on freedom, many placed by lack of awareness and 'conditioning'. Certainly when Kelly uses the term 'choice' he is not suggesting that all individuals have access to all pertinent information before choosing a course of action. We are well aware of limitations on cognitive processing and stated versus 'real' reasons for behaviour (see Nisbett & Wilson, 1977). We simply cannot know everything about ourselves and the world around us to state categorically and correctly why we choose one act over another. Also, once chosen, we must accept the consequences of an act which clearly limit freedom. An individual does appear free, for whatever conscious or less than conscious reasons, to enact and to reenact a wide variety of behaviours, offensive ones included. Why would an individual choose the actions of a 'pervert' or 'killer', or why would a person act in a manner that appeared to be both self-injurious and injurious to others? The answer may be ultimately an individual one – it depends on his/her own experience and past efforts to construe personal experience – but it can also be a simple, shared one – it depends on perceived construct extension and definition. Pain, whether through physical injury, humiliation, or negative descriptors, can be self-confirming and hence very positive. Being physically injured and/or humiliated during what one construes as a sexual act can confirm one's identity as a sexual masochist. The pain, in effect, is pleasure for that individual. In the same way, a painful or negative label like 'heartless killer' or 'rape hound' can, when reinforced by the experience of homicide or sexual assault, or even being told that one is such a creature, provide a reassurance of identity.

Kelly (1955) and other PCT theorists say little about the origins of constructs, especially as applied to oneself. The origins of self-referents, negative and otherwise, undoubtedly lie in personal experience – whether a childhood desire to hurt a parent through shame, or possibly a desire to please friends in a particular deviant peer group who provided a nonnormative definition of the term – and the origins might well be lost to everyone forever. It is also probable that the social environment (e.g., family, peer groups) is responsible for the initial application of these descriptions (see Mead, 1934/1977). Often, offenders can remember, perhaps because of the emotional impact, an incident in which a parent or school-mate called them 'Sicko' or 'Bastard'. The acceptance of such labels may be instantaneous or very gradual, but their impact may be profound. Even well-intentioned formal or professional labels, such as 'paranoid schizophrenic', 'psychopath', or 'homo-sexual paedophile', also lead to negative behaviour. Many offenders accept personal labels quite freely in an attempt to interpret their own bewildering and harmful acts. Many of these self-referents, however tentative in application, only appear to exacerbate the situation, making reoffence more likely. While it appears important for individuals to assume responsibility for their own behaviour in spite of personal trauma and experience, it is equally important that they are not forced to shoulder the demands of others' constructions of them. What is needed is support, guidance, and some insights into existing constructs, and possible alternatives, that would allow these individuals to recreate them-selves. If we grant ourselves creative and recreative powers, why not grant the same abilities to criminal and civil offenders?

Deviant values, fantasy, and personal constructs

Kelly (1955) emphasized that everyone has a unique set of personal constructs but, in his commonality corollary, that people some-times adopt very similar constructs. People who exhibit similar significant behaviours in the same situations are expected to possess similar constructs, and sexual behaviour is likely significant enough to produce some shared or similar constructs among people. Those who interact sexually with children would probably be expected to employ different constructs from those who interact with adults. At the very least they would employ similarly-labelled constructs in very different ways. As well, given heterogeneity among various offenders (see Quinsey, 1977; Knight, 1989; Knight, Carter, & Prentky, 1989), systematic differences in construct systems among various categories of offender are likely. Concerning a gross factor like victim gender, for example, heterosexual child molesters might think more in terms of 'dominant–submissive' than homosexual offenders (Howells, 1979; Horley, 1988). More refined offender typologies are being developed, but construal tends to be deemphasized if considered at all in these approaches. Knight et al. (1989), for example, have focused on offence details or offender behaviour prior to a sexual offence, although they mentioned that fantasies play some role in the identification of half of their six types on their 'amount of contact' axis (i.e., single versus repeated). Holmes and DeBurger (1987), at least, try to distinguish among different types of serial killers by examining gross intents or themes in their homicidal acts. This point raises the issue of how various constructs used by therapists and researchers who traditionally work with offenders, whether from a biomedical or other perspective (e.g., social learning theory), would fit within PCT. These constructs include values and fantasy.

Like learning theorists, Kelly (1955) would accept that behaviour is an important consideration; unlike most learning theorists, even social learning theorists, PCT would emphasize construal processes. Emphasis on behaviour can lead to a difficult position in some learning formulations (e.g., Abel, Becker, Cunningham-Rathner, Rouleau, Kaplan & Reich, 1984). If distorted cognitions function largely to rationalize and to justify deviant behaviour, why should cognitions become a focus of therapy with offenders? The only justification for this position, and I think a correct one, is that thought generally precedes behaviour and, hence, plays an important role in behavioural production and regulation (Laws & Marshall, 1990). As Marshall (1999) noted recently, "we consider what [sexual] offenders think has more to do with offending than does genital arousal" (p. 657). Laws (1989) stressed this position in his relapse prevention model of sexual offending. As a statement of the concerns of this relapse model, Jenkins-Hall (1989) discussed the pivotal role that thought plays in the maintenance of deviant sexual behaviour, and she suggested a cognitive restructuring technique for changing deviant cognitions. It is worth noting that

Jenkins-Hall and other promoters of relapse prevention rely on the cognitive-behavioural work of Meichenbaum (1977), a clinician and theorist who drew much of his inspiration and theoretical framework from Kelly (1955).

With respect to the foregoing discussion of the relationship between cognition and behaviour, personal construct theory makes the explicit and fundamental assumption that cognitions, or personal constructs, form the hypotheses which guide behavioural experiments conducted by everyone in everyday settings. Kelly (1955, 1970) does not deny the reinforcement of behaviour – in fact, probably all successful behavioural experiments are inherently reinforcing – but he is more concerned with a question such as "What validations of predictions does an individual reap?"

Values, attitudes, and beliefs have been described by some theorists and clinicians (e.g., Abel et al., 1984; Andrews & Bonta, 1998; Salter, 1988) as key to understanding offenders. Kelly (1955) did use these terms in the formulation of PCT – at one point describing values as comprehensive, superordinate constructs – but the exact role of these terms in the theory is far from clear. I have argued (Horley, 1991) that values and attitudes can be seen as core constructs, or those personal constructs that provide a sense of identity by capturing in a few distinct terms what an individual accepts as true of him/her. Beliefs, on the other hand, can be seen as peripheral constructs, or constructs concerned with matters of mundane existence that do not involve the self. This position implies that the rep grid is a legitimate technique in the assessment of values, attitudes, and beliefs. A second implication is that traditional value, attitude, and belief assessment techniques can be used profitably and without compromise by construct researchers. It also opens other issues and areas, such as consideration of lifestyle factors (see Horley, 1992; Horley, Carroll, & Little, 1988), for examination by psychologists, forensic and otherwise.

In light of my formulation, the seven types of distorted beliefs about sex with children presented by Abel et al. (1984) can be seen as personal constructs, or based on constructs (e.g., 'likes sex–doesn't like sex'), although whether we are concerned with ordinary beliefs or values and attitudes is debatable. Most likely, given the importance of sexual relations and functioning to most people in terms of self-definition, we are dealing with values and attitudes. The function of distorted beliefs, or 'bizarre constructs', can be seen in terms of guilt avoidance. Guilt is defined in PCT as displacement from core role, or those core constructs that give definition to social relations. Therefore, as one example, if a man has a core role construct of 'good father–bad father' and he has sex with his child, he can avoid guilt, or displacement from his core role, by interpreting the sexual activity as what a good father does insofar as good fathers provide sex education and form intimate relationships with their children. In addition, although the 'good father' in this example might not turn to his neighbour for validation of his view of family relations, each pleasurable sexual encounter with his child is likely to provide validation for his view, thereby entrenching it more deeply.

Not only can Abel et al.'s cognitive distortions be interpreted in terms of values and beliefs, but they can also be construed in terms of attributions that serve as explanations for behaviour. Attribution theories, such as those presented by Kelley (1973), appear unable to account for such explanations because of the particular set of conditions necessary before the theories are applicable. PCT, on the other hand, as a comprehensive theory or even metatheory, focuses on attributions in that characteristics ascribed to people or causal explanations of events are the result of the construal of elements. Kelly (1955, 1969), as a clinician, was concerned with personal but unique attributions, but a social psychology arising from PCT might look to attributional processes of groups of individuals as Harold Kelley (1973) did. Certainly the sociality corollary from personal construct theory is compatible with existing attribution theories – "theories" that should be seen as "principles" (Ross & Fletcher, 1985) – but the social psychological elaboration of personal construct theory has not proceeded this far yet, and it is beyond the scope of this chapter and book.

Fantasies and imaginary rehearsal appear to play a role in many offenders' acts. Sexual fantasy, even wild and whimsical fantasy, appears vital to understanding the offensive acts of sexual offenders. Fantasy is interpretable in light of PCT. Among other purposes, though perhaps first and foremost, fantasies serve as "experimental planning" or "try-outs" (MacCulloch, Snowden, Woods, & Mills, 1983), with the constructions of self and others forming the bases of the plan and directing the imaginary script. Constructs, the hypotheses behind everyday behavioural experiments, are safer when confined to the imagination so that variations of behaviour can be tried out with little fear of failure, let alone arrest (Kelly, 1955, 1970).

About this book

This book is not intended as the first word on the forensic relevance of PCT – as noted, a number of writers have provided articles and books for a number of years – but neither is it intended as the last word. There are a number of areas within forensic psychology, such as psychology and the law, where PCT or constructivism generally has not provided any significant contribution. It is also difficult to imagine how a psychological theory might impact or inform, say, jurisprudence, although with respect to courtroom procedure it is clear that the 'facts' of any criminal proceeding, for example, would be viewed by a Kellian as simply the evidence in support of a theory provided by the defence or the state. What this book is intended to provide is a summary, a state-of-the-art assessment, of work that supports, either directly or indirectly, our contention that PCT or at least constructivism supports a serious, beneficial option in forensic practice.

All of the chapters in this book are written by practising forensic psychologists. While all of the contributors are not strict PCT 'adherents', it would be fair to describe all contributors as inspired by constructivism. Each chapter in this book provides a review of the relevant literature in a variety of substantive areas while attempting to make an argument for a PCT or constructivistic explanation. Reviews are followed by or include some case studies, personal research, clinical tips, and insights for the forensic practitioner. While we are aware of and refer often to the clinical and various research literatures, a primary concern is to make the material presented accessible and usable for the average forensic psychologist. Indeed, other forensic professionals, such as psychiatrists and social workers, might find some helpful insights in our presentations.

The book begins with David Winter's examination of violent offenders, although leaving aside offenders with sexual motives for the moment. If all types of assaultive individuals are included here, violent offenders make up the majority of criminal offenders. Sexual offenders, considered by most as a special subtype of violent offender, are treated separately in my following chapter. These offenders are not the most numerous but are often the most challenging ones encountered by forensic psychologists, indeed by all forensic practitioners. Next, issues concerned with mentally disordered offenders, including so-called 'personality disordered' ones, are discussed by Julia Houston. Like sexual offenders, mentally disordered offenders typically present a real challenge to forensic workers. The following chapter by Winter considers some issues and problems while considering stress and police work. The last two chapters of the book examine the different settings of the community and the institution, in which forensic psychology is practiced. Community-based programmes have very particular circumstances and challenges to consider, just as institution-based programmes, including prisons and forensic hospitals, have unique concerns. Some of these issues will be addressed by Anthony Eccles and William Walker. Finally, Jody Bennett and I tackle the topic of providing psychotherapy to offenders in forensic institutions.

While the book was assembled with the interests of practitioners firmly in mind, it should also appeal to forensic theorists and researchers alike. The research generated by PCT and constructivism in the field of forensic psychology, limited at present, is growing. We hope to provide a background for further growth with this book. We hope, too, that all readers will approach this book with curiosity and openness, which were part of our efforts in writing it.

References

Abel, G. G., Becker, J. V., Cunningham-Rathner, J., Rouleau, J. L., Kaplan, M., & Reich, J. (1984). *The treatment of child molesters.* Atlanta: Behavioral Medicine Laboratory.

Adams-Webber, J. R. (1979). *Personal construct theory: Concepts and applications.* Chichester: John Wiley & Sons.

Andrews, D. A., & Bonta, J. (1998). *The psychology of criminal conduct.* Cincinnatti: Anderson.

Bandura, A. (1986). *Social foundations of thought and action: A social cognitive theory.* Englewood Cliffs, NJ: Prentice Hall.

Bartol, C. R., & Bartol, A. M. (1999). History of forensic psychology. In A. K. Hess & I. Weiner (Eds.), *The handbook of forensic psychology* (pp. 3–23). New York: John Wiley & Sons.

Brigham, J. C. (1999). What is forensic psychology anyway? *Law and Human Behavior, 23,* 273–298.

Bonarius, J. C. J. (1965). Research in the personal construct theory of George A. Kelly. In B. A. Maher (Ed.), *Progress in experimental personality research* (Vol. 2, pp. 1–46). New York: Academic Press.

Ellis, A. (1962). *Reason and emotion in psychotherapy.* New York: Lyle Stuart.

Eysenck, H. J. (1977). *Crime and personality* (2nd ed.). London: Routledge & Kegan Paul.

Fransella, F., & Bannister, D. (1977). *A manual for repertory grid technique*. London: Academic Press.

Hess, A. K. (1999). Defining forensic psychology. In A. K. Hess & I. Weiner (Eds.), *The handbook of forensic psychology* (pp. 24–47). New York: John Wiley & Sons.

Holmes, R. M., & DeBurger, J. (1987). *Serial murder*. Newbury Park, CA: Sage.

Horley, J. (1988). Cognitions of child sexual abusers. *Journal of Sex Research, 25*, 542–545.

Horley, J. (1991). Values and beliefs as personal constructs. *International Journal of Personal Construct Psychology, 4*, 1–14.

Horley, J. (1992). A longitudinal examination of lifestyles. *Social Indicators Research, 26*, 205–219.

Horley, J. (2000). Cognitions supportive of child molestation. *Aggression and Violent Behavior: A Review Journal, 5*, 551–564.

Horley, J., Carroll, B., & Little, B. R. (1988). A typology of lifestyles. *Social Indicators Research, 20*, 383–398.

Houston, J. (1998). *Making sense with offenders: Personal constructs, therapy and change*. Chichester: John Wiley & Sons.

Howells, K. (1979). Some meanings of children for pedophiles. In M. Cook & G. Wilson (Eds.), *Love and attraction* (pp. 519–526). Oxford: Pergamon.

Jenkins-Hall, K. D. (1989). The decision matrix. In D. R. Laws (Ed.), *Relapse prevention with sex offenders* (pp. 159–166). New York: Guilford Press.

Kelly, G. A. (1955). *The psychology of personal constructs* (2 vols.). New York: Norton.

Kelly, G. A. (1969). Ontological acceleration. In B. Maher (Ed.), *Clinical psychology and personality: The selected papers of George Kelly* (pp. 7–45). New York: John Wiley & Sons.

Kelly, G. A. (1970). Behavior is an experiment. In D. Bannister (Ed.) *Perspectives in personal construct theory* (pp. 255–269). London: Academic Press.

Kelley, H. H. (1973). The processes of causal attribution. *American Psychologist, 28*, 107–128.

Knight, R. A. (1989). An assessment of the concurrent validity of a child molester typology. *Journal of Interpersonal Violence, 4*, 131–150.

Knight, R. A., Carter, D. L., & Prentky, R. A. (1989). A system for the classification of child molesters: Reliability and application. *Journal of Interpersonal Violence, 4*, 3–24.

Laws, D. R. (Ed.) (1989). *Relapse prevention with sex offenders*. New York: Guilford Press.

Laws, D. R., & Marshall, W. L. (1990). A conditioning theory of the etiology and maintenance of deviant sexual preference and behavior. In W. L. Marshall, D. R. Laws, & H. E. Barbaree (Eds.), *Handbook of sexual assault* (pp. 209–230). New York: Plenum.

McCreary, C. P. (1975). Personality differences among child molesters. *Journal of Personality Assessment, 39,* 591–593.

MacCulloch, M. J., Snowden, P. R., Wood, P. J. W., & Mills, H. E. (1983). Sadistic fantasy, sadistic behavior, and offending. *British Journal of Psychiatry, 143,* 20–29.

Marshall, W. L. (1999). Diagnosing and treating sexual offenders. In A. K. Hess & I. B. Weiner (Eds.), *The handbook of forensic psychology* (pp. 640–760). New York: John Wiley & Sons.

Marshall, W. L., & Barbaree, H. E. (1990). An integrated theory of the etiology of sexual offending. In W. L. Marshall, D. R. Laws, & H. E. Barbaree (Eds.), *Handbook of sexual assault* (pp. 257–278). New York: Plenum.

Marston, W. H. (1917). Systolic blood pressure symptoms of deception. *Journal of Experimental Psychology, 2,* 117–163.

Marston, W. H. (1921). Psychological possibilities in the deception tests. *Journal of the American Institute of Criminal Law and Criminology, 11,* 551–570.

Mead, G. H. (1977). Self. In A. Strauss (Ed.), *George Herbert Mead: On social psychology* (pp. 199–246). Chicago: University of Chicago Press. (Original work published 1934)

Meichenbaum, D. M. (1977). *Cognitive-behavior modification: An integrative approach.* New York: Plenum.

Munsterberg, H. (1908). *On the witness stand: Essays on psychology and crime.* New York: Doubleday, Page & Company.

Needs, A. (1988). Psychological investigation of offending behavior. In F. Fransella & L. Thomas (Eds.), *Experimenting with personal construct psychology* (pp. 493–506). London: Routledge & Kegan Paul.

Neimeyer, R. A. (1985). *The development of personal construct psychology.* Lincoln, Nebraska: University of Nebraska Press.

Nisbett, R. E., & Wilson, T. D. (1977). Telling more than we can know: Verbal reports on mental processes. *Psychological Review, 84,* 231–259.

Quinsey, V. L. (1977). The assessment and treatment of child molesters: A review. *Canadian Psychological Review, 18,* 204–220.

Ross, M., & Fletcher, G. J. O. (1985). Attribution and social perception. In G. Linzey & E. Aronson (Eds.), *Handbook of social psychology* (Vol. 2, pp. 73–122). New York: Random House.

Salter, A. C. (1988). *Treating child sex offenders and victims: A practical guide.* Beverly Hills, CA: Sage.

Scully, D., & Marolla, J. (1984). Convicted rapists' vocabulary of motive: Excuses and justifications. *Social Problems, 31,* 530–544.

Stam, H. J. (1990). Rebuilding the ship at sea: The historical and theoretical problems of constructivist epistemologies in psychology. *Canadian Psychology*, *31*, 239–253.

Taylor, L. (1972). The significance and interpretation of replies to motivational questions: The case of the sex offender. *Sociology*, *6*, 24–39.

Terman, L. M. (1917). A trial of mental and pedagogical tests in a civil service examination for policemen and firemen. *Journal of Applied Psychology*, *1*, 17–29.

Warren, B. (1998). *Philosophical dimensions of personal construct psychology*. New York: Routledge.

Weeks, J. (1995). History, desires, and identities. In G. P. Parker & J. H. Gagnon (eds.), *Conceiving sexuality: Approaches to sex research in a postmodern world* (pp. 33–50). London: Routledge.

Wigmore, J. H. (1909). Professor Munsterberg and the psychology of testimony. *Illinois Law Review*, *3*, 399–445.

Winter, D. A. (1992). *Personal construct psychology in clinical practice: Theory, research and applications*. London: Routledge.

Chapter 2

A credulous approach to violence and homicide

David A. Winter

George Kelly (1955) urged the personal construct psychologist to take a "credulous approach" to his or her clients, attempting to see the world through the client's eyes and thereby, as Kelly described in his Sociality Corollary, being able to play a constructive role in relation to the client. In describing the credulous approach, he stated that "From a phenomenological point of view the client – like the proverbial customer – is always right. This is to say that his words and his symbolic behaviour possess an intrinsic truth which the clinician should not ignore" (Kelly, 1955, p. 322).

But what if one's client is a murderer or has committed some other violent offence? In such cases, even the most ardent personal construct psychologist may find his or her credulity strained to its limits. Even if he or she does manage to pass beyond any initial revulsion and begins to adopt a credulous attitude, an increasing degree of threat may be experienced as the initial fleeting glimpses of the world through the client's eyes develop into a clearer vision. As Kelly (1955, p. 505) described, from the perspective of Landfield's (1954) exemplification hypothesis of threat, "People are threatened by evildoers" because they may exemplify what we might all too readily become if only we dared or were less vigilant. Such threat may be alleviated by adopting an attitude towards the evildoer which is punitive rather than credulous. To quote Kelly again, the evildoer's

> behavior has been threatening to those whose own morality is insecure; and as long as he is seen as having exemplified the tempting way of life, there are those who will need to punish him as a prophylaxis for their own temptations.
>
> (Kelly, 1955, p. 507)

A strikingly similar view is taken by the infamous 'Moors Murderer', Ian Brady, who killed five children and young people in England in the 1960s. He has written that:

> law-abiding souls must have their victims, too, experiencing no guilt at how pleasurable it feels to punish others for crimes they themselves have contemplated or succeeded in getting away with. Further, in punishing others for these crimes, they actually feel they are making retribution of some sort for their own.
>
> (Brady, 2001, p. 48)

By contrast, attempting to understand the offender may be a less comfortable option in that it may require acknowledgement, by others if not by oneself, of one's own potential criminal tendencies: Brady (2001, p. 72), discussing forensic psychiatrists, states that "loudly proclaiming they have some special psychological insight into the 'criminal mind'" may be seen as "inadvertent admission that they themselves possess more criminal traits and characteristics than average". A focus on understanding rather than solely punishment of the offender is also one which is likely to elicit little public sympathy, the less so the more apparently heinous the crime: witness, for example, the reactions to people who, following the events of September 11th 2001, have attempted to see the world through the eyes of those responsible rather than to clamour for retributive bombing.

Despite these hazards, this chapter will attempt, following Kelly's Sociality Corollary, to 'construe the construction processes' of the violent offender. As well as reviewing research findings and presenting clinical material, it will draw upon the accounts of Ian Brady and others who have committed acts of extreme violence.

Pathways to violence

A personal construct theory perspective on violence will share Megargee's (1970, p. 146) view that this should not be viewed as "a unitary, homogeneous mode of behaviour" but rather that "efforts should be directed at differentiating meaningful subtypes or syndromes of violent individuals". We shall now explore whether Kelly's diagnostic constructs and other aspects of his theory may provide the basis for such a taxonomy of violence and of those who commit it. Several possible pathways to violence will be proposed, but these will not be regarded as mutually exclusive.

Violence as an outcome of tight construing

Some indication that tight, 'cognitively simple' construing may be associated with a greater likelihood of committing violent offences was provided by Chetwynd's (1977) study of prisoners, which found that, by contrast, the offences of cognitively complex prisoners were more likely to have been of a fraudulent nature. Topcu (1976) obtained similar findings in a psychiatric population, and I have provided some evidence that police officers who engage in violent acts or break the law are characterized by tight construing (Winter, 1993). In this study, officers with tighter, more logically consistent construct systems also tended to be more extrapunitive. Although there have also been case studies of violent offenders whose construct systems were very tight (e.g., Landfield, 1971), research evidence in this area is not entirely consistent. For example, neither Noble (1970), studying delinquents, nor Howells (1983), investigating one-off violent offenders, were able to demonstrate an association between tight construing and offences of violence.

If tight construing were related to a higher likelihood of violence towards others, why might this be? Some clues are provided by a number of studies, largely using measures of cognitive complexity, which indicate the interpersonal difficulties likely to be faced by the tight construer. Although again there are some inconsistencies, most of which have been reviewed in Winter (1992), the research findings suggest that people who are cognitively simple (and are therefore likely to be tight construers) may be deficient in their ability to anticipate the construing and behaviour of others; in their capacity to integrate conflicting information about others; and in their communicational ability. In addition, cognitive simplicity in the use of psychological constructs has been related to Machiavellianism (Delia & O'Keefe, 1976).

There is also research evidence that invalidation of construing might pose particular hazards for the person who has a very tight construct system since such a system, in which most constructs are strongly interrelated, is brittle and vulnerable to structural collapse (Lawlor & Cochran, 1981). Invalidation of predictions derived from any construct is thus likely to reverberate to core constructs and to lead to threat, defined by Kelly (1955, p. 489) as "the awareness of imminent comprehensive change in one's core structures".

Faced with a person who behaves in a way which is inconsistent with their anticipations or who challenges their view of events, the tight construer may have difficulty in taking this person's perspective and may be threatened by the invalidation with which they are confronted. For such an individual, the only available option may appear to be violence in an attempt to remove the source of the threat. Hallschmid, Black and Checkley (1985) have suggested that this is often the case in situations of interspousal violence, where the threat is occasioned by situations which require reconstruction of the self–other boundary.

Violence as slot rattling

A process which may be particularly characteristic of the person who construes tightly, and which may lead to violence, is what Kelly (1969a, p. 231) termed "slot rattling", in which the self, some other person, or an event is reconstrued at the opposite pole of a construct to that to which it had previously been assigned. Slot rattling may be associated with 'lopsided' construing, in which people or events are not evenly assigned to the poles of constructs, and which Widom (1976), using repertory grids, has found to characterize individuals diagnosed as primary psychopaths. The operation of a process of slot rattling was also suggested in another repertory grid study, by Howells (1983), of 'one-off' violent offenders, whose offences, mostly committed against family members or close acquaintances, were characterized by extreme violence. Their grids indicated a 'positivity bias' in their construing of others. This bias was particularly evident in a comparison of the construing of their victims by one-off and multiple offenders, the former victims, all of whom had died, being viewed in a significantly more positive light. These findings are consistent with the notion that offences of extreme violence are characteristic of the individual who is generally overcontrolled in regard to expression of anger (Blackburn, 1968; Megargee, 1966). Howells' interpretation, from a personal construct theory perspective, is that the 'negative' poles of the one-off offender's constructs are submerged, being at a low level of awareness. He considers that "Such a person would live in a world in which he perceived only evidence of people's niceness and friendliness, until his perceptual system was undermined" (Howells, 1983, p. 127). This undermining may result from a severe difficulty in a relationship, and violence may occur either at the point of threat before the collapse of the offender's system or after temporary slot rattling in the offender's construction of the victim. However, in a case described by Landfield and Epting (1987), whose repertory grid had shown exclusively positive descriptions, this undermining, and consequent slot rattling to a homicidal state, appeared to be occasioned by reading about degradation and murder in Oscar Wilde's novel, *The Picture of Dorian Gray*!

Slot rattling in construing of the self may also be relevant to the commission of acts of violence. For example, I have found that slot rattling from law enforcer to lawbreaker, in several instances including acts of violence, may occur in police officers as a response to invalidation, particularly in those who construe tightly and may therefore have few, if any, options of reconstruing (Winter, 1993). In other individuals, including some murderers, acts of violence may be a manifestation of slot rattling, sometimes accompanied by sexual arousal, from a view of the self as weak and impotent to one characterized by considerable power. For example, when interviewed while on 'Death Row', Andrei Chikatilo described how "impotence has hounded me all my life" (Cullen, 1999, p. 265) and how "All my life, I've felt humiliated" (p. 266). His slot rattling from this position involved killing and mutilating at least 53 people. Similar histories of sexual humiliation are found in some other serial killers, including Peter Sutcliffe and Reginald Christie, whose sexual failures in his teens led to him being given the nickname 'Reggie No-Dick'.

Similarly, slot rattling may be observed in the commonly reported pattern of the victim of abuse who comes to abuse others (Adshead, 1994; Kempe & Helfer, 1980; Rivera & Widom, 1990; Widom, 1989a, 1989b). For example, Pollock and Kear-Colwell (1994) present two case studies employing repertory grids of women with histories of repeated sexual abuse, each of whom had stabbed her boyfriend. Using Ryle's (1990) procedural sequence object relations model, they view these women's interactions as being characterized by reciprocal roles of abuser and abused. However, they also point out that, despite their histories of abuse, the women had habitually perceived themselves as abusers, suggesting that an explanation of their violence in terms of slot rattling may be too superficial.

Violence as absolution of guilt

For the women described by Pollock and Kear-Colwell (1994), being an abuser appeared, in personal construct theory terms, to be part of their core roles. Any dislodgement from such a role, as by therapists trying to persuade them that they were victims, would be expected to elicit guilt in the sense that this was defined by Kelly (1955). The guilt might only be relieved by acts of violence which affirm their original self-constructions. Similarly, Kelly (1990) has indicated that being an offender may be the only viable core role for some individuals, and one which is reinforced by the individual being labelled as, for example, 'delinquent'.

At first sight it might appear paradoxical that a violent offence may in some cases be seen as a means of absolving oneself of guilt. Indeed, some offenders, namely those labelled as psychopathic, have been regarded in traditional psychiatry as incapable of experiencing guilt. However, if such a person's core role involves, for example, being a sadist, guilt may be experienced if the person acts in a humane fashion, and may lead to further sadistic acts in order to reduce this uncomfortable dislodgement. To view the violent offender as having no sense of morality or capacity for guilt is to display preemptive construing, in that the person is seen as nothing but a violent offender, or constellatory construing, in which lack of moral qualms is part of one's stereotype of such individuals. Again, Ian Brady (2001) takes a position which is not inconsistent with that of personal construct theory, namely that "every intelligent individual, whether predominantly good or evil, possesses a mostly idiosyncratic moral gyroscope which reminds him whether he is in conflict with his *own* moral and ethical convictions or merely those of others" (p. 37, italics in original). He points out that the serial killer is in many respects no different from any other individual: "Serial killers, like it or not, can possess just as many admirable facets of character as anyone else, and sometimes more than average" (p. 64). For example, in his own case, loyalty is clearly part of his core role, and he condemns in no uncertain terms those who do not display this quality, presumably including his partner in crime, Myra Hindley, whose disloyalty involved attempting to gain parole by claiming that Brady was totally responsible for the murders which they committed, and her sister, who betrayed him to the police. Indeed he would murder such a person with no compunction or guilt. Thus, he writes that "I regard personal disloyalty as the worst crime of all, and have killed some guilty of it without a qualm" (p. 64).

In his account of his life after being imprisoned for murder, Reg Kray, the notorious gang leader from the East End of London, also provides many indications that he is far from lacking in moral scruples. For example, he describes his resentment at being asked to acquire a knife for a prisoner who wanted to stab a fellow inmate in order to be certified insane, stating that "it was against my principles to be involved in anything so fundamentally immoral" (Kray, 2000, p. 74). That this does not imply that he had eschewed violence at that time is indicated by such other episodes as an occasion when, on seeing one prisoner trying to "take a liberty" with another, whom Kray 'looked after', he "scuffed the fellow by the neck, slung him against the wall and butted him in the face" (p. 150). Presumably the distinction between these two incidents is that in the latter, but not the former, the victim was construed by Kray as deserving to be attacked and the attack itself as launched on the basis of noble motives of loyalty towards, and protection of, a friend. In such cases, violence can be perpetrated without guilt. Houston (1998) similarly points out that violent offenders, including most of those who have committed violence against children, may construe their victim and their own actions in such a way that their guilt is minimized. Such a pattern has also been observed in soldiers who have participated in atrocities (Glover, 1985). Even if the offenders hold a negative stereotype of violent offenders in general, they might also avoid guilt by dissociating themselves from this stereotype (Fransella, 1977), a pattern which Fransella and Adams (1966) and Winter (1992) have observed in repertory grid case studies of arsonists.

The co-existence of strong moral principles with the capacity to commit murder may in some cases seem as paradoxical and inexplicable to the murderer as it is to the outside observer. For example, the serial killer Dennis Nilsen, a former soldier and policeman, wrote that:

I like to see people in happiness.
I like to do good.
I love democracy.
I detest any criminal acts.
I like kids.
I like all animals.

I love public and community service.
I hate to see hunger, unemployment, oppression, war, aggression, ignorance, illiteracy, etc.
I was a trades union officer.
I was a good soldier and N.C.O.
I was a fair policeman.
I was an effective civil servant.
STOP. THIS ALL COUNTS FOR NOTHING when I can kill fifteen men (without any reason) and attempt to kill about nine others – in my home and under friendly circumstances.
Am I mad? I don't feel mad. Maybe I am mad.

(Masters, 1986, pp. 168–169)

Violence as shame avoidance

Extending Kelly's definitions of emotions, McCoy (1977, p. 121) described shame as "Awareness of dislodgement of the self from another's construing of your role". Therefore, while violence in the service of guilt-reduction may be seen as involving behaving in a way which conforms with one's own expectations of oneself, violence in the service of shame-reduction involves behaving in a way which conforms with the expectations of another person. In many instances, these two sets of expectations will be very similar.

Episodes of violence before an audience, as in gang fights, may be particularly motivated by the avoidance of shame. For example, a participant in a gang fight described how his friend told him, "You know we with you, baby. Go ahead and dust him" (Toch, 1992, p. 22). He also stated that "everybody was struggling for a reputation, recognition. You get a reputation, you go where you want, nobody messes with you, you get your understanding". In order to preserve this reputation he was left with no apparent option but violence in response to a perceived slight. He admitted that had there been no audience the episode would probably not have eventuated in violence. Some incidents of violence towards the police may also occur because an individual who is challenged by a police officer in front of his peers may feel that his reputation is being tested. It may be that such a challenge, particularly if insensitively made, "confirms and reinforces the individual's role as a defender of principle and a champion of his kind. He can then in good conscience fight the officers on behalf of his role" (Toch, 1992, p. 54). Again, the only alternative may be to experience shame.

Violence as a dedicated act

While Kelly did not attempt to make distinctions between different types of violence towards others, he did do so in relation to types of violence towards the self (Kelly, 1961, p. 260). Some of the categories concerned have parallels in types of other-directed violence. For example, he described suicide as a "dedicated act" as "designed to validate one's life, to extend its essential meaning rather than to terminate it". This may be so, for example, in the case of the suicide bomber, who commits violence both to self and others as a dedicated act. In some such individuals, their act may also allow them to avoid guilt and shame, and indeed, if it reflects a shared construction in a particular social group, to go to their deaths knowing that they will receive acclaim from their peers.

Others who approach murder as a dedicated act do so more idiosyncratically and indeed in some cases may be considered to be labouring under delusions. For example, discussing his crimes with Ian Brady, Peter Sutcliffe, the 'Yorkshire Ripper', described how "The mission I'd been given was to kill all prostitutes. I was under God's protection" (Brady, 2001, p. 159). In an interesting manifestation of slot rattling, he later transferred responsibility for his murders from God to the Devil.

Hostile violence

The above heading will appear tautological from the perspective of the lay conception of hostility. However, in terms of Kelly's (1955, p. 510) definition of hostility as "the continued effort to extort validational evidence in favor of a type of social prediction which has already proved itself a failure", not all violence is hostile nor are all hostile acts violent. Although anger, which may be a more common concomitant of acts of violence, was regarded by McCoy (1977, p. 121) as "awareness of invalidation of constructs leading to hostility", this definition has not gone unchallenged. For example, Cummins (1997) views anger as "an emotional experience of invalidation", not necessarily culminating in hostility, and Warren (2001) also notes that "*hostility* is not *anger*, and neither might lead to *aggression*".

However, violence may in some cases be an attempt to make the world fit with one's constructions and thus may be an expression of hostility. Consider, for example, the person whose construction of members of another race as inferior and weak is constantly invalidated by seeing these people enjoying prosperity and power. One way to provide some, albeit limited, validation of the construction may be to reduce members of the race concerned to submission by means of acts of violence. A further illustration may be provided by Toch's (1992) account of the person who is involved in a confrontation with police officers and who "may finally resort to violence as a last-ditch effort to establish his premise of inviolability in the face of a conclusive demonstration of its invalidity" (p. 48). Toch provides several similar examples of the violent 'games' in which an individual, essentially displaying Kellian hostility, may involve others. Such games may also be apparent in situations of marital violence where, as Doster (1985) describes, the couple may enter a vicious cycle consisting of several phases, including the "eruption of hostility and violence . . . as an accelerated effort to impose on one another already invalidated constructs" (p. 227). In his view, the construct systems of such couples tend to be fragmented, with different subsystems operating in the different phases of the cycle and self-construal during the 'eruption' phase often being seen as a 'not me' experience, perhaps involving slot rattling.

Aggressive violence

Again, this heading may seem surprising to the reader who is not familiar with the personal construct theory view of aggressiveness as "the active elaboration of one's perceptual field" (Kelly, 1955, p. 565). Aggressiveness is sometimes regarded by personal construct theorists in a more favourable light, being associated with adventurousness, than is hostility. However, as Kelly pointed out, it may be uncomfortable to those with whom the aggressive individual comes into contact, and this may be particularly so if aggressiveness involves extending one's field to include criminal acts. Such an individual may take the view of Ian Brady (2001, pp. 42–43) that "sometimes it's a most stimulating experience to do something you don't want to do, don't approve of, and are legally proscribed from experiencing – just to discover new aspects of yourself and others".

Violence and dilation

Broadening of the perceptual field also occurs in the strategy which Kelly termed dilation, but in this case "in order to reorganize it on a more comprehensive level" (Kelly, 1955, p. 564) and thereby attempt to remove "incompatibilities" in construing. It is evident in some people who are labelled paranoid, who increasingly elaborate some particular theme. For example, as Ian Brady (2001, p. 162) describes, for Peter Sutcliffe eventually "a woman only had to *look* like a prostitute in order to qualify as a victim". Sutcliffe's capacity for dilation was perhaps indicated in a notice affixed inside the lorry which he drove. This read, "In this truck is a man whose latent genius, if unleashed, would rock the nation, whose dynamic energy would overpower those around him. Better let him sleep?" (Brady, 2001, p. 166).

Violence as constriction

In contrast to dilation, Kelly (1955) regarded constriction as a strategy by which a person minimizes apparent incompatibilities in construing by narrowing their perceptual field. In effect, the individual limits their attention to predictable events, which do not present such incompatibilities. Kelly viewed suicide as the ultimate constriction, and similarly homicide may be regarded as a constrictive act if seen as an attempt to remove permanently from the perceptual field an individual who causes one to experience inconsistencies in construing. Such an analysis, as well as one in terms of the avoidance of shame, may be applied to Reg Kray's murder of Jack 'The Hat' McVitie, a criminal associate of the Kray brothers whose behaviour was becoming increasingly unpredictable. Explaining why McVitie "had to go", Freddie Foreman, who helped dispose of the body, described how:

> there was so many things that he was doing wrong he was embarrassing them, cos he wouldn't take no notice of what they said. I mean, they've got to have a bit of respect. The man's got to do as he's told. But he disregarded everything they said. He was undermining them, he was making them a fucking laughing stock, so they had to act, and the only way to hold credibility was to fucking do him.
>
> (Foreman & Lambrianou, 2001, p. 107)

Violence as escape from chaos

Kelly's (1961) taxonomy of suicide included suicides in conditions of indeterminacy and chaos, in which "everything seems so unpredictable that the only definite thing one can do is to abandon the scene altogether" (p. 260). This is the course of action described by Antonin Artaud when he wrote that:

> If I commit suicide, it will not be to destroy myself but to put myself back together again. Suicide will be for me only one means of violently reconquering myself, of brutally invading my being, of anticipating the unpredictable approaches of God. By suicide, I reintroduce my design in nature, I shall for the first time give things the shape of my will.
>
> (Hirschman, 1965, p. 56)

Just as killing oneself can be a means of reintroducing one's design in nature, so can killing another. While violence can remove a specific source of chaos, as in the murder of Jack McVitie, it can also be committed in the service of a grander design. In Ian Brady's (2001) analysis, this was so in the case of Graham Young, the 'St. Albans Poisoner', whose ambition was to be "the greatest poisoner of all time" (p. 137). Elaborating on his 'interviews' with Young, Brady states that "The serial killer, essentially conceiving life as meaningless and death as nothingness, is consequently not afraid to die or kill in a final vainglorious attempt to introduce some degree of design" (p. 136). Clearly, for Brady, "It was difficult not to empathise with Graham Young" (p. 137). The similarity between this view of serial killing and the notion of chaotic suicide is apparent in another passage in Brady's book:

> the serial killer *has* confronted the chaos or absurdity of exist-ence . . . and is trying to impose upon it some meaning and order of his own. . . . That is why, in this primarily meta-physical context, some can often regard destruction as an act of creation – an 'act of God'.
>
> (Brady, 2001, p. 102, italics in original)

As Brady points out, unlike many 'domestic killers', the primary motivation of the serial killer is often not murder, but rather power and, as in Artaud's description of suicide, the urge to give things the shape of one's will.

In the case of Dennis Nilsen, who invited young, often homeless, men back to his flat because he was lonely and then kept their bodies "for company" for several days after killing them, at least some of the murders appear to have given him a sense of creating a beauty and meaning in death out of people whose lives were chaotic. Thus, describing one of the bodies, which he had carefully washed and dried, he wrote that:

> He looked really beautiful like one of those Michelangelo sculptures. It seemed that for the first time in his life he was really feeling and looking the best he ever did in his whole life. . . . I just lay there and a great peace came over me. I felt that this was it, the meaning of life, death, everything.
>
> (Masters, 1986, p. 130)

In some cases he also "may have felt that I applied a relieving pressure on life as a benevolent act, in that the subjects were ultimately freed from life's pain" (p. 143). For Nilsen, it seems that his murders did allow him to solve some of the puzzles of life, and that this purpose having been served he would no longer feel it necessary to kill. Thus, he writes that:

> I could not kill now because I now know myself and my past. I now have some kind of identity (even though it be one that I would rather not have). There are no longer any mysteries about me to trouble me. Knowing yourself is everything.
>
> (Masters, 1985, p. 267)

It is perhaps the 'medical killer' who best exemplifies the use of murder as part of a scheme of imposing meaning and order on the mysteries of existence. When Dr Harold Shipman was found guilty of murdering 15 of his patients, of whom he is suspected of killing as many as 1,000 more, he attained the dubious distinction of being the most prolific British serial killer. The coroner who investigated his case described him as someone who "enjoyed power and control" (Sitford, 2000, p. 249). He was, however, only one of many doctors and other health care professionals whose career has involved slot rattling from being a life saver to a killer, demonstrating a degree of power and control over life and death perhaps only matched by that of the Roman emperor indicating with his thumb the fate of vanquished gladiators.

Violence as a way of life

That violence or murder may allow some relief from chaos is similar to Kelly's (1955, p. 366) view that "psychological symptoms may frequently be interpreted as the rationale by which one's chaotic experiences are given a measure of structure and meaning". As Fransella (1970) has described, the symptom in effect becomes the person's 'way of life', which will not be relinquished until an alternative is available which offers a similar degree of structure and meaning. Such views draw upon Kelly's Choice Corollary, which asserts that we choose those courses of action which offer greater opportunities for extending and defining our construct systems, and therefore ultimately for predicting our world. For some individuals, the courses of action concerned may be violent ones. For example, the serial killer may be regarded as having chosen actions designed to extend the construct system, or, as Ian Brady (2001, p. 82) puts it, not "to exist as a grey daub on a grey canvas" but rather "as an existential riot of every colour in the spectrum". Furthermore, the more the identity of serial killer is elaborated, as by the increasing media attention given to this phenomenon, the more attractive a choice it may become for the individual who has no other well elaborated identity. For some such people, killing may also develop an addictive quality (Gresswell & Hollin, 1997; Sitford, 2000), which Brady (2001, p. 88) describes as "addiction to hedonistic nihilism".

In the case of Reg Kray (2000), whose last autobiographical account was entitled *A Way of Life*, violence had been his profession (Pearson, 1977). After his death, his wife wrote that:

> The past for Reg was a place of violence. As a young man he moved in unremittingly vicious circles and answered like with like. It was a brutal way of life, the appeal of which had begun to pall even before he went to prison.
>
> (Kray, 2000, p. 299)

Kray's situation was, of course, similar to those of many individuals with careers in organized crime, for whom violent crime is their principal means of organizing and anticipating the world. In a research project on men serving life imprisonment after having killed, Brennan (1997) was told by one of her interviewees that being good made her "act stupid", in contrast to him:

I'm a career criminal, I got a good house, all paid for, couple of cars, ditto, money in the bank, I've got respect, I've got friends, my kids don't want for nothing, I got no worries. I always have the advantage on you.

(Brennan, 1997, unpublished paper)

As has been indicated in various studies of Vietnam veterans, a career in legitimized violence such as warfare, perhaps particularly if it has involved participation in atrocities (Hiley-Young et al., 1995), may also lead to the individual developing 'combat addiction' (Nadelson, 1992; Solursh, 1989) and continuing to live their life in 'survival mode' even after discharge from the armed forces. Hodge (1997) suggests that in some such cases violent behaviour may be mediated by symptoms of post-traumatic stress disorder which allow the individual to re-experience the 'high' of combat.

Violence as a shared construction

Gresswell and Hollin (1997) report on an interview with a murderer who idolized the Kray twins, and described how he had "seen violence as a kid [at home, in the street] and I've grown up feeling that violence is a natural thing. I've got a right" (p. 158). This individual, like his heroes the Krays, is a product of a subculture of violence (Wolfgang & Ferracuti, 1967), in which socially shared constructions lead to a climate which is permissive of, and conducive to, violent acts. Cross-cultural studies (e.g., Riches, 1986) perhaps most clearly demonstrate such possible links between social constructions and violence.

Violent acts which emerge from constructions shared by a particular social group may be committed collectively, ranging in scale from warfare to riots or football hooliganism. At a more micro level, as Procter (1981) has indicated, families or couples may be regarded as having shared construct systems, and in some cases these may lead to acts of violence committed as a joint enterprise. This is the case in those murders which have been viewed, somewhat inaccurately, as manifestations of 'folie à deux'. As Masters (1997) points out, the original meaning of this term involved the adoption of one person's delusion by another, but it is now also used to describe, for example, the sharing of a person's sadistic behaviour, and associated constructions, by someone who falls under their influence. This was the case with Ian Brady and his partner in murder, Myra Hindley, who wrote that "He had a powerful personality, a magnet-like charisma into which my own personality, my whole self, became almost totally subsumed" (Masters, 1997, p. 382). It was not only Hindley whose personality was thus subsumed since, not long after meeting him, her brother-in-law was writing in his journal that "Murder is a hobby and a supreme pleasure" (Brady, 2001, p. 5). However, Brady himself considers that, in cases of 'folie à deux', "an individual can only be corrupted if the seeds of corruption are already within and predisposed to flower" (p. 253).

Another murderous British couple who have been regarded as "a perfect textbook example" (Wilson & Wilson, 1995, p. 526) of 'folie à deux' are Fred and Rosemary West, the occupants of the Gloucester 'House of Horror'. Although the extent of Rosemary's guilt has been questioned (Masters, 1997), they are generally considered to have been responsible for at least 10 sadistic murders, and in Fred's case more than this. His prison journal, which makes no mention of his offences, has been analysed from a personal construct perspective, and indicates that "he construed himself as a decent hardworking family man who would do anything to maintain his family – including killing 12 people" (Moser, 2001a, p. 103). In Moser's (2001b) view, his relationship with his family provided West with a constant source of validation, the loss of which after his arrest led to his suicide in prison.

Violence as an outcome of deficient sociality

In the report of his innovative study in which violent offenders were interviewed by fellow offenders, Toch (1992, pp. 33–34) describes a "remarkable gentleman" who has "a complete blindness to the other person's point of view". A common feature of this gentleman's episodes of violence is that he

> has a habit of placing other people into the most awkward situations without appearing to realize what he's doing – without anticipating the obvious reactions to his tactless opening moves. He isn't aware, for instance, that when you cohabit with a woman you just can't come in one evening and simply announce your imminent departure, and then expect to spend a congenial evening with her.
>
> (Toch, 1992, pp. 33–34)

Responding to the other person's reaction to him as an attack, he "can then be quite brutal while viewing it all blandly as an act of self-defense" (Toch, 1992, p. 34). The gentleman described by Toch is clearly limited in sociality, the capacity to construe another person's construction processes, which Kelly (1955) viewed as being the basis of a relationship with that person. Deficiencies in the ability to take another's perspective may be one reason for finding one's interpersonal world chaotic and unpredictable and may, as we have seen, lead to violence directed at the removal of a person whose construing cannot be predicted. Such deficiencies might also be expected to result in a greater propensity for violence if they are manifested in a lack of empathy for the potential victim of a violent act. They are often apparent in situations of spouse battering, where the batterer, as described by Hallschmid et al. (1985), may have difficulty in construing not only their partner's, but also their own, construction processes.

In a repertory grid study, Widom (1976) provided some evidence of deficient sociality in mentally disordered offenders diagnosed as psychopaths in that they tended to misperceive the construing of other people, assuming it to be similar to their own construing, which was idiosyncratic. This misperception was particularly apparent in relation to the construct 'dull–exciting', psychopaths wrongly anticipating that other people, like themselves, would construe most situations as dull.

Violence as foreshortening of the circumspection-preemption-control cycle

Moser's (2001b) analysis of Fred West's murders views them as involving failure to complete the Circumspection-Preemption-Control (CPC) Cycle, the decision-making process in which a person considers the issues involved, focuses on one of these, and then chooses one pole of the construct concerned as a basis for action. The person who acts impulsively, for example in an attempt to solve a particular problem, tends to foreshorten this cycle by foregoing, or only minimally engaging in, its Circumspection phase. Moser considers that the major problems faced by West were "construing crises" in his relationships with females, and that he tended to solve these problems by removing the female concerned from the context of the crises. Murder can be considered the ultimate such removal.

One of the principal distinctions made in the literature between types of violence is that between instrumental and reactive violent acts, the former being goal-directed and the latter responses to perceived provocation (Berkowitz, 1993). Instrumental violence has been related to the lack of social standards and of concern and respect for others which has been associated with psychopathy (Cornell et al., 1996). Reactive violence, on the other hand, may be considered to be generally a manifestation of foreshortening of the CPC Cycle. Although such foreshortening might therefore not be expected to characterize the violent offender who is labelled psychopathic, a different view was taken by Thomas-Peter (1992) in a repertory grid study which tested the hypothesis that mentally disordered offenders diagnosed as psychopaths display greater impulsivity than normal controls. While he did find faster reaction times in the former group, closer examination of the data indicated that this was only when making the moderate judgements involved in applying less extreme ratings to particular grid elements. The psychopathic group made relatively few such judgements, tending to view other people in extreme terms, and extreme judgements such as these were made quickly in both groups of research participants. Thomas-Peter therefore concluded that his hypothesis was "not supported for the majority of judgements made in the present task" (p. 127). However, the "moderate response deficit" which he demonstrated in his psychopathic group did indicate to him that for such individuals the interpersonal world is very significant, perhaps reflecting, as Blackburn and Lee-Evans (1985) have suggested, a high level of vigilance regarding potential threats to self-esteem. He also considered that since so many of the psychopathic person's judgements are extreme, and therefore made quickly, the person may develop a habit of making all their judgements, even the moderate ones, at high speed.

The violent offender's reaction to their offence

The above analysis of features of construing which are associated with violent offending would suggest that the perpetrators of such offences differ in the extent to which their actions are consistent with their view of themselves and of the world. From a personal construct theory perspective, it is only when this consistency is lacking that the offender would be expected to experience such 'negative emotions' as guilt following their offence. In terms of the distinction between reactive and instrumental violent offenders, this is more likely in the former, namely people whose violence is a result of loss of control following provocation, than the latter, whose violence is planned and unprovoked. For example, in the case of Ian Brady, who may be regarded as exemplifying the instrumental offender category, he presents his murders as an expression of his philosophical position, and makes clear that his book "is not an apologia" (Brady, 2001, p. 44). While he has admitted that he "chose the wrong path" (p. 32), this would appear to be because it resulted in life imprisonment rather than because of any acknowledgement that his actions were "wrong". However, as Colin Wilson has noted in his Introduction to Brady's book, there are indications that even Brady is not immune from remorse. For example, Brady (2001, p. 18) now considers that he was "attacking myself" when he violently assaulted another child killer in prison. He also could not bring himself to read letters written to him by the mothers of two of his child victims since "I have to keep mental blocks tightly shut and keep control. . . . Remorse for my part in this and other matters is axiomatic, painfully deep" (p. 18). Another instrumental violent offender, diagnosed as a psychopath, was a poisoner described by Howells (1978) as showing no remorse for his actions. In his repertory grid, he chose a famous poisoner as "a person I consider successful", and, unlike any other member of a sample of violent offenders, he saw no difference between himself and his ideal self. He viewed himself and the famous poisoner as abnormal and responsible, explaining that this differentiated them from most other violent offenders, whose crimes are unplanned and who do not accept the consequences of these. It was apparent from his grid that he valued being abnormal and going one's own way, and that poisoning allowed him to construe himself in these terms. The constructs concerned appeared to be central to a construct system which was very tightly structured, and more so than those of any members of the comparison group.

The relationship between the instrumental–reactive distinction and response to one's violent acts has been investigated by Pollock (1999), who has drawn upon Meichenbaum's (1996) constructive narrative approach to post-traumatic stress disorder (PTSD). This considers that the narratives of people who suffer from PTSD generally include a view of the traumatic event as being unforeseeable, uncontrollable, and as reflecting their culpability. It is not inconsistent with the personal construct theory model of PTSD, which views this as reflecting the 'constructive bankruptcy' experienced by the individual who does not have an elaborated system of constructs which can be applied to the traumatic event (Sewell, 1997). Although the victims of violence might more commonly be viewed as being at risk of PTSD than are its perpetrators, in fact there have been several reports of traumatic stress in offenders following their violent acts, with prevalence rates ranging from 15 to 32 per cent (Collins & Bailey, 1990; Dutton, 1995; Kruppa, Hickey & Hubbard, 1995; Steiner, Garcia & Matthews, 1997). In some of these cases, it is reported that the individuals appeared also to be suffering from PTSD prior to their offences. Frazer (1988) observed an "abnormal grieving reaction" in 62 per cent of psychiatric in-patients who had killed a loved one, while Pollock's (1999) study of men who had committed homicide found that 52 per cent met PTSD criteria, and that 82 per cent of these reported their offence to have been traumatizing. Consistent with his predictions, he found PTSD symptoms to be more pronounced in those who had committed reactive violent offences than in those who had committed instrumental violent offences. Such symptoms were also less apparent in offenders classified as primary psychopaths, whereas offence-related trauma was most often reported by offenders who, in terms of Blackburn's (1993) taxonomy, were overcontrolled. While this is explained by Pollock on the basis of cognitive formulations of PTSD (Brewin, Dalgleish & Joseph, 1996), it is equally consistent with a personal construct theory formulation in terms of the overcontrolled perpetrator of homicide being more likely to experience guilt, due to dislodgement from their core role, and anxiety, due to their actions being largely unconstruable. Interestingly, Pollock's study provided evidence of a higher frequency of reports of previous traumas in psychopathic offenders and that those offenders with no such prior traumas were more likely to suffer from symptoms involving the re-experiencing of the trauma associated with their homicide. It can be speculated that the individual with no history of trauma is less likely to have developed an elaborated system of constructs concerning such situations and that 're-experiencing' symptoms reflect the individual's consequent difficulty in construing the current trauma.

The development of PTSD in murderers whose crimes were unplanned is illustrated by three men described by Harry and Resnick (1986), who killed women during altered mental states. In one case, the murderer described how it was "just like seeing a murder on TV and all of a sudden it stopped for a commercial. Time seemed to go very fast once I started stabbing her and could not stop" (p. 609). For another, "It took me years to reconstruct what happened" (p. 610). A further case of PTSD in a man who killed his wife is described by Hambridge (1990), while Thomas, Adshead and Mezey (1994) report on the development of PTSD symptoms in a woman who killed her children during a psychotic episode, and Bradley and Chesterman (1995) give an account of PTSD in a man who stabbed his mother to death. Rynearson (1984) has indicated that such reactions are more extreme when the offender is emotionally involved with the victim. However, in some spouse murders, where the victim is construed as culpable by the killer, PTSD symptoms may be less persistent (Curle, 1989). Another murderer, who at first sight does not appear to fit the pattern which emerged from his research, was described by Pollock (2000). This individual, a member of a terrorist organization who had a long history of violence and who had committed a planned shooting, showed no remorse but nevertheless experienced symptoms of PTSD following the murder. He described how his victim

was crying, begging, talking about his children . . . I was becoming more agitated listening to him, then I looked straight into his face and shot him in the head . . . blood spurted on my suit, he fell, I had to step over him and slipped in the blood and fell on top of him, I panicked and ran.

(Pollock, 2000, p. 179)

It was this situation of being emotionally influenced by, and also touched by the blood of, his victim that appeared to cause anxiety to the murderer, presumably contrasting with the more predictable and business-like nature of his previous offences. It may be that the use of blindfolds and gags allows some murderers to reduce any such personalization of their victims by avoiding their gaze and their cries. A similar depersonalization of the enemy may be achieved in such socially sanctioned violence as warfare, but this does not prevent soldiers (Bartemeier et al., 1946; Hendin & Pollinger Haas, 1991; Keane et al., 1985), as indeed police officers (Danto, 1981), presenting with PTSD related to killing, particularly if they have been involved in atrocities (Breslau and Davis, 1987; Glover, 1985, 1988; Laufer, Gallops & Frey-Wouters, 1984).

Assessment of the violent offender

Psychological assessment of the violent offender has generally focused upon normative prediction of the potential for future violence (Rosenblatt & Rosenblatt, 1998), often with minimal consideration of the personal meaning of the offender's acts. As we have seen, this meaning may be vividly captured by interviews with, or narratives written by, offenders, but in some cases the use of more formal personal construct assessment techniques (Neimeyer, 1993) may further help to elucidate features of construing relevant to the offence. Repertory grid technique is one such method which has been used to provide valuable insights into the content and structure of the construct systems of individual violent offenders (Houston, 1998; Howells, 1978; Landfield, 1971; Landfield & Epting, 1987; Needs, 1988; Winter, 1992). However, that the value of personal construct techniques in this area is by no means limited to the grid is indicated by reports of the use of the self characterization, laddering, pyramiding, and Tschudi's (1977) ABC technique (Houston, 1998; Winter & Gould, 2000).

Treatment of the violent offender

Reducing the likelihood of future violence

If violence can be regarded as an outcome of particular modes of construing, personal construct psychotherapy may be effective in reducing the offender's likelihood of committing future violent acts. It is a technically eclectic approach (Winter, 1992), in which therapeutic techniques will be selected based upon a diagnostic assessment, perhaps including the use of the personal construct assessment methods described above, of the pathways of construing which may be implicated in the actions of a particular violent offender. These techniques will therefore differ from case to case, and in some cases may be diametrically opposed. For example, while techniques aimed at tightening of construing may be employed with the offender whose violence is viewed as an attempted escape from chaos, such an approach is likely to be the last thing which is needed by the offender whose violence is an outcome of construing which is already very tight. Such an approach, in which techniques are tailored to particular features of the client's construing, has been used effectively with people who have done violence to themselves (Winter et al., 2000).

There have now been several reports of the use of therapeutic approaches derived from personal construct theory in the treatment of individuals who have committed, or are at risk of committing, violent offences. While some of these reports describe individual psychotherapy (e.g., Houston, 1998), it has not been uncommon for the therapy to be conducted in a group format, and this may be particularly appropriate for those offenders who show deficient sociality. For example, Cummins (1997), who criticizes cognitive-behavioural approaches to anger management on the basis of their essentially negative view of anger, has run 'coping with anger' groups. These have employed methods such as the ABC technique, which delineates the advantages and disadvantages of anger, to clarify the part which anger plays for each group member. Cummins reports that the group allows members to replace their belief that anger is the only way to achieve such goals as to keep control and be powerful, and to develop the capacity to display aggression in Kelly's sense of this term. A principal part of this process, in his view, is the development of better sociality, facilitated by such techniques as asking group members to describe how their partners would construe them and to give their responses to these constructions. Goold and Kirchhoff (1998) report on group psychotherapy aimed at validating new construing in the area of interpersonal relationships in hospitalized men diagnosed as schizophrenic who had committed acts of violence. They provide a case study of one of the group members in which repertory grid technique revealed that his construing became less unidimensional over the course of therapy and that the person whom he had attempted to kill became less salient to him. Laming's (2001) SHED project uses groups run from a personal construct theory perspective to help men who have been violent to women or children to develop constructive alternatives to violence and abuse. The groups include the employment of such personal construct assessment techniques as self-characterization, laddering, and the ABC technique, as well as fixed role therapy, a technique devised by Kelly (1955) in which a client steps into a new role for two weeks as an experiment which may lead to reconstruing. In addition to these group approaches with adults, there have been reports of effective personal construct group therapy with juvenile offenders (e.g. Viney, Henry & Campbell, 1995). These groups have employed a range of structured approaches, including inter-personal transaction group methods (Landfield & Rivers, 1975), in which the group members interact in dyads using topics provided by the therapist.

Treatment of reactions to the offence

The acknowledgement that some violent offenders suffer post-traumatic stress disorder or other forms of distress related to their offence has led to questions as to whether the symptoms concerned should be treated or left to act as a constant reminder of the offence and deterrent to further offending. However, it has generally been argued that the latter course of action, as well as being inhumane (Bradley & Chesterman, 1995), is likely to result in a lower likelihood of effective rehabilitation (Kruppa et al., 1995). There have now been reports of the treatment of PTSD in homicide perpetrators by behaviour therapy (Kruppa, 1991; Rogers et al., 2000), pharmacotherapy (Thomas et al., 1994), and eye movement desensitization and reprocessing (Pollock, 2000); and indications that the successful treatment of PTSD in such individuals does not reduce feelings of guilt and remorse for their actions (Kruppa, 1991). The personal construct theory model of post-traumatic stress (Sewell, 1997) would suggest that personal construct psychotherapy might also be effective in such cases. An example of this approach, taken from Winter and Gould (2000), will now be provided.

Paul arrived for his first therapy session with a self-characterization which I had asked him to write after seeing him for assessment. The self-characterization, to which he had attached his curriculum vitae, was headed formally with his name, address, and telephone numbers, and it set out matter-of-factly his reasons for seeking help. He chose to write it in the first person, rather than my suggestion of it being written as if by a sympathetic friend. It read as follows (spelling and grammar as in the original):

> Where do we start, how about birth, ok. I was born in . . . on . . . I don't remember the birth, perhaps I was too young or maybe I had my eyes closed, I don't know.
> I went to a nursery . . . then went on to . . . Primary school before going on to . . . Comprehensive school where . . . my studies were interrupted by an unforseen event.

I killed my father. I don't really know why, my memory of the event has doesn't appear full. I was a little screwed up afterwards and probably still am today. I ran off immediately afterwards and a few days later was found by the police . . . Mercifully I was kept in the cells most of the trial and the time I was present in the court apart from when I was in the dock I believe I was crying . . . I am not even sure how long I was in the Dock.

A fitfull night in the cells later I was sentenced to 6 or 10 months meaning I could be released immediately. Which I was. And found myself home again . . .

And here I am.

This is the briefest of Synopsis. I have found it very difficult to get to write this lilltle bit and even had Sunday set aside to do it, but failed to. A foreboding has come over me that makes me nervous and distracted just thinking about this and the meeting tomorrow where I will have to talk about my Infamy and try to bring reason to it, where I know it is a painful subject that I can bottle up reasonably well with the odd histerical alcohol induced breakdown and odd week off due to an lethargic despondency that saps the will to due anything but read and sleep. I guess you need the full monty and replaying that record is not an easy thing to do at the best of times let alone trying to grasp it for reasoning.

And it misses a lot . . .

Paul – Pensive at Midnight

At his first session, he said that he still did not know why he did what he did. He used a series of metaphors, saying that he had "bottled it up extremely well", "locked it up and thrown away the key", and "encapsulated it and put it on a shelf". However, he now suffered from panic attacks, nightmares, and flashbacks, and was afraid of losing control if he experienced strong emotions, particularly anger.

Paul told me how difficult it would be to talk about what he had done, and that he did not want "anyone who didn't know what they were doing fiddling about with my mental processes". It later transpired that he had looked me up on the internet to check my credentials. Rather than leaping into exposure-based therapy, I made it clear to Paul that it was entirely his choice whether we took

Figure 2.1   Positive and negative implications for Paul of taking the 'big event' 'off the shelf' (as identified by Tschudi's (1977) ABC technique).

what he called the "big event" down from the shelf and I suggested that we explore this choice using Tschudi's (1977) ABC technique. The positive and negative implications of taking the event off the shelf and, conversely, of leaving it there are shown in Figure 2.1. He used a metaphor from his major hobby, computing, to describe the advantages of taking it off the shelf, saying that he could thereby develop a "programming patch", rather than continuing to have "faulty reasoning". He anticipated that it would also make him more "proactive", in contrast to his present "directionless" life, which resulted from "a big block of bad goo sitting in my brain". However, the disadvantages of taking the event off the shelf included his life reaching a "dead end", perhaps literally, in that he might take his life. After discussing these implications, he said that he still knew that he had to risk looking at the event. I explored with him the sources of support which might be available to him when he did so, and we identified one friend to whom he felt that he might be able to turn.

In subsequent sessions, as a preliminary step in exploring the "big event", we completed two repertory grids. The first of these, which used people as elements, revealed a tight construct system, which in discussing the grid results he related to a difficulty which he experienced in "thinking about people at different levels". Also of interest in this grid were his unelaborated constructions of himself and the other members of his family (as indicated in their proximity to the origin of the plot shown in Figure 2.2), apart from his father, who was construed very negatively. It was apparent in his grid that one of his superordinate constructs concerned trust. He discussed his difficulties in trusting other people and therefore, drawing upon the work of Rossotti (1995), I introduced the notion of dispersion of trust, suggesting that he might place trust in different people concerning particular areas of his life. This contrasted with his previous preemptive ("all or nothing") view of trust, which was coupled with the anticipation that if he revealed one aspect of himself to another person this would inexorably lead to the revelation of all aspects, including the "big event". We devised various experiments in trusting others which he agreed to perform as homework assignments.

The other grid was the Life Events Repertory Grid (Sewell et al., 1996), in which the elements were positive and negative events from different periods of his life. In the session at which we began this procedure, he mentioned a feeling of "impending doom" and a "black cloud", which I related to the fact that the grid would require him to construe the "big event". As indicated in Figure 2.3, this event was, in fact, construed very extremely, being given the most extreme rating on all but one of his constructs, but it was not construed as dissimilar to other negative events in his life. The grid was subjected to a HICLAS analysis (De Boeck, 1986), which provides a measure of the extent to which construing of each event is elaborated in terms of the number of 'construct classes' which are related to it. In Paul's grid, the relationship of the "big event" to only two construct classes indicated that its level of elaboration was low.

In the next session, we agreed on a strategy for exploration of the "big event" in which we would gradually approach it through

Figure 2.2 Plot of elements in construct space in Paul's pre-treatment repertory grid. Cpt. I = First component from prinicpal compenent analysis of the grid. Cpt. II = Second component.

discussion of recollections of his childhood prior to this time. Since his memory of childhood events was hazy, I suggested that he discuss them with members of his family. Although he was unwilling to do this, he agreed to talk to a childhood friend about his memories of Paul's family. We considered the possibility that he may never be able to know exactly what had happened in his childhood, and I suggested that in any case memories are no more

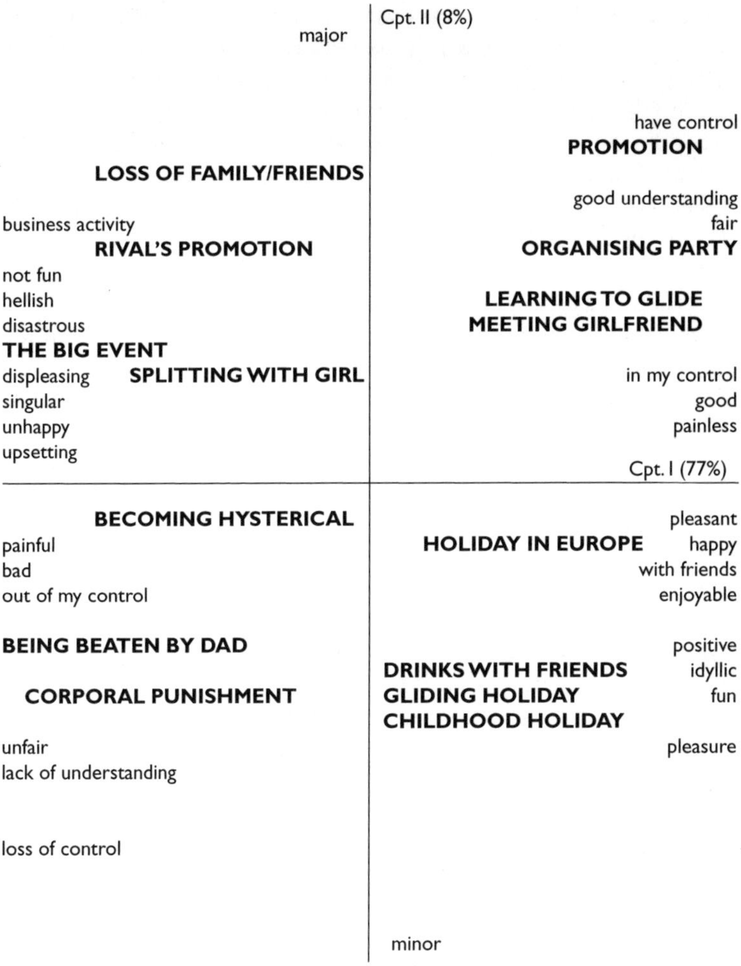

Cpt. II (8%)

major

have control
PROMOTION

LOSS OF FAMILY/FRIENDS

good understanding
fair

business activity
RIVAL'S PROMOTION   **ORGANISING PARTY**

not fun
hellish   **LEARNING TO GLIDE**
disastrous   **MEETING GIRLFRIEND**
THE BIG EVENT

displeasing   **SPLITTING WITH GIRL**   in my control
singular   good
unhappy   painless
upsetting

Cpt. I (77%)

BECOMING HYSTERICAL   pleasant
painful   **HOLIDAY IN EUROPE**   happy
bad   with friends
out of my control   enjoyable

BEING BEATEN BY DAD   positive
                              DRINKS WITH FRIENDS   idyllic
CORPORAL PUNISHMENT   **GLIDING HOLIDAY**   fun
                              CHILDHOOD HOLIDAY
unfair   pleasure
lack of understanding

loss of control

minor

Figure 2.3 Plot of elements in construct space in Paul's pre-treatment
Life Events Grid. Cpt. I = First component from principal component
analysis of the grid. Cpt. II = Second component.

than constructions of the events concerned. This he found disheart-
ening in that if it were not possible to access the truth about the past
he could never fully understand, or make reparation for, his actions.

As the weeks passed, he began to recall childhood events
involving his father's violence towards his mother and himself. An
episode that occurred between therapy sessions in which he

unexpectedly burst into tears after witnessing a violent argument between a friend and her husband provided an opportunity to explore the possible continuing impact of such childhood events. Eventually, he decided that the time had come to "launch into" an account of the "big event", and he proceeded to give his recollection of what had happened on the fateful day. He said that as he spoke, he was constantly telling himself that "logic must prevail". There were several gaps in his account, not least what had precipitated his actions, and we therefore agreed to obtain newspaper reports of his crime, as well as the file of his court case, since these might enable him to fill the gaps. The court file included a mention of an incident on the day of the "big event" which he had forgotten, and I explored with Paul whether this incident might be the missing precipitating factor since it might have evoked memories of his father's violence towards him.

Although he appeared somewhat disappointed that his reaction to reliving of the "big event" was not more intense, this reliving enabled us to explore issues concerning guilt and enabled him to talk about the event with a friend. We also discussed differences between his current and his childhood situation which might now provide him with additional options, and therefore allow him to complete the Circumspection-Preemption-Control Cycle, rather than acting impulsively, when he feels very angry with someone. Over the course of therapy, he made major changes both in his professional and in his personal life, suggesting that taking the event off the shelf had indeed allowed him to become more proactive. When we repeated the Life Events Repertory Grid, one of the new constructs which was elicited concerned the extent to which other events were "linked to the big event". This construct suggested that the "big event" may have become better integrated in his construct system, and this impression was confirmed by HICLAS analysis of the grid, which indicated that the number of construct classes related to the "big event" had doubled since the first grid. His construing of life events was also much less tight than at the initial assessment.

Conclusions

This chapter has demonstrated that personal construct theory may provide an understanding of violent offending and of the offender's reaction to his offence; as well as a means of assessing and treating the violent offender. As Scimecca (1977, 1985) has indicated, it avoids the determinism apparent in labelling theory and radical criminological approaches to the violent offender by, for example, examining the choices made by, and the self-construction of, such an individual. However, it may be questioned whether in attempting to view violence from the offender's perspective, the personal construct theorist is adopting a moral relativism similar to that espoused by Ian Brady (2001). As Warren (1992) has argued, some personal construct theory views of optimal functioning may be considered too neutral as they might even regard the serial killer as functioning optimally if their actions are in the service of elaborating their construct system. Warren proposes that this problem can be resolved by introducing as one aspect of optimal functioning an egalitarian outlook, in which others are seen as equals and there is an attempt to understand, and show tolerance of, their view of the world. Such an outlook is not compatible with violence towards other people or their constructions, but nor is it incompatible with taking a credulous attitude to the construing of the violent offender. Indeed, it could be argued that only by taking such an attitude can any effective attempt be made to identify those at risk of committing violent offences, and to facilitate reconstruing in the offender which might reduce the risk of future violence.

A further debate concerns whether such reconstruing is best achieved by a therapeutic regime or one which is primarily punitive. There are some indications in the literature that effective interventions for offenders are those which focus on antisocial attitudes and values, which de-emphasize punishment, which match treatment approaches to the offender's learning style, which employ clinicians who can relate sensitively and constructively to the offender, and which allow the offender to be exposed to "prosocial activities" incompatible with the criminal network (Gendreau & Paparozzi, 1995). These features of effective interventions are not inconsistent with a personal construct theory approach. By contrast, Norris (1977), in a repertory grid study, has found that a Detention Centre regime was accompanied by a 'downgrading' in young offenders' ideal selves and a greater aspiration to break rules, which increasingly came to be seen as associated with independence. These findings were in contrast to the more favourable changes in construing which she observed in a therapeutic community regime for clients who were mostly diagnosed as psychopathic (Norris, 1983). A further indication of the possibly negative effects of a punitive regime on construing was provided by a study which demonstrated that the construing of "cognitively simple" prisoners became increasingly consistent, and presumably tighter, during solitary confinement (Ecclestone, Gendreau & Knox, 1974). As we have seen that very tight construing may be a pathway to violence, this may not be the most beneficial of outcomes. In Toch's (1992) view, "There are no advantages to settings with custodial orientations. To multiply such facilities under the assumption that they can change Violent Men (other than by making them more bitter) is unrealistic" (p. 222). Ian Brady also has no doubt of the harmful effects of punitive prison regimes, which by providing a setting in which there is commonality of modes of construing associated with criminality, may do no more than to validate and elaborate such construing in prisoners. As Brady writes,

> What better circumstances and material could a resentful, hopeless prisoner ask for to school in the study of crime and revenge? He has at his constant disposal a veritable army of budding psychopaths and psychotics serving short sentences ardent for knowledge and instruction, eager to re-enter the community and try out their new-found ideas of social justice.
>
> (Brady, 2001, p. 44)

And, more chillingly, "common sense should caution that if you indifferently isolate criminals and pretend you cannot identify with them even in human terms – when freed they will isolate you, with extreme prejudice" (Brady, 2001, p. 92).

A construct of punitive versus therapeutic may, in any case, not be the most productive way of viewing appropriate interventions for violent offenders or people with this potential. It may, for example, be more useful to consider the establishment of training programmes in nonviolence, involving not only offenders but also others whom they involve in violent interactions (Toch, 1992). Attention might also productively be turned to fostering the development of a society with an egalitarian outlook. To conclude with another quote by Kelly (1969b), "I don't think that either punishment or treatment has much to do with man's basic undertaking, and it is unfortunate that these should be the only apparent alternatives for dealing with the more urgent matters of personal conduct" (p. 185).

References

Adshead, G. (1994). Damage: Trauma and violence in a sample of women referred to a forensic service. *Behavioral Sciences and the Law, 12,* 235–249.

Bartemeier, L. H., Kubie, L. S., Menninger, K. A., et al. (1946). Combat exhaustion. *Journal of Nervous and Mental Disease, 104,* 358–389.

Berkowitz, L. (1993). *Aggression: Its Causes, Consequences, and Control.* Philadelphia: Temple University Press.

Blackburn, R. (1968). Personality in relation to extreme aggression in psychiatric offenders. *British Journal of Psychiatry, 114,* 821–828.

Blackburn, R. (1993). *The Psychology of Criminal Conduct.* Chichester: John Wiley & Sons.

Blackburn, R., & Lee-Evans, M. (1985). Reactions of primary and secondary psychopaths to anger evoking situations. *British Journal of Clinical Psychology, 24,* 93–100.

Bradley, C., & Chesterman, P. (1995). A case report of post traumatic stress disorder in a perpetrator. *Journal of Psychiatric Case Reports, 1,* 43–47.

Brady, I. (2001). *The Gates of Janus: Serial Killing and its Analysis.* Los Angeles: Feral House.

Brennan, J. (1997). Hard constructs: talking with lifers about their lives. Paper presented at 12th International Congress of Personal Construct Psychology, Seattle.

Breslau, N., & Davis, G. (1987). Post traumatic stress disorder: the stressor criterion. *Journal of Nervous and Mental Disease, 175,* 255–257.

Brewin, C. R., Dalgleish, T., & Joseph, S. (1996). A dual representation theory of post-traumatic stress disorder. *Psychological Review, 103,* 670–686.

Chetwynd, J. (1977). The psychological meaning of structural measures derived from grids. In P. Slater (Ed.), *The Measurement of Intrapersonal Space by Grid Technique. Vol. 2. Dimensions of Intrapersonal Space.* London: John Wiley & Sons.

Collins, J. J., & Bailey, S. L. (1990). Traumatic stress disorder and violent behavior. *Journal of Traumatic Stress, 3,* 203–220.

Cornell, D. G., Warren, J., Hawk, G., Stafford, E., Oram, G., & Pine, D. (1996). Psychopathy in instrumental and reactive violent offenders. *Journal of Consulting and Clinical Psychology, 64,* 783–790.

Cullen, R. (1999). *The Killer Department.* London: Orion.

Cummins, P. (1997). Know what really makes me mad: A reconstruction of anger. Paper presented at 12th International Congress of Personal Construct Psychology, Seattle.

Curle, C. (1989). An investigation of reactions to having killed amongst male homicide patients resident in a maximum security hospital. Unpublished Ph.D. thesis, University of London.

Danto, B. L. (1981). Psychiatric management of the cop who kills. *The Peace Officer*, *24*, 31–37.

De Boeck, P. (1986). *HICLAS Computer Program: Version 1.0*. Leuven: Psychology Department, Katholieke Universiteit Leuven.

Delia, J. G., & O'Keefe, B. J. (1976). The interpersonal constructs of Machiavellians. *British Journal of Social and Clinical Psychology*, *15*, 435–436.

Doster, J. A. (1985). Marital violence: a personal construct assessment. In F. Epting & A. W. Landfield (Eds.), *Anticipating Personal Construct Psychology*. Lincoln: University of Nebraska Press.

Dutton, D. G. (1995). Trauma symptoms and PTSD-like profiles in perpetrators of intimate abuse. *Journal of Traumatic Stress*, *8*, 299–316.

Ecclestone, C. E., Gendreau, P., & Knox, C. (1974). Solitary confinement of prisoners: an assessment of its effects on inmates' personal constructs and adrenocortical activity. *Canadian Journal of Behavioral Science*, *6*, 178–191.

Foreman, F., & Lambrianou, T. (2001). *Getting it Straight: Villains Talking*. London: Sidgwick and Jackson.

Fransella, F. (1970). Stuttering: not a symptom but a way of life. *British Journal of Communication Disorders*, *5*, 22–29.

Fransella, F. (1977). The self and the stereotype. In D. Bannister (Ed.), *New Perspectives in Personal Construct Theory*. London: Academic Press.

Fransella, F., & Adams, B. (1966). An illustration of the use of repertory grid technique in a clinical setting. *British Journal of Social and Clinical Psychology*, *5*, 51–62.

Frazer, K. (1988). Bereavement in those who have killed. *Medicine, Science and the Law*, *28*, 127–130.

Gendreau, P., & Paparozzi, M. A. (1995). Examining what works in community corrections. *Corrections Today*, *57*, 28–31.

Glover, H. (1985). Guilt and aggression in Vietnam veterans. *American Journal of Social Psychiatry*, *59*, 15–18.

Glover, H. (1988). Four syndromes of post-traumatic stress disorder: Stressors and conflicts of the traumatized with special focus on the Vietnam combat veteran. *Journal of Traumatic Stress*, *1*, 57–78.

Goold, P., & Kirchhoff, E. (1998). Personal construing, fuzzy logic and group psychotherapy amongst men with schizophrenia in Broadmoor Hospital: an illustrative case study. *Criminal Behaviour and Mental Health*, *8*, 51–65.

Gresswell, D. M., & Hollin, C. R. (1997). Addictions and multiple murder: a behavioural perspective. In J. E. Hodge, M. McMurran, & C. R. Hollin (Eds.), *Addicted to Crime?* Chichester: John Wiley & Sons.

Hallschmid, C., Black, E. L., & Checkley, K. L. (1985). The core boundary:

a conceptual analysis of interspousal violence from a construct-systems perspective. *Comparative Criminology, 29*, 15–34.

Hambridge, J. A. (1990). The grief process in those admitted to Regional Secure Units following homicide. *Journal of Forensic Sciences, 35*, 1149–1154.

Harry, B., & Resnick, P. J. (1986). Posttraumatic stress disorder in murderers. *Journal of Forensic Sciences, 31*, 609–613.

Hendin, H., & Pollinger Haas, A. (1991). Suicide and guilt as manifestations of PTSD in combat veterans. *American Journal of Psychiatry, 148*, 586–591.

Hiley-Young, B., Blake, D. D., Abueg, F. R., Rozynko, V. et al. (1995). Warzone violence in Vietnam: An examination of premilitary, military and postmilitary factors in PTSD in-patients. *Journal of Traumatic Stress, 8*, 125–141.

Hirschman, J. (Ed.) (1965). *Antonin Artaud Anthology*. San Francisco: City Lights.

Hodge, J. E. (1997). Addiction to violence. In J. E. Hodge, M. McMurran, & C. R. Hollin (Eds.), *Addicted to Crime?* Chichester: John Wiley & Sons.

Houston, J. (1998). *Making Sense with Offenders: Personal Constructs, Therapy and Change*. Chichester: John Wiley & Sons.

Howells, K. (1978). The meaning of poisoning to a person diagnosed as a psychopath. *Medicine, Science and Law, 18*, 179–184.

Howells, K. (1983). Social construing and violent behavior in mentally abnormal offenders. In J. W. Hinton (Ed.), *Dangerousness: Problems of Assessment and Prediction*. London: Allen and Unwin.

Keane, T. M., Fairbank, J. A., Caddell, J. M., Zunering, R. T., & Bender, M. E. (1985). A behavioural approach to assessing and treating PTSD in Vietnam veterans. In L. Figley (Ed.), *Trauma and its Wake*. New York: Brunner-Mazel.

Kelly, D. (1990). A personal construct psychology perspective on deviance. In P. Maitland & D. Brennan (Eds.), *Personal Construct Theory Deviancy and Social Work*. London: Inner London Probation Service and Centre for Personal Construct Psychology.

Kelly, G. A. (1955). *The Psychology of Personal Constructs*. New York: Norton. (Reprinted by Routledge, 1991.)

Kelly, G. A. (1961). Theory and therapy in suicide: the personal construct point of view. In M. Farberow & E. Shneidman (Eds.), *The Cry for Help*. London: McGraw-Hill.

Kelly, G. A. (1969a). Personal construct theory and the psychotherapeutic interview. In B. Maher (Ed.), *Clinical Psychology and Personality: The Selected Papers of George Kelly*. London: John Wiley & Sons.

Kelly, G. A. (1969b). Sin and psychotherapy. In B. Maher (Ed.), *Clinical*

Psychology and Personality: The Selected Papers of George Kelly. London: John Wiley & Sons.

Kempe, C. H., & Helfer, R. (1980). *The Battered Child Syndrome*. Chicago: University of Chicago Press.

Kray, R. (2000). *A Way of Life: Over 30 Years of Blood, Sweat and Tears*. London: Pan Books.

Kruppa, I. (1991). Perpetrators suffer trauma too. *The Psychologist, 4*, 401–403.

Kruppa, I., Hickey, N., & Hubbard, C. (1995). The prevalence of post traumatic stress disorder in a special hospital population of legal psychopaths. *Psychology, Crime and Law, 2*, 131–141.

Laming, C. (2001). SHED TOOLS – Constructing alternatives to violence and abuse and making constructive life choices. Workshop presented at 14th International Congress of Personal Construct Psychology, Wollongong.

Landfield, A. W. (1954). A movement interpretation of threat. *Journal of Abnormal and Social Psychology, 49*, 529–532.

Landfield, A. W. (1971). *Personal Construct Systems in Psychotherapy*. Lincoln: University of Nebraska Press.

Landfield, A. W., & Epting, F. R. (1987). *Personal Construct Psychology: Clinical and Personality Assessment*. New York: Human Sciences Press.

Landfield, A. W., & Rivers, P. C. (1975). An introduction to interpersonal transaction and rotating dyads. *Psychotherapy: Theory, Research, and Practice, 12*, 366–374.

Laufer, R. S., Gallops, M. D., & Frey-Wouters, E. (1984). War stress and trauma: The Vietnam experience. *Journal of Health and Social Behavior, 25*, 65–85.

Lawlor, M., & Cochran, L. (1981). Does invalidation produce loose construing? *British Journal of Medical Psychology, 54*, 41–50.

McCoy, M. M. (1977). A reconstruction of emotion. In D. Bannister (Ed.), *New Perspectives in Personal Construct Theory*. London: Academic Press.

Manolias, M. B., & Hyatt-Williams, A. (1993). Effects on postshooting experience on police-authorized officers in the United Kingdom. In J. P. Wilson & B. Raphael (Eds.), *International Handbook of Traumatic Stress Syndromes*. New York: Plenum.

Masters, B. (1986). *Killing for Company: The Case of Dennis Nilsen*. London: Coronet.

Masters, B. (1997). *She Must Have Known*. London: Corgi.

Megargee, E. I. (1966). Undercontrolled and overcontrolled personality types in extreme antisocial aggression. *Psychological Monographs, 80*, Whole No. 611.

Megargee, E. (1970). The prediction of violence with psychological tests.

In C. Spielberger (Ed.), *Current Topics in Clinical and Community Psychology*. New York: Academic Press.

Meichenbaum, D. (1996). *A Clinical Handbook for Assessing and Treating Adults with Post-Traumatic Stress Disorder*. Chichester: John Wiley & Sons.

Moser, K. (2001a). The personal constructs of serial killer Frederick West. Paper presented at 14th International Congress of Personal Construct Psychology, Wollongong.

Moser, K. (2001b). Construing crisis: The journal of serial killer Frederick West. Paper presented at 14th International Congress of Personal Construct Psychology, Wollongong.

Nadelson, T. (1992). Attachment to killing. *Journal of the American Academy of Psychoanalysis, 20*, 130–141.

Needs, A. (1988). Psychological investigation of offending behaviour. In F. Fransella & L. Thomas (Eds.), *Experimenting with Personal Construct Psychology*. London: Routledge & Kegan Paul.

Neimeyer, R. A. (1993). Constructivist approaches to the measurement of meaning. In G. J. Neimeyer (Ed.), *Constructivist Assessment: A Casebook*. London: Sage.

Noble, G. (1970). Discrimination between different forms of televised aggression by delinquent and non-delinquent boys. *British Journal of Criminology, 10*, 172–180.

Norris, M. (1977). Construing in detention centres. In D. Bannister (Ed.), *New Perspectives in Personal Construct Theory*. London: Academic Press.

Norris, M. (1983). Changes in patients during treatment at the Henderson Hospital therapeutic community during 1977–81. *British Journal of Medical Psychology, 56*, 135–144.

Pearson, J. (1977). *The Profession of Violence: The Rise and Fall of the Kray Twins*. London: Granada.

Pollock, P. H. (1999). When the killer suffers: Post-traumatic stress reactions following homicide. *Legal and Criminological Psychology, 4*, 185–202.

Pollock, P. H. (2000). Eye movement desensitization and reprocessing (EMDR) for post-traumatic stress disorder (PTSD) following homicide. *The Journal of Forensic Psychiatry, 11*, 176–184.

Pollock, P. H., & Kear-Colwell, J. J. (1994). Women who stab: A personal construct analysis of sexual victimization and offending behaviour. *British Journal of Medical Psychology, 67*, 13–22.

Procter, H. G. (1981). Family construct psychology: an approach to understanding and treating families. In S. Walrond-Skinner (Ed.), *Developments in Family Therapy*. London: Routledge & Kegan Paul.

Riches, D. (Ed.) (1986). *The Anthropology of Violence*. Oxford: Blackwell.

Rivera, B., & Widom, C. S. (1990). Childhood victimization and violent offending. *Violence and Victims*, *5*, 19–35.

Rogers, P., Gray, N. S., Williams, T., & Kitchiner, N. (2000). Behavioral treatment of PTSD in a perpetrator of manslaughter: a single case study. *Journal of Traumatic Stress*, *13*, 511–519.

Rosenblatt, A., & Rosenblatt, J. A. (1998). Perpetrators of physical violence and abuse. In A. S. Bellack & M. Hersen (Eds.), *Comprehensive Clinical Psychology, vol. 9. Applications in Diverse Populations*. Amsterdam: Elsevier.

Rossotti, N. (1995). An elaboration on the theme of trust. Paper presented at 11th International Congress of Personal Construct Psychology, Barcelona.

Ryle, A. (1990). *Cognitive-Analytic Therapy: Active Participation in Change: A New Integration in Brief Therapy*. Chichester: John Wiley & Sons.

Rynearson, E. K. (1984). Bereavement after homicide: A descriptive study. *American Journal of Psychiatry*, *141*, 1452–1454.

Scimecca, J. A. (1977). Labeling theory and personal construct theory: Toward the measurement of individual variation. *Journal of Criminal Law and Criminology*, *68*, 652–659.

Scimecca, J. A. (1985). Toward a theory of self for radical criminology. *Psychology, A Quarterly Journal of Human Behavior*, *22*, 27–35.

Sewell, K. W. (1997). Posttraumatic stress: Towards a constructivist model of psychotherapy. In G. J. Neimeyer & R. A. Neimeyer (Eds.), *Advances in Personal Construct Psychology*, Vol. 4. Greenwich, JT: Jai Press.

Sewell, K. W., Cromwell, R. L., Farrell-Higgins, J., Palmer, R., Ohlde, C., & Patterson, T. W. (1996). Hierarchical elaboration in the conceptual structure of Vietnam combat veterans. *Journal of Constructivist Psychology*, *9*, 79–96.

Sitford, M. (2000). *Addicted to Murder*. London: Virgin.

Solursh, L. P. (1989). Combat addiction: Overview of implications in symptom maintenance and treatment planning. *Journal of Traumatic Stress*, *2*, 451–462.

Steiner, H., Garcia, I. G., & Matthews, Z. (1997). Posttraumatic stress disorder in incarcerated juvenile delinquents. *Journal of American Academy of Child and Adolescent Psychiatry*, *36*, 357–365.

Thomas, C., Adshead, G., & Mezey, G. (1994). Case report: traumatic responses to child murder. *Journal of Forensic Psychiatry*, *5*, 168–176.

Thomas-Peter, B. A. (1992). Construct theory and cognitive style in personality disordered offenders. In P. Maitland & D. Brennan (Eds.), *Personal Construct Theory Deviancy and Social Work*. London: Inner London Probation Service and Centre for Personal Construct Psychology.

Toch, H. (1992). *Violent Men: An Inquiry into the Psychology of Violence*. Washington, DC: American Psychological Association.

Topcu, S. (1976). Psychological concomitants of aggressive feelings and behaviour. Unpublished Ph.D. thesis, University of London.

Tschudi, F. (1977). Loaded and honest questions: a construct theory view of symptoms and therapy. In D. Bannister (Ed.), *New Perspectives in Personal Construct Theory*. London: Academic Press.

Viney, L. L., Henry, R. M., & Campbell, J. (1995). An evaluation of personal construct and psychodynamic group work in centre-based juvenile offenders and school-based adolescents. Paper presented at 11th International Congress of Personal Construct Psychology, Barcelona.

Warren, W. G. (1992). Personal construct theory and mental health. *International Journal of Personal Construct Psychology*, *5*, 223–237.

Warren, W. G. (2001). Philosophical writing on anger and violence and its relation to personal construct psychology. Paper presented at 14th International Congress of Personal Construct Psychology, Wollongong.

Widom, C. S. (1976). Interpersonal and personal construct systems in psychopaths. *Journal of Consulting and Clinical Psychology*, *44*, 614–623.

Widom, C. S. (1989a). Child abuse, neglect, and adult behavior: Research design and findings on criminality, violence, and child abuse. *American Journal of Orthopsychiatry*, *59*, 355–367.

Widom, C. S. (1989b). Does violence beget violence? A critical examination of the literature. *Psychological Bulletin*, *106*, 355–367.

Wilson, C., & Wilson, D. (1995). *A Plague of Murder: The Rise and Rise of Serial Killing in the Modern Age*. London: Robinson.

Winter D. A. (1992). *Personal Construct Psychology in Clinical Practice: Theory, Research and Applications*. London: Routledge.

Winter, D. A. (1993). Slot rattling from law enforcement to lawbreaking: A personal construct theory exploration of police stress. *International Journal of Personal Construct Psychology*, *6*, 253–267.

Winter, D., Bhandari, S., Metcalfe, C., Riley, T., Sireling, L., Watson, S., & Lutwyche, G. (2000). Deliberate and undeliberated self-harm: theoretical basis and evaluation of a personal construct psychotherapy intervention. In J. W. Scheer (Ed.), *The Person in Society: Challenges to a Constructivist Theory*. Giessen: Psychosozial-Verlag.

Winter, D., & Gould, C. (2000). Construing the unthinkable. In J. M. Fisher & N. Cornelius (Eds.), *Challenging the Boundaries: PCP Perspectives for the New Millennium*. Farnborough: EPCA Publications.

Wolfgang, M. E., & Ferracuti, F. (1967). *The Subculture of Violence: Towards an Integrated Theory of Criminology*. London: Tavistock.

Chapter 3

Sexual offenders

James Horley

Individuals who commit sexually deviant or anomolous acts are designated sexual offenders. The range of offensive acts varies from so-called 'nuisance' or indecent behaviours like exposing genitalia in public, although such experiences may leave lasting trauma for some victims (Cox & Maletzky, 1980), to more serious offences like rape. The number of incarcerated sexual offenders appears to be rising in many countries (see Borzecki & Wormith, 1987), although this is likely to be due to an increase in reporting, adjudication, and longer custodial sentences imposed by courts rather than an actual increase in incidence. The vast majority of sexual offenders are male, and relatively little is known about women who are convicted of sexual offences (but see O'Conner, 1987, for some case studies of female offenders); thus, most of the studies and comments in this chapter pertain only to men but may apply to women.

Sexual offenders do not represent a homogeneous group psycho-logically, and even subgroups of sexual offenders (e.g., men who molest children) are very heterogenous (Prentky & Knight, 1991; Quinsey, 1977, 1986). Perhaps partly due to this important consideration being ignored by early researchers and clinicians, we have no generally acceptable theories of sexual abuse despite many attempts (e.g., Johnston & Ward, 1996; Marshall & Barbaree, 1990). Most clinicians who work with sexual offenders today adopt a cognitive-behavioural approach (Houston, Thomson & Wragg, 1994), and perhaps with very good reason. Treatment efficacy of such programmes has been demonstrated (Marshall, Jones, Ward, Johnston, & Barbaree, 1991). The question is: What is meant by cognitive-behavioural? This designation can cover everything from rational-emotive therapy (Ellis, 1962) to social learning theory (Bandura, 1982), among others. Some of us (e.g., Horley, 2000;

Winter, 1988) concerned with personal construct theory (PCT) and sexual behaviour, normal and deviant, have certainly suggested that PCT can and should be seen as a viable theoretical basis for understanding sexual function and dysfunction.

This chapter will consider the thoughts and behaviours of sexual offenders by providing a review of explicitly PCT-informed research, as well as work that can be viewed through a PCT lens. Following an examination of material relevant to different types of sexual offenders, discussions of germane issues in assessment and psychotherapy for these offenders will be presented. It is important to keep in mind that, given PCT's avoidance of diagnosis and labeling, I am not describing the "paraphilias", or the "love disorders" from Axis I of *DSM-IV* (American Psychiatric Association, 1994), especially given that rape does not appear in the *DSM* as a sexual or any type of mental disorder.

Varieties of sexual deviation

Child molestation

A comprehensive theory of child sexual abuse could explain and connect the various observations concerning child molesters' thoughts, feelings, and actions. As many authors (e.g., Howells, 1981; Lanyon, 1986; Quinsey, 1986) have noted, however, there is no generally accepted theory of child molestation. Overarching personality theories, even psychosexual ones such as psychoanalysis, have been embraced by relatively few investigators. Freud, for example, had remarkably little to say about molestation after discarding his "seduction" hypothesis (Masson, 1984). Freud (1905/1975) did note that "the sexual abuse of children is found with uncanny frequency among school teachers and child attendants" (p. 14). He concluded, rather weakly, that "the impulses of sexual life are among those which, even normally, are the least controlled by the higher activities of the mind" (p. 15). At least one subsequent psychoanalytic writer (Fraser, 1976) provided an account of child sexual abuse from a Freudian perspective. In a very creative and well-crafted book, Fraser described child molesters as the result of a dominant yet distant mother and an absent, weak or "despised" father. The unresolved Oedipal strivings of a young male in such a family produces a "narcissistic inversion" in which the individual, as he ages, "remains deeply in love with the child he was then" (p. 20). He concluded, perhaps correctly, that the major problem faced by men who molest children is their obsessive preoccupation with their sexually deviant behaviour. Fraser draws widely from English literature to support his case. His account, however, is unconvincing. Not only does Fraser relate homosexuality to child sexual abuse, but he fails to account adequately for adult males who molest young females, the wrong sex to be "the child he was then". His argument is weakened, too, by his failure to consult research literatures seriously.

Perhaps the most popular theory, at least until recently, used to explain child sexual abuse is social learning theory (e.g., Abel, Becker, Cunningham-Rathner, Rouleau, Kaplan & Reich, 1984). From a social learning perspective, a number of theorists (e.g., Abel et al., 1984; Laws & Marshall, 1990) have argued that children can be exposed to models and experience some early arousal to non-normal stimuli which, when combined with inappropriate masturbatory fantasies during the adolescent years, lead to child molestation. At the same time, in line with more recent work in social learning theory (e.g., Bandura, 1982, 1986), cognitions in the form of "self-descriptions which may guide or limit . . . behavior" (Laws & Marshall, 1990, p. 220) are recognized as significant in the acquisition and maintenance of adult sexual interest in children. There has, however, been little explicit use of social learning theory over the past several years. This is surprising given the concern of cognitive social learning theory (Bandura, 1986) on the regulation of behaviour.

PCT is one personality-clinical theory – or a cognitive-behavioural theory, although Kelly (1955) eschewed the term 'cognition' because of its typical contrast with 'affect' – similar in emphasis and intent if not form to social learning theory (see Bandura, 1971). Kelly (1970) regarded behaviour as indispensable yet peripheral to a complete understanding of an individual. Kelly (1955) made little reference to sexuality and no reference to deviant sexuality, even in his later writings elaborating on abnormal and clinical themes (e.g., Kelly, 1969), but several writers (e.g., Chin-Keung, 1988; Horley, 2000; Horley & Quinsey, 1995) have suggested that PCT can provide a theoretical and therapeutic basis for child molestation. Chin-Keung (1988) attempted to understand the dynamics of child molestation using PCT. Too many problems with his effort, unfortunately, are evident. Most significantly, Chin-Keung misinterpreted several aspects of personal construct theory, and he appears to view it as both psychological theory and moral theory. In particular, he seems to view PCT as a moral theory that promotes an 'anything goes' position. Horley and Quinsey (1995) suggested that PCT, as a personality-clinical theory that has direct assessment techniques (e.g., role construct repertory grid) and therapeutic techniques (e.g., fixed-role therapy), is ideally suited to provide a framework for an account of child molestation. To date, however, no systematic PCT explanations of child molestation have been advanced, although it could be argued that we at least have an outline of a theory.

A significant portion of the empirical work on child molesters' cognitions has been concerned with fantasy, especially deviant sexual fantasy, and to a somewhat lesser extent on deviant beliefs and attributions. A fairly direct line can be traced back to a New Jersey study of 300 sexual offenders by Ellis and Brancale (1956). This early work did not focus on offenders' cognitions, which is quite surprising given Ellis' (e.g., Ellis, 1962) developing interest in irrational beliefs. These investigators did examine offenders' accounts of their own offences. Among their results, Ellis and Brancale cited nonspecific 'clinical evidence' that exhibitionists and child molesters tend to have difficulty explaining their own motives. They failed, however, to make differential predictions for offender types, with most of their discussion in terms of sex offenders as a single entity.

One early research project that focused on a single child molester was conducted by Bell and Hall (1971). Their extensive case study of a child molester from a psychodynamic perspective examined the dream content of a child molester. Their position was that latent dream symbols are used to represent significant but disturbing thoughts and feelings. These investigators reported that their molester, a single adult male who lived with his mother, had numerous dreams that involved his mother, supportive of the psychoanalytic view that dominant mothers, or at least the perception of a dominant mother, have an important developmental function in child molestation.

The role that fantasy plays in deviant sexuality in general and child molestation in particular was examined by Marshall (1973). Marshall showed that an attempt to control and alter the deviant sexual fantasies of five child molesters was effective in reducing penile responses to child stimuli as well as inappropriate sexual behaviour outside the treatment setting. Marshall and many others (e.g., Marshall & Barbaree, 1988) have included alteration of deviant fantasies in a treatment programme for child molesters. Abel and Blanchard (1974), too, demonstrated the centrality of deviant fantasy, as have others (e.g., MacCullough, Snowden, Woods & Mills, 1983). Perhaps first and foremost, fantasies serve as experimental plans (MacCulloch et al., 1983). Lanyon (1986) and Quinsey (1986) have concluded that an account of sexual fantasy is essential for any adequate explanation of child molestation and any effective treatment programme.

Abel, Becker, and Cunningham-Rathner (1984) have investigated the role that certain beliefs and attitudes play in continued sexual involvement by adults with children. They have focused in particular on seven types of beliefs about children and sex that they term 'cognitive distortions'. These distorted beliefs include: if children fail to resist advances, they must want sex; sexual activity with children is an appropriate means to increase the sexual knowledge of the children; if children fail to report sexual activity, they must condone it; in the future, sex between adults and children will be acceptable if not encouraged; if one fondles rather than penetrates, sex with children is acceptable; any children who ask questions about sex really desire it; and one can develop a close relationship with a child through sexual contact. According to Abel et al., the commonality among all of these 'wrong' views (i.e., inappropriate insofar as children cannot consent meaningfully to sexual interaction) is that child molesters make no attempt to validate them against the experience of others. A number of writers confirm that child molesters do report these and similar sexual attitudes and beliefs about children. Stermac and Segal (1989), for example, reported that child molesters, compared to normals, perceive more benefits for children as a result of adult sexual contact, greater complicity on the child's part, and less responsibility on the adult's part. Hayashino, Wurtele and Klebe (1995) found that extrafamilial molesters, compared to nonoffenders and even incest offenders, report more abnormal beliefs about the nature of adult–child sexual encounters (e.g., children enjoy sex with adults).

Although studies of the attributional processes per se of child molesters are few in number, some sociological and social psychological investigation has examined beliefs and what could be termed social cognition. McCaghy (1967, 1968) showed that the amount of coercion in the sexual activity with children predicted level of denial and attempts to maintain an identity as 'sexually normal'. Interestingly, he also found that, although incarceration and probation had no significant impact on motivational change, the number of psychotherapeutic sessions did affect self-confessed motives. After 11 individual or 21 group sessions (McCaghy, 1967), or roughly 20 sessions of unspecified therapy (McCaghy, 1968), child molesters tended to accept more personal responsibility for their actions, as opposed to blaming an alcohol or drug problem. They also tended to provide many psychodynamic explanations for their behaviour, not surprising given the psychoanalytic orientation of most of their therapists, past and present. Interestingly, McCaghy warned that the label 'child molester' should be avoided lest offenders, or deviants attempting to portray themselves as normal, come to accept such a deviant role as an integral part of themselves.

Taylor (1972) had judges sort motivational accounts into categories on a true-false scale. He found that the sex offenders, including child molesters, invoked 'mental breakdown' reasons for their behaviour much more often than 'social skill deficit' explanations. Judges, however, rated 'social skill deficit' reasons as more credible than 'mental breakdown' reasons. These patterns of attribution, with minimization and denial of deviance, appear consistent with clinical findings concerning offenders' use of denial and minimization (Barbaree, 1989).

Ward, Hudson and France (1994) had incarcerated child molesters complete an attribution scale at three points in time while describing and explaining their most recent sexual offence. They found that sexual needs were reported most often, followed by intimacy needs, especially during their recall of the lapse (stage two) just prior to their sexual assault. Along similar lines, Ward, Loudon, Hudson and Marshall (1995) examined molesters' accounts of the chain of thoughts and feelings that accompanied their most recent offences. The resulting qualitative data led them to propose a nine-stage process for child molesters' offence chains that emphasized distorted beliefs. Earlier, Ward, Hudson and Marshall (1994) found that child molesters who reported a lapse viewed the causes of their deviant behaviour as more uncontrollable than molesters without a lapse.

Child molesters' attitudes have been examined by some investigators. The technique of choice has been the semantic differential technique, first presented by Osgood, Suci and Tannenbaum

(1957). Marks and Sartorius (1967) argued that sexual attitude is an important component in the assessment and treatment of sexual deviation, and they presented a 'sexualized' version of the semantic differential. Their technique included not only bipolar adjectives that Osgood et al. would classify as general evaluative (e.g., kind–cruel, good–bad), but they included sexual evaluative adjectives as well (e.g., seductive–repulsive, erotic–frigid). Factor analysis of the assessment device showed that there was some distinction between the general and sexual evaluative scales, although the two factors were similar. In an examination of the clinical utility of the technique with eight clients who revealed a variety of sexual deviations, they found that attitude change paralleled clinical change. They concluded, therefore, that their version of the semantic differential provided 'useful indicators of clinical progress' (p. 448). For a concise clinical tool, they recommended an abbreviated version of their technique with three sexual evaluative scales (viz., sexy–sexless, seductive–repulsive, and erotic–frigid) and three general evaluative scales (viz., kind–cruel, good–bad, and pleasant–unpleasant).

Quinsey, Bergersen and Steinman (1976) used this brief sexual semantic differential as part of their test battery in a study of change in child molesters over the course of an aversion therapy programme. Together with significant pre- versus post-treatment changes in penile circumference responses and skin conductance responses, Quinsey et al. found that the general evaluative and sexual evaluative scales were highly correlated and that both showed the expected interaction of increased ratings for adults and decreased ratings for children, in line with both penile circumference and skin conductance results. Thus, the semantic differential appears to be a useful paper-and-pencil measure of attitudes that are relevant to the treatment of child molestation. One warning sounded later by Quinsey (1977, 1986), however, concerns the transparency of any devices that include only sex-related dimensions. The ability of respondents, many of whom are highly motivated to dissemble, to appear as they wish to be seen should not be overlooked.

One of the first uses of the semantic differential with child molesters was by Frisbie and colleagues (Dingman, Frisbie & Vanasek, 1968; Frisbie, Vanasek & Dingman, 1967). They described the general technique as "non-threatening" and "relatively ambiguous" (Frisbie et al., 1967, p. 700). They argued further that it and similar psychological assessment techniques are important "because an adult male's selection of a child as a sexual object seems to be related to his perceptions of the self, his role in a given social structure, and his recognition and/or acceptance of ethical values and social expectations" (p. 699). Their research involved an examination of incarcerated and released child molesters' views of themselves and their ideal selves. One bipolar adjective pair, "happy–sad", was found to distinguish incarcerated from community molesters, with community molesters reporting more resemblance between their actual versus ideal selves on this dimension than incarcerated offenders. This finding in part led to the conclusion that released offenders were "better integrated" than incarcerated offenders, but Frisbie et al. correctly noted that this could be a reflection of their different situations rather than personality differences. A one year follow-up of 79 of the released molesters (Dingman et al., 1968) showed that the respondents' views of both their real and ideal selves declined. This finding was described in terms of erosion of morale, and it was related to concern about impending recidivism.

Borrowing from Marks and Sartorius (1967), Frisbie et al. (1967) and others, Horley and Quinsey (1994) developed a semantic differential to examine child molesters' attitudes or thoughts about themselves and other individuals. Child molesters, relative to nonmolesters, described themselves as submissive and sexually unattractive, while they described women as oppressive and unattractive. Examination of the child molester group alone revealed some intragroup differences using Kelly's (1955) role construct repertory grid (rep grid). Responses of molesters who had exclusively victimized girls included significantly more external appearance constructs, while offenders against young boys used more emotional and self-sufficiency terms to describe people. Molesters who had killed their young victims described men and boys as cruel but sexy. Untreated molesters reported more social anxiety than treated offenders (Horley & Quinsey, 1995). A subsequent study (Horley, Quinsey & Jones, 1997), using a revised semantic differential, confirmed that molesters described themselves as less positive sexually than did nonmolesters. Women were seen by molesters more negatively in terms of sexual descriptors than by nonmolesters although, somewhat paradoxically, molesters described women as more trusting and mature than nonmolesters. Molesters also reported a more positive view of women on the

Attitudes Toward Women Scale (Nelson, 1988) than comparison participants. Molesters and nonmolesters also differed in terms of their responses to the Criminal Sentiments Scale (Andrews & Wormith, 1990), with child molesters reporting a more favourable view of the police, courts, and legal process than comparison participants. A similar finding was revealed in ratings of authority figures: child molesters described authorities as kinder and less repulsive, deceitful, and unpleasant than comparisons.

A modest but interesting study by Howells (1979) examined the thoughts of child molesters and nonsex offenders about people in their social environments in terms of personal constructs (Kelly, 1955), or the terms, or even preverbal "hunches" or "intuitions", by which a person interprets personally-experienced events. Howells compared the personal constructs of 10 "mentally disordered" heterosexual child molesters and 10 nonsex offenders using versions of the rep grid. The constructs elicited from Howells' respondents were sorted according to an amended version of Landfield's (1971) categorization scheme, and analyses revealed certain differences between offender groups. Perhaps most importantly, child molesters used more "egoistic" constructs, such as "domineering–passive" and "dominant–submissive", than nonmolesters, with children described as passive and submissive. There was also a suggestion that molesters were concerned with small body parts such as small genitalia. A combination of both offender groups, where constructs elicited using male and female elements were compared, showed that women were construed in terms of sexual and physical appearance while men were interpreted in terms of status and organization.

Wilson and Cox (1983a, 1983b) provided some indirect support for Howells' (1979) egoism finding. In a study of the personality of 77 members of a British child molester organization, Wilson and Cox (1983a) found that child molesters frequently described themselves as shy and attracted to children because of the children's "naive innocence". They concluded that social dominance was a key to understanding a child molester's choice of partner.

A conceptual replication of Howells' work was attempted by Horley (1988), who compared the personal constructs of 10 "mentally disordered", mixed (heterosexual and homosexual) child molesters and 10 "mentally disordered" nonsex offenders. Analyses confirmed the previous findings concerning the tendency of the combined groups to think of women, compared to men, in terms of sexual and physical appearance, but the egoistic construct difference between groups was not found. Neither did there seem to be a preoccupation with small body size among child sexual abusers. Although the failure to replicate between-group findings may be due to differences between the two studies (e.g., heterosexual versus mixed molesters, prison comparison versus mental health comparison), it is also possible that the original egoism finding is attributable to statistical artifact.

More recently, Marshall and colleagues (e.g., Marshall & Mazzucco, 1995) have pointed to a related concern with the self-perception and self-esteem of child molesters. They have argued that low self-esteem leads some adult males to seek sexual relationships with children. Certainly some child molesters report that negative feelings, and negative self-feelings, explain their offending (Ward, Hudson & France, 1994). Ward, McCormack and Hudson (1997) also reported low self-esteem among molesters. Horley et al. (1997), however, suggest that the situation may be more complex, in that child molesters may perceive themselves as inadequate sexually, or not very physically attractive, but they do not show low self-esteem in general. At least two studies with incarcerated molesters support this view (Horley & Quinsey, 1994; Horley et al., 1997). This issue remains to be settled.

An interesting study by Johnston, Hudson and Ward (1997) examined the sexual thoughts, at least the words relevant to children and/or sexual activity, of incarcerated child molesters, especially ability to suppress unwanted or inappropriate thoughts. They concluded that there is both "some hope and some notes of caution" (p. 303) after showing that sexual thoughts could be suppressed but more so by situational offenders than molesters who are obsessed by children. They also concluded that thought suppression techniques alone are insufficient for changing child molesters' behaviour.

Rapists

Relatively little work has been done from a PCT perspective on men who assault adult females sexually; in fact, relatively little work has focused on rapists, period. Whether this has any relation to the "difficult to understand" (Marshall, 1999, p. 643) situation where men who rape are not considered to have a mental disorder

(American Psychiatric Association, 1994), or the evolutionary perspective that rape is "natural" (Malamuth & Heilmann, 1998), is unclear. What is clear is that the situation demands address.

Rada (1978) has argued that rapists suffer from what he terms the "Madonna-Prostitute Complex", or a tendency to think in extreme terms of women as either extremely pure, and not to be touched, or extremely impure, and to be touched whenever desired. This syndrome, or really a particular pattern of construal, was the subject of a case study by Mathis (1971), who used it to explain the puzzling behaviour of a man, recently married, who forced his wife to "talk dirty" during sex and who eventually raped her. Carnahan (1987) investigated this hypothesis from a PCT perspective using a rating grid with incarcerated rapists and a comparison group of incarcerated property offenders. Although he could find no overall support for this form of construal among rapists, Carnahan did find a tendency among rapists, compared to property offenders, to view rape victims as "dirty" versus "pure". Carnahan's sample only included "less serious" rapists (i.e., those sentenced to confinement of two years or less), and it is possible that a group of serious rapists might show such extreme construal. It is important to note the generality of such a hypothesis, however, especially in light of Howells' (1981) warning that rapists seem to have multiple meanings of their actions, actions that seem to be mediated by a wide variety of emotional states. The work of Prentky and Knight (1991) demonstrates too that there are many different subtypes of rapist, with a major dimension to discriminate between them of whether obtaining sex or negative emotional expression is key, suggesting that construal of the act varies widely among the perpetrators of sexual assault.

Scully and Marolla (1984) have argued that "rapists have learned the attitudes and actions consistent with sexual aggression against women" (p. 530) and use their "vocabulary of motive" to explain themselves, especially in terms of normal personal identity. They found in an extensive sociological inquiry involving dozens of convicted rapists that many different types of explanations (e.g., drugs/alcohol involved, denigration of victims) were employed by offenders. One point raised by this research with rapists is that, while there may be larger themes and types of accounts provided by these offenders, the individual and his perspective on his own actions is the very real reference point that should be examined.

Shorts (1985) reported on a single rapist who, over the course of therapy in a forensic hospital, came to view himself as more like men who assault women. His distance from women, however, in terms of both self and ideal self was significant at the beginning and end of treatment. This may reflect what Malamuth and Heilmann (1998) have described as "hostile masculinity", or a very patronizing and aggressive 'machismo', on the part of men who rape. Once again, however, there is a problem in attempting to understand the constructions of rapists as somehow monolithic. While the behaviour may have a common feature, there is no necessary reason why the thinking of the offenders must be common.

Other sexual offenders

There are a variety of other forms of sexual offending, commonly classed as 'nuisance' offences because of a lack of physical contact or at least less physical trauma inflicted on victims. In general, we know little about the offenders. They tend to not be incarcerated for long periods when discovered and adjudicated, and they tend not to step forward on their own for treatment. Thus, very little work from a PCT perspective has been done.

Men who exhibit their genitalia for sexual gratification, so-called 'flashers' or exhibitionists (American Psychiatric Association, 1994), are very seldom studied despite very high offence rates (Mohr, Turner & Jerry, 1964). Landfield and Epting (1987) reported on a single exhibitionist who, when completing a rep grid, had difficulty nominating acquintances, especially women, for specific role titles. Whether this is a common circumstance of these individuals, and whether it is the precursor or effect of the problem, is unknown. One clinical treatment that I (Horley, 1995) conducted with a repeat exhibitionist, only somewhat successfully, showed that this individual viewed himself as a 'pervert' who repeatedly offended in part to strike back at his family. To argue that this personal construal is at the basis of all exhibitionism is premature and facile, and we need to conduct more work in this area.

Those individuals who observe others unknowingly, usually disrobing or engaging in sexual activity, for sexual gratification purposes, or voyeurs (American Psychiatric Association, 1994), are especially difficult to study (i.e., rarely incarcerated or hospitalized). My clients over the years who have engaged in this type of behaviour have never been 'pure types', that is they have had some other form of sexual deviance, especially telephone scatalogia, which is apparently common (Abel, Becker, Cunningham-Rathner, Rouleau, Kaplan & Reich, 1984). My only insight into this sexual deviation is that these men, who view themselves as 'normal' by noting that anyone who consumes 'adult media' (i.e., pornography) or who attends 'exotic shows' (i.e., strip clubs) is voyeuristic, admit to timidity when approaching potential sexual partners. Whether this is the result of a desire for intimidating or domineering partners, or a perceived social deficiency, is not clear to me at this point.

Certainly a number of more exotic forms of sexual deviance, such as frotteurism (American Psychiatric Association, 1994), or the public rubbing against other individuals for sexual gratification, have been examined, albeit infrequently, and rarely from a PCT-perspective. In the case of frotteurism, I (Horley, 2000) have argued that the few frotteurists that I have seen over the years make me wonder about the need for a separate diagnostic category, since these individuals may be timid or would-be rapists. If only to deny a convenient 'medical escape', we should limit such labels until we have more information about the nature of the distinct problem.

Assessment issues with sexual offenders

Assessment of sexual offenders over the past three or four decades has either focused on penile plethysmography or phallometry (Freund & Blanchard, 1989). This psychophysiological assessment technique has proven useful for determination of sexual preference patterns (Quinsey & Earls, 1990), and it provides useful information in some risk assessment strategies (Quinsey, Harris, Rice & Cormier, 1998). Phallometry, however, provides limited information of relevance to general psychological assessment and treatment. Also, as noted by Marshall (1999) and others, it likely distracts attention from psychosocial processes, directing attention to biological processes. While I would not recommend abandoning penile plethysmography, it might be better viewed as an adjunct to other forms of assessment rather than *the* primary assessment tool. The question is: What assessment devices should be used with sexual offenders? A variety of paper-and-pencil questionnaires and scales, with some already mentioned, have been employed in the past for exclusive use with these offenders.

One popular technique for examining the distorted beliefs of child molesters is the Cognition Scale (Abel et al., 1984). Whether the full or modified Cognition Scale, there appear to be some limitations of this device. Horley and Quinsey (1995) failed to find any hypothesized differences using Abel's Cognition Scale because of high top-end loading. Because of the transparency of the items, all expressed very negatively but scored in the reverse, incarcerated molesters in particular may be reluctant to report distortions. This concern and others (see Ward, Hudson, Johnston & Marshall, 1997) led Bumby (1996) to develop a 38-item MOLEST Scale. This assessment of cognitive distortions in child molesters is similar to the Cognition Scale, but items appear to be much more "neutral" in tone (e.g., "Some children can act very seductively.") and may avoid problems encountered by some of those using the Cognition Scale. Preliminary psychometric reports of the internal and test-retest reliabilities of the MOLEST Scale, as well as convergent and discriminative validities, are encouraging (Bumby, 1996), but it is premature to endorse this scale without reservation. Collings (1997), too, has developed a 15-item scale to examine child sexual abuse myths, or really distorted beliefs or cognitions. Again, initial psychometric data for his CSA scale are quite adequate, but further efforts are demanded.

Psychological assessment of rapists has focused on a number of specific issues (e.g., attitudes toward women, belief in rape myths) and has generated development of specific scales and objective techniques. Burt (1980), for example, developed the Rape Myth Inventory, a technique used in many investigations of rapists' particular beliefs and attitudes. With moderate reliabilities and validities, the Rape Myth Inventory appears to be a sound choice *if* an assessor is interested in a narrow range of very specific beliefs concerning rape. It is susceptible, too, like most other scales with high face validity, to deceptive manipulation on the part of the assessee, and needless to say most of the offenders completing such an assessment would have every reason to deceive those interpreting and reading the results of the procedure. A detailed discussion of this issue of deception, and related issue of malingering, is beyond the scope of this chapter (but see Rogers, 1997, for a detailed examination of the problems), but it should concern all forensic psychologists who assess sexual offenders. There appear to be no easy answers at this point in time to counter attempts to deceive.

Use of the Cognition Scale and other specific or narrow focus techniques may be popular, but are they necessarily pointing in the right direction? Broader, more idiographic methods like semantic differentials and rep grids may provide an alternative that requires examination (see Collett, 1980). They appear to suffer from less 'transparency' (i.e., they are more ambiguous and therefore more difficult to fake) than most questionnaires. I have had a very clever offender, an individual not resistant to any psychological assessments in the past, study a rep grid for several minutes, ask me directly what I was looking for, and then refuse to complete the technique – he appeared to have difficulty not in understanding the instructions but rather in reading the intent of the device.

These devices, too, have drawbacks. Both the semantic differential and the rep grid would benefit from more detailed psychometric study (Chambers, 1985), although some writers (e.g., Bannister & Mair, 1968; Fransella & Bannister, 1977) have argued that psychometric criteria such as temporal reliability do not apply to the rep grid because of PCT's assumption concerning the dynamic nature of human personality. The rep grid has been shown to possess moderate reliabilities and validities aside (e.g., Sperlinger, 1976), even with forensic samples (Horley, 1996; Horley & Quinsey, 1995). Such techniques may provide rich, contextualized data in exchange for result complexity and difficulty in interpretation, but this is perhaps one of the problems – many assessors and assessment consumers (e.g., parole boards, judges) are looking for straightforward results that are quick and simple to communicate. Can we assume safely that offenders' constructions about sexual identity and sexual activity – indeed, an individual's personality – are straightforward and simple? If we are only going to look for valid psychological predicates where they are easiest sought, like the proverbial drunk under the street light searching for keys lost elsewhere, it is likely that we will find nothing of value.

Individual and group psychotherapy with sexual offenders

Psychotherapeutic interventions with sexual offenders have varied little over the past half century. Following some tentative treatments based on psychodynamic and humanistic, especially Rogerian, approaches, the majority of the work in this area has becn behavioural since the 1960s. Aversion therapy, systematic desensitization, and satiation techniques are among the behavioural strategies addressing deviant sexual activity. There have been calls for more cognitive perspectives and interventions (Marshall & Barbaree, 1990; Segal & Stermac, 1990), but relatively little work has been done on non-behavioural approaches. In terms of the cognitive work done to date, it appears to be based in general on rationalist approaches – some of the earliest work by Ellis (e.g., Ellis & Brancale, 1956) on rational-emotive therapy was in a correctional setting with sexual offenders from New Jersey. Such rationalist-based forms of therapy, however, are at odds with the constructivist-based treatments (Winter & Watson, 1999).

Constructivist approaches to psychotherapy with sexual offenders, such as those based on PCT (Kelly, 1955), appear to offer much to the field (Horley, 2000; Horley, Quinsey, & Jones, 1997). PCT provided a foundation for a sexual offender treatment programme that I maintained during the early 1990s within the Ontario (Canada) Ministry of Correctional Services. Various forms of psychotherapy consistent with PCT were employed, and an examination of different PCT-related psychotherapies for sexual offenders is in order.

Individual psychotherapy with sex offenders

Fixed-role therapy

The principles of fixed-role therapy (FRT) are well established (Epting, 1984; Kelly, 1955; Winter, 1992), but use of FRT with offenders has not been examined in any detail, even in a recent book on working with offenders from a PCT perspective (Houston, 1998). What will be offered here will be some caveats and warnings about the use of FRT with sexual offenders, particularly in a prison setting.

One difficulty with FRT for sexual offenders involves developing effective fixed-role sketches (i.e., ones that the client can relate to in terms of a workable ideal). Often, offenders' values are difficult for therapists to relate to (i.e., may involve drug abuse, sexual variation, aggression, or other antisocial aspects), although this appears to be less true for sexual offenders who hold less antisocial attitudes than most offenders. To write an effective sketch, however, the client's values need to be considered seriously, although the resulting sketch need not represent an ideal individual. The sketch writer needs to avoid unworkable roles (i.e., those perhaps construed as "straights", "square Johns", or simply "not me, never could be"). Having an experienced 'characterization coach' (e.g., a therapeutic aide or prison trustee, an experienced colleague) to help rough out the basic sketch can be useful, and more than usual feedback from the client while trying out the new character is important. If a very prosocial character with no rough edges is foisted on the client, it will likely result in rejection, either explicit ("Forget it, this isn't anyone I can relate to!") or implicit ("I'm trying, but it's tough getting my head around this guy.").

Another difficulty with FRT in a prison setting, or even certain community-based forensic settings (e.g., half-way house), is limitation of experimentation of the new role. The social and physical environmental conditions of most prisons do not permit the range of experiences that allow for 'behavioural try-outs' of new actions based on new ways of construing. Often, poor substitutes are all that would be available for a client in a prison (e.g., talking to a female guard in an appropriate manner in place of asking a female love interest for a date). In many cases where only poor substitutes were available, especially in maximum-secure facilities, I have relied on imaginary encounters and substantial discussion of how the possessor of the new personality would respond or think.

One critical point to consider when developing and presenting fixed-role sketches is the forensic setting. Some sketches could result in a client's death if enacted in the wrong place, and some prisons are completely the wrong place for someone attempting to become more sensitive to others, concerned about a neighbour's well-being, etc. The 'inmate code', or the unwritten yet prescribed set of acceptable behaviours for prison inmates, needs to be considered. This varies somewhat from facility to facility, but sexual offenders in any facility, even some forensic hospitals, need to conform to the code, especially given their lowly status in the inmate hierarchy. A prudent approach would be to go over the new sketch with the client in extreme detail about possible negative outcomes of implied behaviours from the sketch, expressing warnings wherever necessary. On more than one occasion, I have found it necessary to send a sketch 'home' (i.e., to the street upon release) with a client with a stern warning "Don't try this here". Feedback can then be provided through phone conversations, letters, anonymous communications, or contacts through community-based probation-parole officers or therapists. While this situation is far from ideal, dealing with the frustration on both sides is better than dealing with the death or severe injury that may result from trying to be too therapeutic in an extremely nontherapeutic setting.

Cognitive restructuring

By far the most important and frequent form of individual therapy that I provided to sex offenders in maximum-security facilities was what was termed 'cognitive restructuring'. This term was used in part because offenders saw it as a popular type of treatment and, perhaps more importantly, it was a nonthreatening term. The professional problem with the term is connection with rationalist forms of psychotherapy (e.g., Ellis, 1962), but I tend to use the term 'cognitive' in a broad sense (see Horley, 2000) to include construal processes.

This form of individual psychotherapy is appropriate for situations where FRT or enactment therapies are difficult to use (e.g., maximum-secure facilities) or when clients object to enactment-based approaches. Cognitive restructuring can be an elaborative technique as described by Winter (1992). A client is invited to identify and to explore his own construct system by way of "talking about yourself, your past, and how you think about things". This process inevitably involves addressing a client's inconsistencies, construct system fragments or subsystems, and personal concerns with the intent of allowing him to resolve inconsistencies and to elaborate personal meaning. Clearly there can be some 'slot-rattling' involved, but I do not see changing the use of a particular construct as necessarily insignificant when it comes to personal understanding. Reconstruing oneself as 'thoughtful' versus 'thoughtless' when the outcome might be not raping versus raping another individual is not trivial.

Challenging accounts or understandings of one's life and actions are part of the process of cognitive restructuring but, because this is not a rationalistic therapy, there is no 'name-calling' or 'finger-pointing' with respect to a client's account of events. Indeed, much of my work in this field is spent examining and, in many cases, attempting to disabuse the client of many negative labels or 'names' that others, especially therapists, have placed on him (e.g., homosexual pedophile, psychopath, paranoid schizophrenic). Use of guilt in the Kellian sense, and even displacement from negative core roles (e.g., 'solid con'), can be an important tool in getting an offender to reconstrue himself and relations with others. What is vital is that the offender is allowed to express himself (i.e., his views are respected) and is given hope for change, accepting that both respect and hope are experienced all too seldom in many prisons.

One potential problem in cognitive restructuring involves self-pity. Due to the abuse and violence, emotional as well as physical, of typical correctional settings, and in part due to the victimization experienced by many sexual offenders, there is a tendency to indulge in self-pity and the construction or reconstruction of one-self as victim. This is a difficult line to walk, but allowing a client to express feelings of victimization is important while at the same time keeping the present concern of 'self as victimizer' salient for the client. This can be maintained by pointed questions and comments, and in general by keeping discussion focused on the problems at hand. Often personal abuse experiences that require further attention can be handled by telling the client that such issues can be dealt with upon release or with another therapist.

The problem of self-pity involves a larger issue of directiveness in this therapy. While the client must be left to tell his story and express his perspective, anti-social statements cannot go unchallenged lest silence be construed as validation, and many sex offenders are adept at finding or extorting validation. As described by a number of authors (e.g., Andrews & Bonta, 1998), the most effective forensic counsellors appear to be firm in accepting only prosocial comments. This may seem to compromise a complete acceptance of a client's perspective that PCT expects (Chin-Keung, 1988; Winter & Watson, 1999), but the therapist must also consider the 'other', whether a victim or any potential victim (i.e., all members of society), in a therapeutic encounter. Challenges do not have to be abrupt verbal assaults (e.g., "You're wrong there!") but can be requests to examine particular statements (e.g., "Do you really believe that women like rough sex and like to be forced?"). The distinction here may be fine but important.

Covert sensitization

Since initial development and introduction by Cautela (1966), covert sensitization as a therapeutic technique has been viewed as either strictly behavioural or cognitive behavioural. I would suggest that it can be construed as constructivistic, albeit loosely so. The procedure involves having a client imagine a negative outcome to an event that typically involved positive outcomes. When involving sex offender clients, the technique is often used in conjunction with phallometric assessment as a form of sexual preference reassignment therapy (see Quinsey & Earls, 1990) when the client is aroused by a negative stimulus (e.g., a sexual assault). This does assume that a client is aroused by an inappropriate sexual object (e.g., prepubescent child) or activity (e.g., rape) which includes only a minority of sexual offenders. The client is briefed about his role in the session, and the therapist takes on the role of a 'thought coach' who suggests a number of images or useful ideas. Tactics may expand beyond focusing on the negative outcomes of the imagined situation (e.g., disease, death, incarceration) to include the particular negative feelings and thoughts of the offender in the situation (e.g., embarrassment at return to prison). One approach that appears helpful is use of Kellian guilt in terms of helping the client see how he might feel if he were to engage in offensive acts inconsistent with existing or new core role constructs.

In my work with sex offenders, covert sensitization is useful in particular with developmentally delayed or brain-damaged clients, especially serious solvent and alcohol abusers. The procedure gives them a concrete act (viz., penile arousal to a negative event) and a relatively concrete connecting event. So long as the focus of the procedure is on thoughts or construal processes rather than on genital responses, the technique is available to constructivists. While a therapist may be altering sexual preference patterns by using such a procedure, the underlying change involves a construct shift reinforced or maintained by a negative event.

Group psychotherapy with sex offenders

Problem identification

Developed as a general first step for offenders interested in some help with psychological problems, problem identification is intended to provide a supportive environment for sexual offenders to discuss their lives, personal difficulties, and construct systems in order to receive feedback from therapist(s) and peers. As such, it has been operated as a process-oriented group that is a first step rather than an end in itself. Clients (usually six to eight per rota-tion, closed group) are allowed to speak without fear of attack (i.e., there is no 'hot seat', insults, physical contact), although questioning and challenge is encouraged. Each group member is permitted over two weeks (or eight hours of group time) to 'tell his story' through a detailed and coherent autobiographical account or simply recounting specific episodes that are construed as mean-ingful for some reason. The group composition that seems to work best is a homogenous one with respect to offence – in fact, the more homogeneity the better (e.g., all child molesters with offences involving male victims) – and client background. The pitfall that has been noted with this arrangement is 'alliances' where indi-viduals band together to support each other and to validate each others' deviant perspectives. While this is a real danger, it can be countered by challenges to all potential allies at the first sign of such a possibility.

A problem with any form of group psychotherapy with sex offenders, especially in a correctional institution, is fear of physical retribution by virtue of being identified as a sex offender. This is minimized by the generic and relatively benign title of this group, but the issue of confidentiality of information is important in any group such as this. The main intent of this group is to allow individuals to examine and to 'troubleshoot', usually in very pre-liminary ways, their construct systems (i.e., elaborative technique). A very comfortable environment is required. Dropouts from this group (usually 25 per cent) seem to result from an inability of individuals to feel secure enough with other participants and/or therapists to participate. The main short-term benefits of this group approach to treatment include a sense of not being alone ("I'm not the only one with this kind of problem") and a sense of hope concerning the ability to change. It appears too common that sexual offenders, whatever their particular offences, are labelled negatively by medical authorities, or individuals using medical terminology, that imply a long-term genetic 'etiology' with a poor 'prognosis' for their 'condition' that makes change very unlikely.

Relapse prevention

Relapse prevention is a popular form of therapy, typically in group format, borrowed from the alcohol treatment area. It is used by various therapists, including those who work with sex offenders (see

Laws, 1989). It is described as a cognitive-behavioural approach to helping clients recognize how and why problem behaviours occur and how to avoid repetition. The language or jargon of relapse prevention is extensive, and aspects of different programmes do vary, but I will show how I have approached relapse work.

The relapse prevention group that I have run for sex offenders in a prison setting involved biweekly meetings over a 12-week period. A number of topics for discussion were presented that included the notion of offence chains, the role of negative emotion in sexual offending, victim impact/empathy, developing helping networks, informed decision-making, and avoiding high-risk situations. Homework in the form of mock letters to victims and decision-making exercises was an aspect of the treatment. Most individuals became involved in this group just prior to release; hence it was viewed more as an attempt to consolidate gains made throughout other aspects of their treatment.

My emphasis in relapse prevention is not on behaviour per se, or on the didactic 'information' to prevent reoffence, although there is inevitably discussion of behaviour and reinforcement with a clear didactic emphasis at times. Rather, the discussions about 'thoughts and feelings' in offence chains and concern for oneself rather than others are highlighted and form a central theme throughout the group meetings. Allowing individual offenders in a setting where they can receive prompting as well as support to explore how their own constructions of the world can lead directly to inappropriate actions is the key to relapse prevention. One major problem with this approach can occur if insufficient time is spent exploring the connections between how our views of people and the world lead to behavioural 'experiments' – often relapse prevention becomes a lecture or even harangue about the obvious cues that offenders are unable or unwilling to pick up in order to avoid negative behaviours. Lecturing and berating offenders, whether in a group or individually, is not therapeutic and is unlikely to lead to personal change. A group like relapse prevention needs to proceed with respect for the construal processes of all individuals.

General and concluding comments

A PCT account of the various forms of sexual offending is only now emerging, and much more work, both theoretical and empirical, is demanded. While the studies done to date from formal PCT-informed and related perspectives have not produced consistent findings, at least we have some suggestions of profitable directions of study.

There appears to be increasing agreement concerning some findings in the area of child molesters' cognitions. One robust finding concerns fantasy, especially deviant sexual fantasy. Child molesters appear to fantasize about their offences prior to the actual behaviour. This may be more true for obsessed or preferential molesters than situational or regressed offenders, but such a state-of-affairs has yet to be established. Reduction or elimination of deviant fantasy, and replacement by more appropriate images, should be a target of treatment programmes for child molesters.

The question of child molesters' thoughts about themselves, particularly concerning self-worth and self-esteem, is very much that, a question. Child molesters may see themselves as undesirable or less than adequate individuals, as Marshall and Mazzucco (1995) would argue, but molesters may only perceive and report lack of attractiveness or sexual adequacy, and even this might be more true for molesters with male victims rather than female victims. Whatever the case, negative self-image may provide the basis for the relatively consistent behavioural finding that many child molesters display or report shyness or difficulty in social interaction (Quinsey, 1986; Salter, 1988). The importance of assessing and altering thoughts about inadequacy or lack of social/ sexual efficacy is indicated.

Social cognitive research into child molesters' attributional processes has found, not surprisingly, that molesters tend to have difficulty accounting for their sexually deviant behaviour. Many ascribe their offences to alcohol abuse. In sociological terms, their deviance disavowal is understandable as an attempt to appear more normal sexually than they in fact behave. More detailed studies examining differences among molesters need to be done. Such work may reveal, for example, that practicing heterosexual males who molest young boys need to engage in more 'mental gymnastics', and experience more accompanying anxiety, in order to explain themselves because they have more perceived deviance to disavow or to account for. Assessment of causal attributions of sexually inappropriate behaviour is helpful in programming, and it serves as a specific therapeutic target in treatment.

At this point, it seems clear that many child molesters hold some distorted beliefs about adult–child sex or what constitute appropriate relationships with children. How many molesters who hold what types of unacceptable beliefs, however, is not known. Whether certain types of distorted beliefs about sexuality are more serious, or are more likely to trigger sexually offensive behaviour, than others remains unanswered as well. The types of distorted cognition by types of offender (e.g., male versus female victim, amount of force or sadistic behaviour in assault) demand examination.

The adequacy of some of the techniques we use to assess beliefs, attitudes, values, distorted cognitions, personal constructs, or any number of other cognitive propositions, processes, or products are certainly open to question too. Doubts have been raised about the usefulness of the Cognition Scale, but more work needs to be done on alternatives (e.g., MOLEST Scale, CSA scale). The semantic differential and rep grid are two methodologies, as opposed to specific scales, that have been used in a variety of studies but, because they represent general methodological approaches, specific content needs to be identified. To do this, more informed 'hunches' or clinical insights are needed. The lack of overarching theory, and theoretical hypotheses, however, restrict us here.

Work on rapists and other sexual offenders tends to be very limited. Simple perspectives, such as the Madonna-prostitute complex, are unlikely to provide significant progress. Much more theoretical and methodological consideration must be applied, especially at the level of understanding individual offenders, if we are to realize advances here.

A multimodal approach to treatment programming has been advocated not only within psychotherapeutic circles broadly (e.g., Lazarus, 1971) but within the treatment of sex offenders narrowly (e.g., Marshall & Barbaree, 1988; Quinsey, 1977). This appears particularly appropriate because we should not view categories of sex offenders (e.g., child molesters) as homogenous and requiring a single form of intervention, let alone all sex offenders as homogenous. Offering a variety of different types of psychotherapy can assist clients in addressing a range of personal problems, and it is clear that many factors can influence certain sexual problems (e.g., exhibiting genitalia for sexual gratification). Many of my clients are involved typically in drug and alcohol rehabilitation, life skills' training, and anger management in addition to one or more components of my programme. Although treatment resources are scarce, and this seems to be especially true in forensic settings in most jurisdictions, it appears to be worthwhile to scramble for the resources to provide a range or choice of services to clients who have committed sex offences. These programmes would be particularly welcome at the community level (see Chapter 6, this volume). Community-based programmes seem to be maximally effective (Andrews & Bonta, 1998). Prison-based treatments are hampered by the nontherapeutiveness of the setting – many of my incarcerated clients have pointed out to me that "There is no correction in Corrections!" – and months of therapeutic gains can be wiped out in minutes on a prison range (but see Chapter 7, this volume).

Constructivist psychotherapists, especially PCT psychotherapists, need to enter the field of forensic practice to develop new forms of treatment for sexual offenders for a number of reasons. One important reason concerns the humanization of treatment offered to sexual offenders. Much of what passes for treatment currently (e.g., confrontational groups, forced acceptance of psychiatric labels) is more akin to torture than treatment. Often, it appears to be conducted to exorcize therapists' demons rather than assist clients. Although we may not condone or accept the behaviours of our forensic clients (c.f., Chin-Keung, 1988), we can at least understand their situations, and understand that future victims will only be prevented to the extent that we can reach and help the clients to reorder their lives. Directiveness and prosocial modelling appears to be a part of effective forensic therapy (Andrews & Bonta, 1998), but the extreme directiveness of rationalist therapies (e.g., Ellis, 1962) and confrontational approaches, in contrast to the less directiveness of PCT therapies (see Winter & Watson, 1999), may not be maximally effective. They certainly are not as humane, and we as psychotherapists who work with sexual offenders need to demonstrate humanity to our clients if we are to expect them to demonstrate it later.

References

Abel, G. G., Becker, J. V., & Cunningham-Rathner, J. (1984). Complications, consent, and cognitions in sex between children and adults. *International Journal of Law and Psychiatry*, 7, 89–103.

Abel, G. G., Becker, J. V., Cunningham-Rathner, J., Rouleau, J. L., Kaplan, M., & Reich, J. (1984). *The treatment of child molesters*. Atlanta: Behavioral Medicine Laboratory.

Abel, G. G., Becker, J. V., Cunningham-Rathner, J., Mittelman, M., & Rouleau, J. (1988). Multiple paraphilic diagnoses among sex offenders. *Bulletin of the American Academy of Psychiatry and the Law*, *16*, 153–168.

Abel, G. G., & Blanchard, E. B. (1974). The role of fantasy in the treatment of sexual deviation. *Archives of General Psychiatry*, *30*, 467–475.

American Psychiatric Association (1994). *Diagnostic and statistical manual* (4th edition). Washington: American Psychiatric Association.

Andrews, D. A., & Bonta, J. (1998). *The psychology of criminal conduct*. Cincinnatti, OH: Anderson.

Andrews, D. A., & Wormith, J. S. (1990). *A summary of normative, reliability, and validity statistics on the Criminal Sentiments Scale*. Unpublished manuscript, Carleton University, Ottawa.

Bandura, A. (1971). Psychotherapy based upon modeling principles. In A. E. Bergin & S. L. Garfield (Eds.), *Handbook of psychotherapy and behavior change: An empirical analysis* (pp. 241–279). New York: John Wiley & Sons.

Bandura, A. (1982). Self-efficacy mechanism in personal agency. *American Psychologist*, *37*, 122–147.

Bandura, A. (1986). *Social foundations in thought and action: A social cognitive theory*. Englewood Cliffs, NJ: Prentice-Hall.

Bannister, D., & Mair, J. M. M. (1968). *The evaluation of personal constructs*. London: Academic Press.

Barbaree, H. (1989). *Denial and minimization among adolescent and adult sexual offenders*. Invited paper presented at the Conference on the Adolescent Sexual Offender, Vancouver, November.

Bell, A. P., & Hall, C. S. (1971). *The personality of a child molester: An analysis of dreams*. Chicago: Aldine.

Borzecki, M., & Wormith, S. J. (1987). A survey of treatment programmes for sex offenders in North America. *Canadian Psychology*, *28*, 30–44.

Bumby, K. M. (1996). Assessing the cognitive distortions of child molesters and rapists: Development and validation of the RAPE and MOLEST scales. *Sexual Abuse: A Journal of Research and Treatment*, *8*, 37–54.

Burt, M. R. (1980). Cultural myths and supports for rape. *Journal of Personality and Social Psychology*, *38*, 217–230.

Carnahan, T. E. (1987). *Rapists' perceptions of women: A repertory grid study*. Unpublished B.A. (Honours) thesis, University of Guelph, Guelph, Canada, April.

Cautela, J. R. (1966). Treatment of compulsive behavior by covert sensitization. *Psychological Record*, *16*, 33–41.

Chambers, W. V. (1985). Measurement error and changes in personal constructs. *Social Behavior and Personality*, *13*, 29–32.

Chin-Keung, L. (1988). PCT interpretation of sexual involvement with children. In F. Fransella & L. Thomas (Eds.), *Experimenting with personal construct psychology* (pp. 273–286). London: Routledge & Kegan Paul.

Collett, P. (1980). The repertory grid in psychological research. In G. P. Ginsburg (Ed.), *Emerging strategies in social psychological research* (pp. 225–252). London: John Wiley & Sons.

Collings, S. J. (1997). Development, reliability, and validity of the child sexual abuse myth scale. *Journal of Interpersonal Violence, 12,* 665–674.

Cox, D. J., & Maletzky, B. M. (1980). Victims of exhibitionism. In D. J. Cox & R. J. Daitzman (Eds.), *Exhibitionism: Description, Assessment, and Treatment* (pp. 289–293). New York: Garland STM Press.

Dingman, H. F., Frisbie, L., & Vanasek, F. J. (1968). Erosion of morale in resocialization of pedophiles. *Psychological Reports, 23,* 792–794.

Ellis, A. (1962). *Reason and emotion in psychotherapy.* New York: Lyle Stuart.

Ellis, A., & Brancale, R. (1956). *The psychology of sex offenders.* Springfield: Thomas.

Epting, F. R. (1984). *Personal construct counseling and psychotherapy.* New York: John Wiley & Sons.

Fransella, F., & Bannister, D. (1977). *A manual for repertory grid technique.* London: Academic Press.

Fraser, M. (1976). *The death of Narcissus.* London: Secker & Warburg.

Freud, S. (1975). *Three essays on the theory of sexuality.* New York: Basic Books. (Original work published 1905)

Freund, K., & Blanchard, R. (1989). Phallometric diagnosis of pedophilia. *Journal of Consulting and Clinical Psychology, 57,* 100–105.

Frisbie, L. V., Vanasek, F. J., & Dingman, H. F. (1967). The self and the ideal self: Methodological study of pedophiles. *Psychological Reports, 20,* 699–706.

Hayashino, D. S., Wurtele, S. K., & Klebe, K. J. (1995). Child molesters: An examination of cognitive factors. *Journal of Interpersonal Violence, 10,* 106–116.

Horley, J. (1988). Cognitions of child sexual abusers. *Journal of Sex Research, 25,* 542–545.

Horley, J. (1995). Cognitive-behavior therapy with an incarcerated exhibitionist. *International Journal of Offender Therapy and Comparative Criminology, 39,* 335–339.

Horley, J. (1996). Content stability in the repertory grid: An examination using a forensic sample. *International Journal of Offender Therapy and Comparative Criminology, 40,* 26–31.

Horley, J. (2000). Cognitions supportive of child molestation. *Aggression and Violent Behavior: A Review Journal, 5,* 551–564.

Horley, J., & Quinsey, V. L. (1994). Assessing the cognitions of child molesters: Use of the semantic differential with incarcerated offenders. *Journal of Sex Research, 31*, 187–195.

Horley, J., & Quinsey, V. L. (1995). Child molesters' construal of themselves, other adults, and children. *Journal of Constructivist Psychology, 8*, 193–211.

Horley, J., Quinsey, V. L., & Jones, S. (1997). Incarcerated child molesters' perceptions of themselves and others. *Sexual Abuse: A Journal of Research and Treatment, 9*, 43–55.

Houston, J. (1998). *Making sense with offenders: Personal constructs, therapy and change.* Chichester: John Wiley & Sons.

Houston, J., Thomson, P., & Wragg, J. (1994). A survey of forensic psychologists' work with sex offenders in England and Wales. *Criminal Behaviour and Mental Health, 4*, 118–129.

Howells, K. (1979). Some meanings of children for pedophiles. In M. Cook & G. Wilson (Eds.), *Love and attraction* (pp. 519–526). Oxford: Pergamon.

Howells, K. (1981). Adult sexual interest in children: Considerations relevant to theories of aetiology. In M. Cook & K. Howells (Eds.) *Adult sexual interest in children* (pp. 55–94). London: Academic.

Johnston, L., & Ward, T. (1996). Social cognition and sexual offending: A theoretical framework. *Sexual Abuse: A Journal of Research and Treatment, 8*, 55–80.

Johnston, L., Hudson, S. J., & Ward, T. (1997). The suppression of sexual thoughts by child molesters: A preliminary study. *Sexual Abuse: A Journal of Research and Treatment, 9*, 303–319.

Kelly, G. A. (1955). *The psychology of personal constructs* (2 vols.). New York: W. W. Norton.

Kelly, G. A. (1969). Ontological acceleration. In B. Maher (Ed.), *Clinical psychology and personality: The selected papers of George Kelly* (pp. 7–45). New York: John Wiley & Sons.

Kelly, G. A. (1970). Behavior is an experiment. In D. Bannister (Ed.) *Perspectives in personal construct theory* (pp. 255–269). London: Academic Press.

Landfield, A. W. (1971). *Personal construct systems in psychotherapy.* Chicago: Rand McNally.

Landfield, A. W., & Epting, F. R. (1987). *Personal construct psychology: Clinical and personality assessment.* New York: Human Sciences.

Lanyon, R. I. (1986). Theory and treatment in child molestation. *Journal of Consulting and Clinical Psychology, 54*, 176–182.

Laws, D. R. (Ed.) (1989). *Relapse prevention with sex offenders.* New York: Guilford Press.

Laws, D. R., & Marshall, W. L. (1990). A conditioning theory of the etiology and maintenance of deviant sexual preference and behavior. In

W. L. Marshall, D. R. Laws, & H. E. Barbaree (Eds.), *Handbook of sexual assault* (pp. 209–230). New York: Plenum.

Lazarus, A. A. (1971). *Behavior therapy and beyond.* New York: McGraw-Hill.

McCaghy, C. H. (1967). Child molesters: A study of their careers as deviants. In M. Clinnard & R. Quinney (Eds.), *Criminal behavior systems: A typology* (pp. 75–88). New York: Holt, Rinehart, Winston.

McCaghy, C. H. (1968). Drinking and deviance disavowal: The case of child molesters. *Social Problems, 16,* 43–49.

MacCulloch, M. J., Snowden, P. R., Wood, P. J. W., & Mills, H. E. (1983). Sadistic fantasy, sadistic behavior, and offending. *British Journal of Psychiatry, 143,* 20–29.

Malamuth, N. M., & Heilmann, M. F. (1998). Evolutionary psychology and sexual aggression. In C. Crawford & D. L. Krebs (Eds.), *Handbook of evolutionary psychology: Ideas, issues, and applications* (pp. 515–542). Hove, UK: Lawrence Erlbaum Associates Ltd.

Marks, I. M., & Sartorius, N. H. (1967). A contribution to the measurement of sexual attitude. *Journal of Nervous and Mental Disease, 145,* 441–451.

Marshall, W. L. (1973). The modification of sexual fantasies: A combined treatment approach to the reduction of deviant sexual behavior. *Behaviour Research and Therapy, 11,* 557–564.

Marshall, W. L. (1999). Diagnosing and treating sexual offenders. In A. K. Hess & I. B. Weiner (Eds.), *The handbook of forensic psychology* (pp. 640–760). New York: John Wiley & Sons.

Marshall, W. L., & Barbaree, H. E. (1988). An outpatient treatment program for child molesters. In R. A. Prentky & V. L. Quinsey (Eds.), *Human sexual aggression: Current perspectives* (pp. 205–214). New York: Annals of the New York Academy of Sciences.

Marshall, W. L., & Barbaree, H. E. (1990). An integrated theory of the etiology of sexual offending. In W. L. Marshall, D. R. Laws, & H. E. Barbaree (Eds.), *Handbook of sexual assault* (pp. 257–278). New York: Plenum.

Marshall, W. L., & Mazzucco, A. (1995). Self-esteem and parental attachments of child molesters. *Sexual Abuse: A Journal of Research and Treatment, 7,* 279–285.

Marshall, W. L., Jones, R., Ward, T., Johnston, P., & Barbaree, H. E. (1991). Treatment outcome with sex offenders. *Clinical Psychology Review, 11,* 465–485.

Masson, J. M. (1984). *The assault on truth: Freud's suppression of the seduction theory.* New York: Farrar, Straus, and Giroux.

Mathis, J. L. (1971). The madonna-prostitute syndrome. *Medical Aspects of Human Sexuality, 5,* 202–209.

Mohr, J. W., Turner, R. E., & Jerry, M. B. (1964). *Pedophilia and Exhibitionism*. Toronto: University of Toronto Press.

Nelson, M. C. (1988). Reliability, validity, and cross-cultural comparisons for the simplified Attitudes Toward Women Scale. *Sex Roles, 18*, 289–296.

O'Conner, A. (1987). Female sex offenders. *British Journal of Psychiatry, 150*, 615–620.

Osgood, C. E., Suci, G. J., & Tannenbaum, P. (1957). *The measurement of meaning*. Urbana, IL: University of Illinois Press.

Prentky, R. A., & Knight, R. A. (1991). Identifying critical dimensions for discriminating among rapists. *Journal of Consulting and Clinical Psychology, 59*, 643–661.

Quinsey, V. L. (1977). The assessment and treatment of child molesters: A review. *Canadian Psychological Review, 18*, 204–220.

Quinsey, V. L. (1986). Men who have sex with children. In D. N. Weisstub (Ed.), *Law and mental health: International perspectives* (Vol. 2, pp. 140–172). New York: Pergamon.

Quinsey, V. L., & Earls, C. (1990). The modification of sexual preferences. In W. L. Marshall, D. R. Laws, & H. E. Barbaree (Eds.), *Handbook of sexual assault* (pp. 279–293). New York: Plenum Press.

Quinsey, V. L., Bergersen, S. G., & Steinman, C. M. (1976). Changes in physiological and verbal responses of child molesters during aversion therapy. *Canadian Journal of Behavioural Science, 8*, 202–212.

Quinsey, V. L., Harris, G. T., Rice, M. E., & Cormier, C. A. (1998). *Violent offenders: Appraising and managing risk*. Washington: American Psychological Association.

Rada, R. T. (1978). Psychological factors in rapist behaviour. In R. T. Rada (Ed.), *Clinical aspects of the rapist* (pp. 21–58). New York: Grune & Stratton.

Rogers, R. (Ed.) (1997). *Clinical assessment of malingering and deception*. New York: Guilford Press.

Salter, A. C. (1988). *Treating child sex offenders and victims: A practical guide*. Beverly Hills, CA: Sage.

Scully, D., & Marolla, J. (1984). Convicted rapists' vocabulary of motive: Excuses and justifications. *Social Problems, 31*, 530–544.

Segal, Z. V., & Stermac, L. E. (1990). The role of cognition in sexual assault. In W. L. Marshall, D. R. Laws, & H. E. Barbaree (Eds.), *Handbook of sexual assault* (pp. 161–176). New York: Plenum.

Shorts, I. D. (1985). Treatment of a sex offender in a maximum security forensic hospital: Detecting changes in personality and interpersonal construing. *International Journal of Offender Therapy and Comparative Criminology, 29*, 237–250.

Sperlinger, D. J. (1976). Aspects of stability in the repertory grid. *British Journal of Medical Psychology, 49*, 341–347.

Stermac, L. E., & Segal, Z. V. (1989). Adult sexual contact with children: An examination of cognitive factors. *Behavior Therapy*, *20*, 573–584.

Taylor, L. (1972). The significance and interpretation of replies to motivational questions: The case of the sex offender. *Sociology*, *6*, 24–39.

Ward, T., Hudson, S. M., & France, K. G. (1994). Self-reported reasons for offending behavior in child molesters. *Annals of Sex Research*, *6*, 139–148.

Ward, T., Hudson, S. M., & Marshall, W. L. (1994). The abstinence violation effect in child molesters. *Behavior Research and Therapy*, *32*, 431–437.

Ward, T., McCormack, J., & Hudson, S. M. (1997). Sexual offenders perceptions of their intimate relationships. *Sexual Abuse: A Journal of Research and Treatment*, *9*, 57–74.

Ward, T., Hudson, S. M., Johnston, L., & Marshall, W. L. (1997). Cognitive distortions in sex offenders: An integrative review. *Clinical Psychology Review*, *17*, 479–507.

Ward, T., Louden, K., Hudson, S. M., & Marshall, W. L. (1995). A descriptive model of the offense chain for child molesters. *Journal of Interpersonal Violence*, *10*, 452–472.

Wilson, G. D., & Cox, D. N. (1983a). Personality of paedophile club members. *Personality and Individual Differences*, *4*, 323–329.

Wilson, G. D., & Cox, D. N. (1983b). *The child-lovers: A study of paedophiles in society*. London: Peter Owen.

Winter, D. A. (1988). Reconstructing an erection and elaborating ejaculation: Personal construct theory perspectives on sex therapy. *International Journal of Personal Construct Psychology*, *1*, 42–53.

Winter, D. A. (1992). *Personal construct psychology in clinical practice: Theory, research and applications*. London: Routledge.

Winter, D. A., & Watson, S. (1999). Personal construct psychotherapy and the cognitive therapies: Different in theory but can they be differentiated in practice? *Journal of Constructivist Psychology*, *12*, 1–22.

Chapter 4

Mentally disordered offenders

Julia C. Houston

Introduction

The term "mentally disordered offenders" is a generic one, used in both clinical and legal settings to describe offenders with a mental illness, psychopathic or other severe personality disorder, or learning disability. This umbrella term clearly describes heterogeneous groups of individuals. The chapter therefore addresses mental illness and personality disorder separately, beginning by discussing the relationship with offending. The chapter reviews the research on the personal construct theory (PCT) perspective on mental illness and personality disorder, focusing on what is known about both the structure and content of construing of those individuals. For those who go on to offend, the PCT approach is particularly useful in understanding the meanings of their behaviour. Clinical applications of the PCT approach with these client groups are discussed, with one particular case example illustrated in detail.

Offenders diagnosed with a mental disorder have historically been treated differently by the legal system compared to those who are considered to be 'responsible' for their behaviour, and many such offenders receive a psychiatric or non-custodial disposal at court to reflect this. In most Western and many other countries, the provision of secure hospital facilities for mentally disordered offenders is well established. In the UK, about 2000 mentally disordered offenders are detained in the four maximum security ('Special') hospitals and there are also about 2000 beds in smaller, medium secure psychiatric units. Other mentally disordered offenders are managed in open psychiatric hospitals, therapeutic communities, specialist hospital wings in prison, or in the community.

Similar provision for mentally disordered offenders is found in North America (Kerr & Roth, 1986) and Europe (Koenraadt, 1992). Assessment and treatment facilities vary in the degree to which they are specialized in either mental illness or personality disorder, or accept both client groups under the generic 'mental disorder' umbrella. However, as will be discussed in the rest of the chapter, individuals who are diagnosed with the two different labels have widely differing difficulties and treatment needs, and this is increasingly reflected in treatment provision.

Mental illness and offending

The relationship between different kinds of mental disorder and criminal or violent behaviour is complex, and early studies were fraught with definitional and methodological problems. The relationship between current and specific symptoms of mental illness is now recognized to be more relevant in contributing to the relationship with violence, rather than diagnosis per se (Monahan, 2000). However, the recent review by Blumenthal and Lavender (2000) concluded that although some researchers have found symptoms associated with threat, the overriding of personal controls or thought insertion to account for violence by individuals with severe mental disorder, other studies are inconclusive. Social, interpersonal, and environmental factors are also recognized as dynamic risk factors which contribute to the likelihood of future violence, and substance abuse is a more robust predictor than mental illness. It is therefore important for clinicians working with mentally ill offenders not to assume a sole causative relationship between the mental illness and the offending, and to assess the contributory role of relevant personality factors.

The PCT perspective on mental illness

Kelly (1955/1991) was very critical of the medical model. He did not construe clients' difficulties in terms of pathology or traditional nosological categories as he considered this to represent pre-emptive construing by professionals (i.e., assumptive and rigid). However, he accepted that clients' difficulties *could* be construed in physical terms, as well as psychological, and suggested that clinicians might be more effective if they routinely applied both psychological and physiological construct systems at the outset of assessment, rather than applying one only after the other has been shown to be inadequate. His view was that the primary determinant of whether a problem should be approached physiologically or psychologically should be pragmatic, and relate to the client's likely response to the different types of intervention.

The PCT perspective not does not therefore discount the potential contribution of physiology or biochemistry to symptoms which are considered diagnostic of mental illness. However, personal construct theorists emphasize the ways in which the structure and content of a person's construing have led to them behaving in such a way as to be diagnosed as mentally ill. The PCT approach to understanding mental illness has a long tradition, dating back to the pioneering work of Bannister and colleagues in the 1960s, focusing on clients diagnosed with schizophrenia. Personal construct theory suggests a theoretical model of thought disorder, developed from Kelly's original proposal that the thinking of some clients diagnosed as schizophrenic is characterized by loose construing. Loose constructs are those which lead to variable predictions, and schizophrenic thought disorder is seen as a state in which constructs have largely ceased to have strong stable relationships with each other. This means that 'meaning' is changeable and verbal labels simply become 'noise'. Bannister (1962) states that the lack of any pattern in construing means that "the thought-disordered schizophrenic is left occupying a fluid, undifferentiated, subjective universe" (p. 833). The lack of constellation between constructs means that it is difficult for the person with schizophrenia to make useful unidirectional predictions about future events. However, this very looseness also means that the person cannot be wrong, as the lack of association between constructs means that apparent inconsistencies can always be 'explained' or accommodated.

The PCT perspective has also been applied to other diagnoses of mental illness. For example, clients diagnosed as paranoid have been viewed as having a structural disorder involving *dilation* of the construct system (Winter, 1992). Dilation is a means by which a person deals with apparent incompatibilities in their construing, by broadening their view of the world, and seeing new links between events or aspects of their life (Kelly, 1955/1991). However, this is only possible if the person has an existing superordinate structure in their construct system which can accommodate the new dilated field. The delusions of people who are diagnosed as paranoid may therefore represent a sweeping elaboration of a persecutory or grandiose construction. In other words, as proposed by Kelly (1955/1991), the so-called fictitious perception of the client may often turn out to be a distorted construction of something that really does exist.

Patterns of construing in people with a mental illness

There is a large body of research on the *structure* of construing in people diagnosed with schizophrenia, and this is comprehensively reviewed by Winter (1992) and Pierce, Sewell and Cromwell, (1992). The origin of this work was in the series of studies carried out by Bannister and Fransella (Bannister, 1960, 1962; Bannister & Fransella, 1966, 1967), which defined thought disorder operationally in terms of repertory grid methodology. Most of this work used the Bannister-Fransella Grid Test which required subjects to rank eight photographs of people on six supplied constructs (e.g., kind, selfish) and then to repeat the task again as if they were doing it for the first time. The grids of thought disordered subjects were characterized by both low correlations between constructs and low consistency of the pattern of relationships between constructs when the grids were repeated. Thought disorder was therefore defined as grossly loosened construing, with the inevitable and simultaneous lowering of both *Intensity* (i.e., how tightly the construct system is organized) and *Consistency* (i.e., the relationship between constructs over time). Later studies indicated that looseness of construing was more evident with psychological constructs (e.g., 'Trusting vs Not trusting') compared to non-psychological (e.g., 'Old vs Young') and that it is particularly *people*, rather than objects, that the thought disordered person finds difficult to understand and predict (McPherson, Blackburn, Daffan & McFayden, 1973).

Having established that loose construing was a characteristic feature of thought disorder, Bannister (1963, 1965) then used the Grid Test to test his *serial invalidation* hypothesis of how people become thought disordered. He found that if a person is faced with repeated invalidation of part of their construct sub-system for viewing people, they begin to alter and eventually loosen the pattern of relationships between their constructs. Conversely, repeated validation (i.e., confirmation of expectations) leads to an intensification of the linkages between constructs until the system becomes simple and monolithic. Bannister and Fransella (1986) noted that the serial invalidation hypothesis could be related to those psychological theories of the origins of schizophrenic thought disorder which emphasize the role of inconsistent and incompatible messages within the family (e.g., Lidz, 1964). The serial invalidation hypothesis could also be considered relevant to the more recent emphasis on the role of expressed emotion (EE) in families as a predictor of schizophrenic relapse (e.g., Kavanagh, 1992).

Winter (1992) reviews the subsequent debate in the literature which has focused on Bannister's interpretation of his results in terms of loose construing. Although many studies have since supported his earlier work, critics have suggested that the performance of thought disordered schizophrenics on the Grid Test is merely a reflection of their inconsistency of performance on all cognitive tasks due to attentional deficits (Harrison & Phillips, 1979). Other authors have suggested that thought disordered schizophrenics lack the superordinate linkages (i.e., more complex constructs which are higher up in the hierarchical structure) which allow most normal people to resolve inconsistencies in their experiences (Space & Cromwell, 1978). However, despite the differing views of authors about the precise nature of the structural characteristics of construing which contribute to the schizophrenic process, there are areas of agreement which link the different interpretations together. Another important finding from the Bannister studies was that the construct systems of thought disordered schizophrenics were also *socially deviant* in terms of *content*. The clinical histories of the research patients indicated that they had not moved straight from 'normality' to 'thought disorder', but had progressed first through a phase in which they were described as 'paranoid' or 'deluded' or 'manifesting bizarre behaviour', indicating that gross disturbances of content in the construct system had occurred before the final disintegration of the structure. In other words, the nature of the process underlying the development of thought disorder is that the construct system becomes odd before it becomes weak. There are therefore different responses to the experience of invalidation. Some individuals remain at the stage in which merely the content of their construing is altered, and maintain a 'paranoid integration', whilst others proceed to structural breakdown. Lorenzini, Sussaroli and Rocchi (1989) suggest that, in contrast to the thought disordered individual, the construct system of a person who is paranoid tends to become more and more monolithic, or unidimensional, as they experience repeated invalidation. The authors suggest that whereas the client with schizophrenia responds to invalidation with a sense of *threat* (i.e., the awareness of an imminent change in their core role structure), the client who is paranoid responds with *hostility* (i.e., the continuous effort to extort validational evidence for predictions that have already been shown to be a failure) (Kelly, 1955/1991). The choice of a schizophrenic or paranoid 'solution' to predictive failure, may depend on the combination of premorbid personality, type of invalidation, and the existing structural state of the individual's construct system.

There has been less focus on the *content* of construing in people with a mental illness. Early studies found that people with schizophrenia showed a greater tendency to identify with the opposite sex parent than a control group (Space & Cromwell, 1978; Winter, 1975), which is consistent with the suggestion that the families of schizophrenics may be characterized by patterns of construing which are different from the usual social norm (Lidz, 1968). Work by Gara, Rosenberg and Mueller (1987, 1989) on the personal identity of people with schizophrenia, has suggested that such clients have both poorly elaborated views of themselves and stereotyped perceptions of themselves and other people. It has not yet been demonstrated whether these results are specific to people with schizophrenia or indicative of psychopathology in general. More recently, it was found that males diagnosed with a psychotic disorder used fewer positive constructs in their self-construal than women. However, both previous and subsequent studies have found that women diagnosed with schizophrenia construed themselves more negatively (Badesha & Horley, 2000; Walker & Rossiter, 1989).

Information about both the structure and construing of offenders diagnosed with a mental illness can be used to understand the meanings of their offending. However, the only empirical study of construing in mentally abnormal offenders (Howells, 1983) broke down its results in terms of degree of violence perpetrated (i.e., one-off extremely assaultative aggressors compared to multiple moderately assaultative aggressors) rather than in terms of legal category (i.e., 'mental illness' or 'psychopathic disorder', Mental Health Act, 1959), and so specific conclusions cannot be drawn about the meanings of violence for mentally ill offenders. Individual meanings must therefore be understood from case studies and examples. Houston (1998) describes two individual cases which illustrate the different ways in which the offending of a client with a mental illness can be understood, depending on the relative contribution of premorbid patterns of construing. In one example, information from both clinical interview and a repertory grid indicated that a man's violent assault on his neighbour was directly related to the content of his construing, or in psychiatric terms, to his delusional beliefs. The structural features of his construing were also very striking and consistent with the literature (Lorenzini et al., 1989). A repertory grid indicated a very tightly organized, cognitively simple pattern of construing, in which a massive 91 per cent of the variance was accounted for by the first component, primarily reflecting positive versus negative personal characteristics. However, what is more commonly observed in clinical practice, is that relevant aspects of construing predate the onset of mental illness. A second case example is discussed in which these interactions were complex, and regardless of his mental state the individual construed his social contact with others in terms of a "Win vs Lose" situation. In this case, and for other individuals, an interaction between premorbid patterns of construing and the disinhibiting effects of illness may contribute to offending. This may particularly occur when the client is diagnosed as having an affective component to their illness or as being thought disordered, as the consequent loosening of construing may contribute to poor judgement. Furthermore, if the client is diagnosed as having a personality disorder in addition to their mental illness, it is again likely that premorbid characteristics of construing contribute an important part to the understanding of their offending.

Personality disorder and offending

The classificatory system DSM-IV defines personality traits as "enduring patterns of perceiving, relating to, and thinking about the environment and one's self . . . exhibited in a wide range of important social and personal contexts" (Diagnostic and Statistical Manual-IV, 1994, p. 630). All individuals have personality traits, and they only constitute a *disorder* when they are "inflexible and maladaptive and cause either significant impairment in social or occupational functioning or subjective distress" (p. 630). Personality disorders are enduring rather than temporary, present by the time of adolescence and continuing through adulthood. In terms of this definition, a person can have anti-social or paranoid traits, but only receives a diagnosis of personality disorder if the above criteria are fulfilled.

There are three clusters of personality disorders in DSM-IV. Cluster A contains those in which the individuals appear odd or eccentric, such as the paranoid or schizoid personality disorders. In Cluster B, individuals show dramatic, emotional or erratic features, such as the anti-social or borderline personality disorders. Cluster C contains those who appear anxious or fearful, for example obsessive compulsive or passive aggressive personality disorder. However, in offender populations it has been demonstrated that the different personality disorders are not mutually exclusive categories (Blackburn, Crellin, Morgan & Tulloch, 1990; Dolan, 1995), and problems with diagnostic reliability still remain. The usefulness of such diagnoses for the clinician lies in having a framework with which to conceptualize the client's difficulties and therefore to set realistic goals. Most of the clients described in the studies and case examples in this chapter have been diagnosed as having an anti-social or borderline personality disorder. However, other types of personality disorder are also common in offender populations, such as schizoid, dependent and narcissistic disorders, the latter showing some overlap with psychopathy.

There are also many inconsistencies of terminology in this field. In particular, the terms 'anti-social personality disorder', 'socio-path' and 'psychopath' are all commonly used to describe individuals with persistent socially deviant behaviour. However, psychopathy is a specifically defined personality construct, measured by an objective checklist (the Hare Psychopathy Checklist-Revised, 'PCL-R', Hare, 1991) and characterized by "a persistent disregard for social norms and conventions; impulsivity, unreliability and irresponsibility; lack of empathy, remorse and emotional depth; and failure to maintain enduring attachments to people, principles or goals" (Hare, 1991, p. 45). PCL-R scores have been found to be an important predictor of recidivism in general and of violent behaviour in particular (Hart, 1998; Hemphill, Hare & Wong, 1998), although Freedman (2001) has drawn attention to the high false positive rates. Blumenthal and Lavender (2000) also note that although there is the potential for psychopathy to assist in risk assessment, use of the PCL-R can result in pejorative labelling which can have negative consequences for those designated as psychopaths, and should therefore be used with caution and sensitivity.

As well as the clinical definition of psychopathy, there is also a wider *legal* definition. The Mental Health Act for England and Wales (1983) defines 'psychopathic disorder' as "a persistent disability of mind (whether or not including significant impairment of intelligence) which results in abnormally aggressive behaviour or seriously irresponsible conduct". In practice, this means that many of the individuals detained under this category in hospital can be suffering from a range of personality disorders as diagnosed by clinical criteria, or may not completely fulfil strict criteria for any one of the clinical personality disorders. The Mental Health Act (1983) only allows for individuals to be detained if they fulfil the 'treatability' criterion, i.e., if "treatment is likely to alleviate or prevent a deterioration of his condition". However, current proposals for change to mental health legislation have profound implications for offenders diagnosed as personality disordered. A key element of the proposals includes the removal of the "treatability" criterion, so that individuals could be detained for as long as they continue to pose a risk to others. Such legislation on preventive detention already exists in North America and Canada (see Quinsey, Harris, Rice & Cormier, 1998).

The above proposals clearly raise important questions about treatment and its effectiveness. The last major review of the treatment of psychopathic and anti-social personality disorders concluded that the paucity of methodologically sound studies meant that clinicians' pessimism about the treatability of people with personality disorders could not be substantiated empirically (Dolan & Coid, 1993). The authors tentatively concluded that encouraging results have been found from studies of Therapeutic Community treatment, and Blackburn (1993) also suggested that some offenders with personality disorders do appear to change with cognitive-behavioural approaches (Beck & Freeman, 1990; Layden, Newman, Freeman & Morse, 1993). More recently reviews have still concluded that the lack of studies comparing treatments makes it difficult to state that any one treatment consistently demonstrates greater effects than no treatment (Bateman & Fonagy, 2000; Perry, Banon & Ianni, 1999). A comprehensive review of the treatment of personality disorder has also been undertaken but is as yet unpublished (personal communication, Norton, April 2002). However, it is clear from recent guidelines published by the Department of Health, that both general adult forensic services are expected to develop and provide for people with personality disorder (National Institute for Mental Health in England, 2003).

The PCT perspective on personality disordered offenders

Personality disordered offenders are a heterogeneous group who commit a range of different offences. For such individuals, their offending is only one aspect of a wide range of difficulties which may be inter-related and affect all aspects of their lives. They may have additional difficulties with interpersonal relationships, substance abuse, low self-esteem, anxiety and depression or self-harm. Difficulties trusting others or with dependency may be manifested in the therapeutic relationship, which pose challenges for the clinician. Furthermore, apparently persisting with self-destructive or anti-social behaviour, despite the consequences, can make work with these individuals frustrating and lead to feelings of being deskilled. Houston (1998) suggests that the PCT perspective is particularly useful in understanding the thinking and behaviour of these offenders, and that understanding both the structure and content of their construing is important in making sense of their offending. Furthermore, a number of the key concepts in PCT are particularly pertinent to understanding the behaviour of offenders diagnosed with a personality disorder. These are the notions of self-identity and core role structure, threat, anxiety, guilt, hostility, and impulsivity.

Core constructs are those which are essential to a person's sense of identity and the way in which a person's core constructs are inter-related forms that individual's *core role structure* (Kelly, 1955/1991).

For some individuals their childhood and life experiences have led them to develop a deviant self-identity, in which the notion of offending is a central aspect of their core self. Whilst there is no empirical evidence to suggest that deviant self-identity is a causal factor on the development of offending, it is likely that it may be an important contributor to the development and maintenance of the offending of individuals, particularly relevant to adult offenders diagnosed with an anti-social or psychopathic personality disorder.

A person's core role structure is crucial in determining their behaviour as they will want to behave in ways which are consistent with this. Any challenge to their view of themselves would lead to uncertainty and unpredictability, and a sense of *threat* in PCT terms ("the awareness of an imminent comprehensive change in one's core structure", Kelly, 1955/1991, p. 361). For some offenders, particularly those with a personality disorder, although the consequences of their offending behaviour are negative, they are also predictable and therefore unthreatening. The implications of behaving in a different way is also likely to provoke *anxiety* in both the traditional and the Kellian sense ("an awareness that the events with which one is confronted lie mostly outside the range of convenience of one's construct system", Kelly, 1991, p. 365). Change is therefore actively resisted.

Kelly (1955/1991, p. 370) defined guilt as "perception of one's apparent dislodgement from one's core role structure". People suffer from guilt if they do things which are incompatible with their view of themselves. The way in which personality disordered offenders view themselves is therefore crucial in determining whether or not they are likely to feel guilty (in the conventional sense) about their offending. Dalton and Dunnett (1992) also note that if a person has a core role structure in which they have no particular fixed ideas about the kind of person they are, or what beliefs are important to them, or in which 'anything goes', then guilt is unlikely to be a problem. The authors suggest that this might be a description in PCT terms of the psychopathic personality, where whatever a person does is acceptable to them, as long as they construe it as being in their interests.

A further way in which an individual can avoid guilt is to construe events in a *hostile* way in the Kellian sense, i.e., "the continued effort to extort validation or evidence in favour of the type of social prediction which has already been recognised as a failure" (Kelly, 1955/1991, p. 375). People are likely to become hostile when they are in a situation in which they have been shown to be wrong, yet cannot cope with the idea of abandoning their beliefs. For example, offenders diagnosed with a borderline personality disorder are likely to have difficulty trusting others and expect rejection. When faced with a therapist who does not behave in this way, such individuals are likely to try and provoke that behaviour in order to maintain their view of the world.

Finally, impulsivity is one of the diagnostic criteria for anti-social and borderline personality disorders and psychopathy, and it is therefore useful to examine the PCT approach to this concept. This relates to one of Kelly's (1955/1991) hypotheses about the process of change. Kelly describes the *CPC cycle* (circumspection–pre-emption–control) as the process which precedes choice and action in any situation. In the first stage (*circumspection*), the individual considers all the possible options open; secondly, they choose an appropriate construct or dimension of experience (*pre-emption*); and thirdly, they reach a decision point along the chosen dimension (*control*). For example, consider an individual in a situation where they feel that someone else has just insulted them. Most people would consider their options (e.g., ignoring the person, responding assertively, responding aggressively, etc.), choose which is most appropriate in the given circumstances, and then decide how to implement that response (e.g., responding verbally, physically, immediately, later). In practice this process happens fairly quickly, but it is shaped by individuals' previous experience and usual way of responding to similar situations. Impulsiveness can be seen to represent a shortening of the circumspection stage and a related restriction of options e.g., a person would not consider any other options apart from immediate physical aggression.

Clinicians taking a PCT perspective therefore construe offenders who are diagnosed as personality disordered as behaving in ways which are entirely consistent with their own particular construct system. If their construct system is in itself unstable, then the individual may be observed to behave in apparently contradictory ways on different occasions. However, to the individual, their behaviour makes sense. There are therefore interesting links between the PCT perspective and the developments in cognitive treatment approaches which emphasize the role of dysfunctional cognitive schema in the development and maintenance of person-ality disorders (Layden et al., 1993; Safran, 1990; Young, 1999). These approaches originate from the interpersonal theories of personality disorder which conceptualize personality disorders as dysfunctional interpersonal styles supported by biased schemata, which then function as self-fulfilling prophecies through their effects on other people (e.g., Kiesler, 1983).

Patterns of construing in personality disordered offenders

A number of research studies have examined the different ways in which the construing of this group of offenders contributes to their behaviour. However, with one exception (Klass, 1980), the research has all been carried out on patients detained under the legal category of psychopathic disorder, which is a clinically hetero-geneous group. In the outline below the terms used in specific studies are maintained, and it is specified where issues are relevant only to one type of personality disorder.

Compared to PCT research of other types of offenders which has focused on content (e.g., sex offenders, Horley, 1988; Horley & Quinsey, 1994; Houston & Adshead, 1993), there has been comparatively greater interest in the *structural* features of the construing of those diagnosed with a personality disorder. The research indicates that personality disordered offenders often have construct systems which are structured in unusual ways, compared to both non-offenders and other offenders. Although now an old study, Widom's (1976) repertory grid study of primary and secondary psychopaths still has significance today for the under-standing of their construing. Elements of different interpersonal situations were presented to the subjects, including antisocial behaviour, 'good but dull' situations (e.g., giving blood), and those involving risk, alcohol, drugs, and criminal responsibility. Half the situations were those in which the person was playing an active part in the situation (e.g., Getting caught for a crime you com-mitted) and half were those in which the person was on the receiving end themselves (e.g., Getting caught for a crime you didn't commit). The grids were then administered twice, using both elicited and supplied constructs, with the participants being asked to say how both they as an individual and people in general would view those situations. Widom (1976) used a number of measures to examine the structure of the construct systems. There was no difference in the overall *intensity* scores of the psychopaths and controls (i.e., the interrelationship between their constructs, indi-cating how tightly organized the construct system is), or in the type of constructs elicited. However, the most significant difference between primary psychopaths compared to secondary psychopaths and controls was in the *lopsidedness* of their construct systems i.e., that most elements were only assigned to one pole of the con-structs. In this case, the lopsidedness of construing indicated a tendency by the primary psychopaths to construe situations as dull rather than exciting. Lopsidedness or maldistribution is pathological in the sense that, carried to its extreme, it could result in the person's complete inability to make useful conceptual discriminations. This characteristic has also been associated with difficulties in predicting the responses of other people (Hayden, Nasby & Davids, 1977; Winter, 1988) and has been observed in extremely violent offenders who have committed 'one-off' offences (Howells, 1983). However, it is not clear from Howells' study whether there were proportionally greater numbers of patients legally categorized as personality disordered in the 'one-off' group of violent offenders, and as such, whether lopsided construing is a characteristic feature of that client group per se, or of individuals who commit a single, extremely violent offence.

Thomas-Peter (1992) has also described characteristic structural features of construing in personality disordered offenders. His clinical observations were that personality disordered offenders (i.e., those detained in a maximum security hospital under the legal category of psychopathic disorder) made a remarkable number of very extreme judgements, using the ends of constructs rather than mid-range or neutral points, and they also made their judgements very quickly. These observations were confirmed by their performance on a computerized repertory grid task about social judgements. However, whereas the control group made moderate and neutral judgements more slowly, the personality disordered group did not do this, and made all types of judgements equally quickly. Since reaction time is considered to be an analogue of cognitive processing, Thomas-Peter (1992) suggested that the impairment shown by the personality disordered offenders was therefore in making *moderate judgements*. Since both speed and extremity of judgements are associated with their personal meaning (Adams-Webber, 1979), Thomas-Peter (1992) therefore suggested that making an 'impulsive' judgement may reveal the significance of the judgement to the subject. It may be that for personality disordered offenders, judgements of different personal meaning and significance provoke a similar style of shortened circumspection phase of the CPC cycle normally associated with extreme judgements. A cognitive 'habit' may develop from having quickly made many personally significant judgements. Alternatively, unusual construct systems may be dominated by superordinate (i.e., abstract and more generally applicable) constructs, so that the speed of moderate judgements reflects the extremity of those particular constructs.

Finally, although Widom's (1976) empirical study failed to demonstrate that the construing of psychopaths was any more tightly organized than that of non-psychopaths, other authors have suggested that there is a relationship between *cognitive simplicity* and personality disorder (Orford, 1974). Cognitive complexity is "the capacity to construe social behaviour in a multidimensional way" (Bieri et al., 1966, p. 185), and indicates the complexity of a person's thinking processes. People who show cognitively simple or black and white thinking often therefore construe themselves and others in 'all or nothing' terms. This was clearly illustrated in a case study described by Howells (1978), who used a repertory grid to explore the perceptions of a psychopath in a maximum security hospital who had attempted to poison members of his family. The man had a long-standing fascination with poisons and had reported fantasies of poisoning people he knew, maintaining that he had no remorse for his behaviour. Most of his constructs were highly inter-correlated and 80.36 per cent of the total variance was accounted for by the first component of the principal components analysis, described mainly by the constructs 'Accepts authority vs Abnormal' and 'Goes his own way vs Goes society's way' .

Research on the construing of offenders diagnosed with personality disorders has also focused on the *content* of their construct system. A number of studies have highlighted the way in which some people with anti-social personality disorders do not construe any difference between their current (i.e., offending) self and their ideal self, and therefore do not experience guilt in the traditional sense. Maintaining consistency between current and ideal self in the face of continued offending, can either be achieved by construing harm as self-congruent and having a deviant self-identity (e.g., Howells, 1978; Klass, 1980) or by not construing the offending behaviour as harmful (Fransella & Adams, 1966).

Klass (1980) investigated the way in which sociopaths perceive themselves when harming others. This is the only empirical study of an out-patient population of this client group, who were recruited from a methadone maintenance clinic. Those who met a minimum criteria of five antisocial behaviour symptoms over and above their drug abuse were selected as the sociopath sample. Klass compared both 'persons' and 'situations' repertory grids of sociopathic and non-sociopathic methadone users to those of students. As she predicted, the sociopaths had a greater tendency to see *harming others* as consistent with their view of themselves than the non-sociopathic group, and were also significantly more likely to view *harmful acts* as typical of themselves than the students. In addition, the greater the difference between a person's view of themself and their view of harming others, the more negative reaction they expected from others to their anti-social behaviour. This is consistent with social learning theory (Bandura, 1977) which predicts a parallel between perceived self-congruence of transgression and level of actual antisocial activity. The findings are also consistent with Kelly's view (1955/1991) of the importance of self-concept in negative self-reactions i.e., that experiences of guilt are mediated by discrepancies between self-concept and one's actions.

Howells' (1978) repertory grid study of a poisoner provides a further example of the link between self-congruence and anti-social activity. The man construed his actual, ideal and social self, together with the name of a famous poisoner (the person he named to fit the role of "A person I consider successful") all as socially abnormal. He saw no difference between his actual and ideal self. The construct 'Responsible vs Irresponsible' differentiated his actual, ideal, social selves and the famous poisoner from other patients who were also seen as socially abnormal. Therefore although he saw himself as socially abnormal, he also saw himself as responsible. In interview, the man elaborated this, saying that although other patients or criminals may be abnormal or socially unacceptable, he viewed them as "not responsible" because they did not plan and execute their crimes with full knowledge of what they were doing and then accept the consequences. Only himself and the famous poisoner were abnormal and responsible, as their crimes were rational and calculated and they fully accepted the consequences. The famous poisoner was also the element rated closest to his self and ideal, with his parents and brother seen as the total opposite.

In contrast, Fransella and Adams (1966) used repertory grids to study a 39-year-old man referred to a psychiatric hospital from prison, who had committed several acts of arson, but who did *not* see himself as the type of person to commit this kind of offence. In interview he described how tense and aggressive feelings would be temporarily relieved by the calmness which followed fire setting. His personality was described as being characterized by extreme conscientiousness and dislike of change, considerable drive and strongly held opinions regarding sexual and business morality. A number of different grids were administered to the man to test hypotheses about his behaviour. The main construct with which he construed the world was 'As I'd like to be in character vs Not as I'd like to be in character'. The most significant finding was that although he perceived no difference between his current and ideal self, he did not see himself as the sort of person who was likely to commit arson. He construed his current and ideal self, fire-related feelings and feelings of power and hostility at the 'good' pole (i.e., how he would like to be), and people who were immoral, sinful and who commit arson all being deserving of punishment at the 'bad' pole (i.e., not how he would like to be). Over time, the negative relationship between the self and arson constructs increased to the point where his view of himself was almost the direct opposite of the sort of person who commits arson. In his view therefore, when he was setting fires he was not 'committing arson', and further grids were used to test out hypotheses about why he did set fires. These suggested that he saw himself as someone who enjoyed power, who was a 'punisher of wrongdoers', and believed people got the punishment they deserved. These constructs were closely associated with the way he felt when setting fires. Fransella and Adams (1966) therefore suggested that the man may see himself as carrying out a crusade against people who deserve punishment by setting fires, an act which he would not see as wrong or criminal, since he viewed himself as delivering justice. The author did not discuss how the man kept the symbolism of his fire setting separate from the reality. Assuming that he did not *intend* to endanger life, one could hypo-thesize that he might have construed his own fire setting as 'not life-threatening', or that he 'only set small fires' (Houston, 1998).

In contrast to the above cases, Pollock and Kear-Colwell (1994) describe the self-construing of two female offenders diagnosed with borderline personality disorder, who *did* construe themselves as both 'guilty' and as 'perpetrators'. Both women had been seriously violent towards their boyfriends, and also had a history of significant sexual abuse. The study attempted to examine the relationship between sexual victimization and violent offences using Kelly's (1955/1991) concept of core role constructs, and Ryle's (1990) notion of reciprocal role procedures (i.e., that an offender's self-perception as an 'abuser' or a 'victim' are complementary procedures of the same role). The authors' hypothesised that the *sexually abused offender* would construe themselves in the role of an 'abuser' rather than as a 'victim', and repertory grids supported this. This role is associated with intense guilt and self-denigratory feelings, in which the self-perception of being a perpetrator allows the individual to confirm their belief about how bad they are. To perceive the individual as an 'abused victim' rather than a 'guilty abuser' may therefore dislodge them from their core role structure, which would elicit further guilt in the Kellian sense. Both women felt that to see themselves in an abused role highlighted the harmful actions of others, and represented an attempt to blame others for their own offending. Pollock and Kear-Colwell (1994) describe the use of Cognitive-Analytic Therapy (Ryle, 1990) to enable the women to progress towards a rational analysis of both their actions and their guilt.

The above studies have also focused on how individuals with a personality disorder construe other people. Characteristic features of psychopathy include lack of empathy and lack of remorse or guilt. However, in Klass's (1980) study, both sociopathic *and* non-sociopathic drug users expected to react less negatively to harming *disliked victims* compared to those that they liked. In contrast, the student group expected to react equally negatively to harming someone, whatever their attitude towards the victim. Since normal individuals believe that harming another person creates negative feelings even if they dislike the person, Klass (1980) suggests that most people are likely to show self-restraint in a wider range of interpersonal situations than the clinical groups. However, although the fact that an individual client has a lack of regard for other people may help to make sense of their particular behaviour, the evidence to date does not suggest that personality disordered offenders as a group construe other people in more negative ways than other clinical groups. However, the psychopaths in Widom's (1976) study showed a significant amount of misperception about the construct systems of people in general. This group wrongly assumed that people in general would characterize situations in the repertory grid as dull rather than exciting, as they themselves had done. Thus as well as responding physiologically as if stimuli and/or events are dull and unexciting (Hare, 1976), this study suggests that psychopaths are also more likely to perceive situations in that way. In other words, these individuals may not think that other people think differently to themselves, and therefore see no need to modify their own construct systems. Kelly (1955/1991) proposes that the ability to construe the construction processes of other people is essential for successful social relating (*sociality corollary*), and it is therefore likely that individuals who have a deficit in this area will be impaired in their ability to make interpersonal relationships.

The above studies indicate how aspects of the structure and content of an individual's construct system may provide some insight into the meanings of their offending. Case studies have illustrated the construing of personality disordered individuals who do not see their deviant behaviour as harmful (Fransella & Adams, 1966) or even see it as overtly positive (Howells, 1978). What is viewed as exciting to normal individuals is seen as dull by psychopaths, and what elicits unpleasant feelings in the former can elicit pleasant feelings in the latter (Widom, 1976). However, apart from the work by Klass (1980) there has been little published research about the construing of personality disordered offenders other than those detained in a maximum security hospital, and it is therefore inappropriate to assume commonality of construing with other populations or clinical types. The variety of meanings of similar behaviour are illustrated by two case examples of women both diagnosed with a borderline personality disorder and both with a history of fire-setting (Houston, 1998). For one of the women it appeared that she had set fires in the past when she felt stressed, frustrated, angry and unable to communicate how she felt. She had spent many years in a maximum security hospital and was in the process of rehabilitation into the community, now no longer construing herself as the type of person who was likely to set fires. In contrast, another woman had had a number of unsuccessful attempts at moving to a less secure environment than a maximum secure hospital. She had a history of being abused as a child, and one of her significant constructs was 'Been abused vs Normal'. Although she also did not now see herself as the type of person to set fires, she was unable to construe herself as 'normal'. She was terrified of life outside hospital and construed fire-setting as a way of ensuring that she could always return to the psychological security of a secure hospital environment.

Clinical applications of PCT with mentally disordered offenders

Specific clinical applications of PCT with both mentally ill and personality disordered offenders, including suggested elements and constructs to use in repertory grid assessments, have been discussed previously (Houston, 1998). The main contribution of the PCT perspective when assessing and treating an offender with a mental illness is to highlight the importance of individual personality factors, as well as the traditional psychiatric diagnosis. An individual's difficulties can be construed by professionals using both physiological and psychological constructs. These construct systems are likely to have different ranges of convenience (i.e., limits of applicability) and the variety of difficulties presented by the client may not be fully subsumed within only one system.

One of the advantages in using the PCT perspective in clinical work with personality disordered offenders is its emphasis on understanding the meaning of the individual's behaviour, which offers a positive framework with which to conceptualize the frustration that is often generated by this client group. The studies outlined previously suggest that the entrenched patterns of deviant behaviour shown by this group may be, at least in part, accounted for by the fact that the whole structure of their construct systems lacks order. A repertory grid is therefore a particularly useful technique used to assess the tightness of construing, the cognitive complexity and lopsidedness of their construct system and the polarization of elements on individual constructs.

In clinical practice it is common for problems of mental illness and personality disorder (or anti-social personality traits) to co-exist. The following case example illustrates how the PCT approach can both inform the clinical team's perspective in their work and also help the individual client to conceptualize their difficulties and identify future treatment and rehabilitation needs.

Graham was the youngest of three siblings whose parents separated when he was aged 6 years, as a result of both his father's physical violence and an extra-marital affair. After the separation his school performance and his behaviour deteriorated. When he transferred to secondary school he was bullied and refused to attend school. On transfer to another school, although he showed a promising talent for athletics, he also got into fights with older boys and was suspended on a number of occasions. His older brother engaged in a variety of delinquent behaviours and had obtained a "tough reputation" which Graham appeared to emulate. His brother was eventually taken into voluntary care, and at the age of 13 years his mother sent Graham to live with his father. His father was unable to provide any parental supervision and Graham was left largely to his own devices. It was at this point that he started using alcohol and illicit drugs. Over the next few years his own delinquent behaviour also escalated from shoplifting through to other types of theft, including car theft. His drug habit increased substantially and he became a heavy user of heroin, cocaine, ecstasy, and amphetamines. Further non-attendance at school led to a period of home tuition, but he did not take any formal qualifications.

Graham was first convicted of a criminal offence at the age of 17 years. He was convicted of Grievous Bodily Harm following a fight with a stranger in a pub, in which he assaulted the man with a broken chair leg. Graham had consumed large quantities of alcohol and been using crack-cocaine. He was sentenced to three years in a young offenders' institution, and it was at this point that he first developed a mental illness. He showed symptoms of both psychosis and mania, and was transferred to a secure ward of a hospital where he was treated with mood-stabilizing medication. The use of illicit drugs undoubtedly precipitated or exacerbated a deterioration in his mental state but he did not agree that this was a problem and was not compliant with medication when he was in the community. Over the next five years Graham received a further two convictions for increasingly violent offences with the use of available weapons (metal piping, hammer). At sentencing for his third conviction Graham received a hospital order with a restriction order, ensuring that future rehabilitation (including leave into the community and eventual discharge) would need to be approved by the Home Secretary, and that conditions would apply to future discharge plans (such as maintaining contact with mental health services). Graham was detained in a medium secure hospital and received a psychiatric diagnosis of bipolar affective disorder and anti-social personality disorder. Although he refused to complete any formal psychometric testing or a repertory grid (as he construed this as 'finding out too much about me'), he was happy to have assessment interviews with a clinical psychologist and to discuss his childhood, history of violence, and drug abuse and future treatment needs.

The three main aims of assessment with Graham, as with other offenders, were to obtain a psychological formulation of his offending behaviour, i.e., to understand its development, maintenance, and meaning; to assess his suitability for treatment and amenability to change; and to assess the future risk of violent behaviour. As discussed previously (Houston, 1998), using the PCT perspective does not mean abandoning other theoretical frameworks or approaches to assessment, but rather focuses on what is unique about this particular individual. This raises the following specific questions:

- What is the client's understanding of their offending behaviour, and how does this make sense to them? In other words, how do they construe the world in general and their offending in particular, and what is the relationship between the two?
- How do they construe themselves and significant others, including their victims (where relevant)? Is offending or deviant behaviour compatible with their core role i.e., their sense of 'what is me'?
- How does their offending and sense of self link to their childhood experiences and other difficulties in their life – past or present? In what way have those experiences shaped their construing of the world and their role in it?
- Does the client see the need to change or believe that change is possible? In other words, is there a discrepancy between the construing of their 'current self', 'offending self', and 'ideal self'? Do they see their ideal self as a role which it is possible to achieve?
- What are the potential obstacles to change, i.e., ways of construing that enable the client to avoid being invalidated when they offend?

(Houston, 1998, p. 31)

Graham initially construed his most severe past violence as attributable to either drug-induced psychosis or his mental illness, which he therefore saw as lessening his responsibility. However, it soon became clear that, notwithstanding his mental state, he also had a long-standing reputation even as a child and young teenager for being a "tough nut", which he said "followed me like a legacy". Graham then acknowledged that much of his past violence had occurred in the context of 'gang pub fights', and saw this as a response to provocation from others. He therefore distinguished between victims of his violence whom he had assaulted when mentally unwell, and "did not deserve it" and those who "did deserve it" as they had provoked him. For most of his teenage years and early adulthood, violence was therefore part of Graham's core role, defined both by how others saw him, and his view of himself. The fact that both his father and elder brother had behaved in similar ways indicated commonality between their construing, and since these were key figures in his life whom Graham looked up to, they had a clear influence on the development of his own construct system.

Graham acknowledged enjoying his "tough" reputation when younger and behaving in ways which were consistent with that. However, he maintained that he did not now see himself as being a violent person and was keen to change his behaviour, emphasizing that he had a positive side to him which he described as "loving, sincere and caring". It appeared that Graham's construct system was quite fragmented, which may have been how he accommodated apparently inconsistent aspects of his experience and behaviour. For example, he described his childhood as "a good laugh" but also how his parents' separation "devastated me completely". This raised the question of whether a more superordinate construct, such as "Me at home vs Me outside of home" was linking these fragments together. This would also help to account for the differences between Graham's behaviour towards women to whom he was close (i.e., his mother and female partners), which when he was mentally well had always been warm and affectionate, and his behaviour towards his peers, which could be bullying and intimidatory. It also appeared that Graham related differently to men and women, although he was not consciously aware of this, suggesting that this construct may be operating at a *preverbal* level. Graham could however conceptualize an 'ideal self' in which he did not behave in a violent way, as the notion of being "caring towards others" was already part of his construct system. In PCT terms, change would require *dilation* of his construct system, a broadening and expanding process to make links between the way he related to women to whom he was close, and the way he related to his peers and adult male strangers. However, a major obstacle to change was Graham's view of his past alcohol and drug use. He denied that alcohol was a problem for him, construing himself as a "social drinker", and denied ever having been either physiologically or psychologically dependent on drugs, despite his past heavy use. Graham denied urges or cravings for drugs, and maintained that he usually took drugs on impulse when he was in the company of other users. He believed that determination to stay off drugs and limit his drinking was all that was required, and did not see the need to attend drug and alcohol treatment groups. At the point of assessment, he also did not acknowledge any link between his alcohol and drug use and the likelihood of a relapse in his mental state, although he did view himself as having a mental illness and recognized the need for and benefits of mood-stabilizing medication.

At the end of the assessment period it was clear that a number of factors contributed to the development and maintenance of Graham's violence. His history of aggressive behaviour dated back to childhood and may initially have been accounted for by the combination of the consequences of his parent's separation, plus having his father and older brother as significant role models. Graham came to enjoy the reputation that he obtained, and further physical aggression reinforced his image (or in PCT terms, validated his self-identity) and became something that he was good at. Over the years the severity of his physical violence escalated, with his pre-existing justifications disinhibited by alcohol, drugs, and mental illness. In terms of risk, both actuarial (e.g., the Violence Risk Appraisal Guide (VRAG), Quinsey et al., 1998) and clinical assessment indicated that the likelihood of him behaving in a violent way in the future was high, and the degree of harm caused could be severe, depending on the available weapon. Although being in hospital meant that his bipolar affective disorder could be treated, Graham's clinical team were less sure about his ability to change those aspects of his personality which contributed to his offending. Although he consistently expressed motivation to change, it was not clear how easy he would find it to give up his "tough image", and his view of his drug taking left him very vulnerable to future relapse.

The process of rehabilitation for Graham was a long one. He did agree to participate in a series of drug and alcohol awareness sessions, but these made little impact on his views. In the hospital he continued to display both the 'caring and sensitive' aspect of his self (helping out on the ward with elderly patients) but also showed evidence of bullying and intimidatory behaviour towards other male patients. He then suffered a major relapse of his mental illness, displaying psychotic and manic symptoms as well as suicidal ideation, which required a long period of intensive nursing care and supervision, in conditions of greater security within the unit. It emerged that the relapse had most likely been precipitated by Graham taking some cocaine, although he would not disclose how he had obtained this. It took a long time for Graham to respond to medication compared to previous episodes of illness, and this appeared to be a turning point for him with regard to his view of drugs and his future rehabilitation.

As his mental state slowly improved, Graham asked to see the clinical psychologist again, "to get things off my chest". Initially he was only able to concentrate for periods of 10–15 minutes and he was unable to focus on one topic for very long. However, he was keen to talk about some of his past negative experiences, including the drug-related deaths of a number of close friends and previous experiences of physical abuse whilst in prison. He was slowly moving towards the realization that if he wanted to stay mentally well and out of both hospital and prison, he would need to abstain from drugs. The nature of Graham's varying concentration and mental state meant that approaches to changing his cognitions had to be done carefully, initially using gentle *elaborative techniques*, such as encouraging him to imagine the possible outcomes of different alternatives, and *facilitating experimentation*, by working in the "as if" mode (Fransella & Dalton, 1990), encouraging him to approach an event as if his new way of construing it was correct. Over time, Graham established positive relationships with nursing and Occupational Therapy staff, who were encouraging him to develop a new core role which validated his 'caring' self-identity, exploring the possibilities of future voluntary work. As his mental state improved, he began individual sessions with the specialist drug and alcohol worker, and then started to attend a relapse prevention group. His way of construing drugs shifted to "nice but damaging". He continued to meet with the clinical psychologist and started to view himself in terms of the 'old Graham' and the 'new Graham', eventually able to acknowledge how much of his previous behaviour towards men had been motivated by a need to maintain his image. His relationships with the other male patients improved.

After a year of stability in both his mental state and behaviour, the clinical team began to consider moving Graham out of hospital into a hostel. In the context of reviewing the changes that he had made since his admission three years earlier, he agreed to complete a repertory grid. Elements included 'self now', 'self when ill', 'self when taking drugs', and 'ideal self'. Other elements were his family members, a drug-using friend, a non drug-using friend and his current girlfriend, who had a past history of alcohol abuse. Graham had no difficulty in eliciting constructs using the triad method and came up with some complex constructs, as outlined below:

"Sensitive and loving" vs "Hard and doesn't show emotions"
"Supportive" vs "Out of sight, out of mind attitude"
"Bossy and stubborn" vs "Soft and gentle"
"Has a settled life" vs "Has an erratic life"
"Relishes excitement" vs "Wants an easy life"
"Thinks ahead" vs "Walks blindly into things"
"Thinks about self first" vs "Thinks about others' feelings"
"Aggressive and quick tempered" vs "Mellow and understanding"
"Avoids conflict" vs "Takes on conflict"
"Reliable" vs "Unreliable"

Graham rated the elements reasonably quickly but not impulsively, and used the full range of the rating scale. The plot of his 10 × 12 grid is shown in Figure 4.1. There was a strong correlation between constructs describing sensitivity and support, and those describing reliability, stability, and thinking ahead. Forty-six per cent of the variance was accounted for by the first component, consisting of these constructs. A second important way in which Graham discriminated between people was whether they were bossy and stubborn and took on conflict, compared to being soft and gentle and avoided conflict. It was encouraging to note that he rated his 'self now' as very different to both his 'self when ill' and 'self on drugs'. He consistently rated his current self as towards the middle of the constructs making up the first component, and contrasted this with the latter two 'self' elements, whom he rated as hard/not showing emotions, unreliable, walking blindly into things, and having an erratic life. Interestingly, he continued to view himself as only taking on conflict when he was ill, otherwise seeing himself as in the middle of the "Takes on conflict vs Avoids conflict" construct. He also appeared to continue to see his father and brother as role models to some degree, although both now had settled lifestyles. His rating of his girlfriend reflected her own past history of alcohol abuse, and prompted the team to suggest some joint counselling sessions. Interestingly, the construct "Relishes excitement vs Wants an easy life" made up a third component, with Graham rating himself in the middle of this construct. On exploring

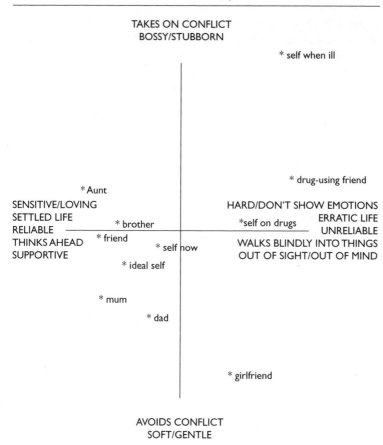

TAKES ON CONFLICT
BOSSY/STUBBORN

* self when ill

* drug-using friend

* Aunt
SENSITIVE/LOVING   HARD/DON'T SHOW EMOTIONS
SETTLED LIFE   ERRATIC LIFE
RELIABLE   * brother   *self on drugs   UNRELIABLE
THINKS AHEAD   * friend   WALKS BLINDLY INTO THINGS
SUPPORTIVE   * self now   OUT OF SIGHT/OUT OF MIND
                  * ideal self

      * mum
            * dad

                        * girlfriend

AVOIDS CONFLICT
SOFT/GENTLE

Figure 4.1   Plot of elements in construct space from Graham's grid.

this further with him he said that he now wanted to try and obtain
excitement in his life by legal means, such as through sport.

Graham moved from hospital into a supported hostel. He
continued to attend the drug and alcohol relapse prevention group
as an out-patient and also to do voluntary work, as well as starting
part-time work with his brother's building business. He was
compliant with medication and had insight into factors which were
likely to trigger a relapse of his illness. Whilst it is still too early to
comment on longer term prognosis and outcome, at six months
after discharge he was still successfully maintaining abstinence
from drugs, had started a controlled drinking programme, and had

not re-offended. For Graham, the PCT perspective provided a way of conceptualizing and verbally labelling his difficulties in a way which was meaningful for him, and for the clinical team it provided an empathic and collaborative way of engaging therapeutically, as well as a unique understanding of Graham's view of the world.

Conclusions

As demonstrated throughout the chapter, the term 'mentally disordered offenders' actually describes two heterogeneous groups of individuals, and so although it may be useful in a *legal* context, the term communicates little information about an individual from a *clinical* perspective. Studies of construing also highlight key underlying differences in these two groups. Although the structure of construing in people with a mental illness has been one of the most widely studied fields within PCT, it is the *content* of construing which may be more useful in understanding why some of those individuals go on to offend. When planning treatment it is therefore useful to distinguish between that construing which is primarily related to their mental state, and that which is primarily premorbid. For other individuals, their symptoms have a loosening effect on their construing, and they interpret events in ways which are not traditionally 'psychotic', but are different from usual. In contrast, for personality disordered offenders, although themselves a heterogeneous group in terms of both personality type and offending behaviour, the available research suggests that the whole *structure* of their construct system is different to that of other people. With psychopaths for example, Widom (1976) suggests that idiosyncrasies in the patterns of their construing are likely to reduce the possibility of effective personal communication and place the individual in a subjectively unusual world in which unpredictable behavioural reactions become more understandable. The PCT perspective enables their behaviour to be seen as entirely consistent with their view of the world, which may go some way towards assisting with the development of appropriate treatment programmes.

The advantages of working within a PCT framework with offenders are even more pertinent when trying to engage those who have also received a diagnosis of personality disorder. These individuals are more likely to be construed by others as 'bad' as opposed to 'mad', and engender feelings of being deskilled in even the most experienced clinicians. This contrasts with offenders diagnosed with a mental illness, whose offending is construed as relating to an 'external cause', and by implication, not one for which the individual is responsible. Personal construct theory offers a framework for understanding how offenders see the world, an understanding of why many individuals show an apparent failure to learn from past experiences, an understanding of resistance to change, a collaborative way of working with the client in which they take some responsibility for the process of change, and techniques such as the repertory grid, for understanding the structure and content of construing, and for measuring change. It is *complementary* to other theoretical approaches and nomothetic forms of assessment, and provides an insight into what is unique about that particular individual.

Finally, it could perhaps be argued that the advantages that PCT has to offer the forensic clinician have not been matched by progress in the research setting. It is notable that many of the key studies of the construing of mentally disordered offenders are now twenty to thirty years old, and whilst time has not diminished the significance of their results, there has been a dearth of more recent publications building on that earlier work. Dolan and Coid (1993) concluded that a lack of methodologically sound studies meant that there was no empirical evidence to support clinicians' pessimism about the treatability of personality disorders, and that further research was urgently required. Several years on, subsequent reviews have reached similar conclusions (Bateman & Fonargy, 2000; Perry et al., 1999). As discussed earlier, the UK Government is currently proposing new legislation for the detention of individuals diagnosed with severe personality disorder who pose a significant risk to others, and removing the 'treatability' criterion from the Mental Health Act. This means that as well as a need for a collaborative and empathic way of working, there is a need for PCT oriented clinicians and researchers (this author included!) to contribute to the published literature about the treatment of this challenging group of individuals.

References

Adams-Webber, J. R. (1979). *Personal Construct Theory: Concepts and Applications*. Chichester: John Wiley & Sons.

Badesha, J., & Horley, J. (2000). Self-construal among psychiatric out-patients: A test of the golden section. *British Journal of Medical Psychology*, *73*, 547–551.

Bandura, A. (1977). *Social Learning Theory*. Englewood Cliffs, NJ: Prentice Hall.

Bannister, D. (1960). Conceptual structure in thought disordered schizophrenics. *Journal of Mental Science*, *106*, 1230–1249.

Bannister, D. (1962). The nature and measurement of schizophrenic thought disorder. *Journal of Mental Science*, *108*, 825–842.

Bannister, D. (1963). The genesis of schizophrenic thought disorder: A serial invalidation hypothesis. *British Journal of Psychiatry*, *109*, 680–686.

Bannister, D. (1965). The genesis of schizophrenic thought disorder: Retest of the serial invalidation hypothesis. *British Journal of Psychiatry*, *111*, 377–382.

Bannister, D., & Fransella, F. (1966). A grid test of schizophrenic thought disorder. *British Journal of Clinical and Social Psychology*, *5*, 95–102.

Bannister, D., & Fransella, F. (1967). *A Grid Test of Schizophrenic Thought Disorder: A Standard Clinical Test*. Barnstable: Psychological Test Publications.

Bannister, D., & Fransella, F. (1986). *Inquiring Man: The Psychology of Personal Constructs* (3rd ed.). London: Croom Helm.

Bateman, A., & Fonagy, P. (2000). Effectiveness of psychotherapeutic treatment of personality disorder. *British Journal of Psychiatry*, *177*, 138–143.

Beck, A. T., & Freeman, A. (1990). *Cognitive Therapy of Personality Disorders*. New York: Guilford Press.

Bieri, J., Atkins, A. L., Briar, S., Leaman, R. L., Miller, H., & Tripodi, T. (1966). *Clinical and Social Judgements*. New York: John Wiley & Sons.

Blackburn, R. (1993). *The Psychology of Criminal Conduct: Theory, Research and Practice*. Chichester: John Wiley & Sons.

Blackburn, R., Crellin, M. C., Morgan, E. M., & Tulloch, R. M. B. (1990). Prevalence of personality disorders in a special hospital population. *Journal of Forensic Psychiatry*, *1*, 43–52.

Blumenthal, S., & Lavender, T. (2000). *Violence and Mental Disorder*. Hay-on-Wye: The Zito Trust.

Dalton, P., & Dunnett, G. (1992). *A Psychology for Living: Personal Construct Theory for Professional and Clients*. Chichester: John Wiley & Sons.

Diagnostic and Statistical Manual of Mental Disorders, Fourth Edition. (1994). Washington, DC: American Psychiatric Association.

Dolan, B. (1995). The attribution of blame for criminal acts: Relationship with personality disorders and mood. *Criminal Behaviour and Mental Health*, *5*, 41–51.

Dolan, B., & Coid, J. (1993). *Psychopathic and Antisocial Personality Disorders: Treatment and Research Issues.* London: Gaskell.

Fransella, F., & Adams, B. (1966). An illustration of the use of repertory grid technique in a clinical setting. *British Journal of Clinical and Social Psychology, 5,* 51–62.

Fransella, F. & Dalton, P. (1990). *Personal Construct Counselling in Action.* London: Sage.

Freedman, D. (2001). False prediction of future dangerousness: Error rates and Psychopathy Checklist-Revised. *Journal of the American Academy of Psychiatry and the Law, 29,* 89–95.

Gara, M. A., Rosenberg, S., & Mueller, D. R. (1987). Personal identity and the schizophrenic process. *Psychiatry, 50,* 267–269.

Gara, M. A., Rosenberg, S., & Mueller, D. R. (1989). Perception of self and others in schizophrenia. *International Journal of Personal Construct Psychology, 2,* 253–270.

Hare, R. D. (1976). Psychopathy. In P. Venables & M. Christie (Eds.), *Research in Psychophysiology.* New York: John Wiley & Sons.

Hare, R. D. (1991). *Hare Psychopathy Checklist-Revised.* Toronto, Ontario: Multi-Health Systems Incorporated.

Harrison, A. & Phillips, J. P. N. (1979). The specificity of schizophrenic thought disorder. *British Journal of Medical Psychology, 52,* 105–118.

Hart, S. D. (1998). The role of psychopathy in assessing risk for violence: Conceptual and methodological issues. *Legal and Criminological Psychology, 3,* 121–137.

Hayden, B., Nasby, W., & Davids, A. (1977). Interpersonal conceptual structures, predictive accuracy and social adjustment of emotionally disturbed boys. *Journal of Abnormal Psychology, 86,* 315–320.

Hemphill, J. F., Hare, R. D., & Wong, S. (1998). Psychopathy and Recidivism: A review. *Legal and Criminological Psychology, 3,* 139–170.

Horley, J. (1988). Cognitions of child sexual abusers. *Journal of Sex Research, 25,* 542–545.

Horley, J., & Quinsey, J. L. (1994). Assessing child molesters' cognitions: Use of the semantic differential with incarcerated offenders. *Journal of Sex Research, 31,* 247–255.

Houston, J. (1998). *Making Sense with Offenders: Personal Constructs, Therapy and Change.* Chichester: John Wiley & Sons.

Houston, J., & Adshead, G. (1993). The use of repertory grids to assess change: Application to a sex offenders' group. In N. Clark & G. Stephenson (Eds.), *Sexual Offenders: Context, Assessment and Treatment. Issues in Criminological and Legal Psychology, 19,* 43–51.

Howells, K. (1978). The meaning of poisoning to a person diagnosed as a psychopath. *Medicine, Science and the Law, 18,* 179–184.

Howells, K. (1983). Social construing and violent behaviour in mentally abnormal offenders. In J. W. Hinton (Ed.), *Dangerousness: Problems of Assessment and Prediction*. London: Allen & Unwin.

Kavanagh, D. J. (1992). Recent developments in expressed emotion and schizophrenia. *British Journal of Psychiatry*, *160*, 601–620.

Kelly, G. (1991). *The Psychology of Personal Constructs* (2 vols). London: Routledge. (Original work published 1955.)

Kelly, G. A. (1969). Hostility. In B. Maher (Ed.), *Clinical Psychology and Personality: The Selected Papers of George Kelly*. New York: John Wiley & Sons.

Kerr, C. A., & Roth, J. H. (1986). Populations, practices and problems in forensic psychiatric facilities. *Annals of the American Academy of Political and Social Science*, *484*, 127–143.

Kiesler, D. J. (1983). The 1982 interpersonal circle: A taxonomy for complimentarity in human transactions. *Psychological Review*, *90*, 185–214.

Klass, E. T. (1980). Cognitive appraisal of transgression among sociopaths and normals. *Cognitive Therapy and Research*, *4*, 353–367.

Koenraadt, F. (1992). The individualising function of forensic multi-disciplinary assessment in a Dutch residential setting: The Pieter Baan centre experience. *International Journal of Law and Psychiatry*, *15*, 195–203.

Layden, M. A., Newman, C. F., Freeman, A., & Morse, S. B. (1993). *Cognitive Therapy of Borderline Personality Disorder*. Boston, MA: Allyn & Bacon.

Lidz, T. (1964). *The Family and Human Adaptation*. London: Hogarth.

Lidz, T. (1968). The family, language and the transmission of schizophrenia. In D. Rosenthal & S. S. Kety (Eds.), *The Transmission of Schizophrenia*. Oxford: Pergamon.

Lorenzini, R., Sassaroli, S., & Rocchi, M. T. (1989). Schizophrenia and paranoia as solutions to predictive failure. *International Journal of Personal Construct Psychology*, *2*, 417–432.

McPherson, F. M., Blackburn, I. M., Daffan, J. W., & McFadyen, M. (1973). A further study of the grid test of thought disorder. *British Journal of Social and Clinical Psychology*, *12*, 420–427.

Mental Health Act (1959). London: HMSO.

Mental Health Act (1983). London: HMSO.

Monahan, J. (2000). Clinical and actuarial predictions of violence. In D. Faigman, D.Kaye, M. Saks, & J. Sanders (Eds.), *Modern Scientific Evidence: The Law and Science of Expert Testimony* (Vol. 1). St. Paul, MN: West Publishing Company.

National Institute for Mental Health in England (2003). Personality disorder: No longer a diagnosis of exclusion. www.doh.gov.uk.

Orford, J. (1974). Simplistic thinking about other people as a predictor of early dropout at an alcoholism halfway house. *British Journal of Medical Psychology*, *47*, 53–62.

Perry, J. C., Banon, E., & Ianni, F. (1999). Effectiveness of psychotherapy for personality disorders. *American Journal of Psychiatry*, *156* (9), 1312–1321.

Pierce, D. L., Sewell, K. W., & Cromwell, R. L. (1992). Schizophrenia and depression: Construing and constructing empirical research. In R. J. Neimeyer & G. J. Neimeyer (Eds.), *Advances in Personal Construct Psychology, Volume 2*. London: JAI Press Limited.

Pollock, P. H., & Kear-Colwell, J. J. (1994). Women who stab: A personal construct analysis of sexual victimisation and offending behaviour. *British Journal of Medical Psychology*, *67*, 13–22.

Quinsey, V. L., Harris, G. T., Rice, M. E., & Cormier, C. A. (1998). *Violent Offenders: Appraising and Managing Risk*. Washington, DC: Americal Psychological Association.

Ryle, A. (1990). *Cognitive Analytic Therapy: Active Participation in Change*. Chichester: John Wiley & Sons.

Safran, J. D. (1990). Toward a refinement of cognitive therapy in the light of interpersonal theory: 1. Theory. *Clinical Psychology Review*, *10*, 87–105.

Space, L. G., & Cromwell, R. L. (1978). Personal constructs among schizophrenic patients. In S. Schwartz (Ed.), *Language and Cognition in Schizophrenia*. Hillsdale, NJ: Lawrence Erlbaum Associates Ltd.

Thomas-Peter, B. A. (1992). Construct theory and cognitive style in personality disordered offenders. In P. Maitland & D. Brennan (Eds.), *Personal Construct Theory, Deviancy and Social Work*. London: Inner London Probation Service/Centre for Personal Construct Psychology.

Walker, E., & Rossiter, J. (1989). Schizophrenic patients' self perceptions: Legal and clinical implications. *Journal of Psychiatry and Law*, *17*, 55–73.

Widom, C. S. (1976). Interpersonal and personal construct systems in psychopaths. *Journal of Consulting and Clinical Psychology*, *44*, 614–623.

Winter, D. (1975). Some characteristics of schizophrenics and their parents. *British Journal of Social and Clinical Psychology*, *14*, 279–290.

Winter, D. (1988). Towards a constructive clinical psychology. In G. Dunnett (Ed.) *Working With Young People: Clinical Uses of Personal Construct Psychology*. London: Routledge.

Winter, D. (1992). *Personal Construct Psychology in Clinical Practice: Theory, Research and Application*. London: Routledge.

Young, J. (1990). *Cognitive Therapy for Personality Disorders: A Schema-Focused Approach* (3rd ed.). Sarasota, FL: Professional Resource Press.

Chapter 5

Stress in police officers: A personal construct theory perspective*

David A. Winter

After walking out of a supermarket with his coat pockets bulging with goods, John was surprised to find himself apprehended by a store detective. Responding to her request that he empty his pockets, he produced an assortment of foodstuffs and other items, many of which he would normally have no use for.

This is a common enough situation, but what distinguishes John's story from many similar incidents is that he was a police officer. Even this, however, is not altogether uncommon. This chapter will consider, from a personal construct theory perspective, why it might be that some individuals who are charged with the responsibility of enforcing the law may on occasion act in a way which contrasts markedly with this role. More broadly, it will examine how personal construct theory may contribute to under-standing and amelioration of the stress faced by police officers in the course of their work, as well as to the selection and training of police officers.

The nature of stress in police work

Hans Selye (1978), the pioneer of stress research, regarded policing as "one of the most hazardous professions, even exceeding the formidable stresses and strains of air traffic control" (p. 7). While it might seem self-evident that the primary stressors involved in this work are life-threatening situations, there is evidence (Lawrence, 1984) that police officers may, in fact, perceive such situations as

---

* Revised and expanded from Winter, D. A. (1993). Slot rattling from law enforcement to lawbreaking: A personal construct theory exploration of police stress,
International Journal of Personal Construct Psychology, 6, 253–267.

less bothersome than they do incidents, for example involving administrative procedures or relationships with the courts, that Kroes, Margolis and Hurrell (1974, p. 154) describe as involving a threat to their "self-image and professionalism". In an attempt to elucidate the nature of these stressors, we shall consider them, from the personal construct theory perspective, in terms of the emotions which they are likely to evoke.

The police officer as emotional labourer

As Cornelius (2000) has indicated, the police are amongst the professions which may be regarded as "emotional labourers", in the sense that they "need to engage *proactively* with their emotions in order to get their job done, and specifically, it is essential for the primary task" (p. 42). While there have been attempts to delineate various dimensions of emotional labour (Smith, 1998), some of which are particularly relevant to certain professions, Cornelius (2000) considers that police work spans most of these dimensions and thus requires "a great deal of emotional labouring dexterity" (p. 45).

George Kelly (1955) viewed emotions as being associated with the awareness of transitions in construing. Elaborating on this view, McCoy (1981) differentiated between "negative emotions", which "follow unsuccessful construing", and "positive emotions", which "follow validation of construing" (p. 97). It is the former which are most likely to be implicated in police officers' experience of stress, and three of the major emotions concerned will now be considered.

Threat

For Kelly (1955), stress was the awareness of potential threat, or in other words awareness of the potential for an imminent comprehensive change in one's core structures, those constructs which are central to the individual's identity. The possibility of imminent death, which police officers not infrequently have to contemplate, is in these terms generally threatening because it is perceived as likely to entail fundamental changes in core constructs. However, there are numerous other aspects of the police officer's work which, though less dramatic, may be no less threatening.

That interaction with criminals may be threatening, regardless of whether this involves any physical danger, is indicated by

Landfield's (1954) exemplification hypothesis of threat, which suggests that another person may pose threat if he or she causes one to experience self-uncertainty by exemplifying how one once was and all too easily could become again. Drawing upon this hypothesis, Kelly (1955) wrote that:

> The 'evildoer' exemplifies what we might do if we dared, or what we might be if we behaved childishly, or what we would have been if we had not tried so hard to do better. We dare not interact with him on common ground lest we step back into the unwanted ways. In order to take protective steps against the threat that his presence arouses within us we take symbolic measures called 'punishment' against him. By such measures we either destroy or symbolize the destruction of the core role relationship of the 'evildoer' with ourselves. That may make us feel a little safer from the looming shadow of ourselves as 'evildoers'. . . It helps to clarify our stand as nonevildoer by making it clear that the evildoer is not one of us.
>
> (Kelly, 1955, pp. 505–506)

Although police officers and evildoers may be regarded as polar opposites, the contrast between them is not so great, as indicated by research evidence that criminals often admire the police and have thought of joining the force themselves (Samerow, 1984) and that habitual criminals are similar in personality to 'supercops', officers who are highly productive in terms of arrests (Reming, 1988). The latter study is considered to provide support for the notion that 'it takes a thief to catch a thief'. Its findings may be explicable if high levels of attributes such as risk-taking or fearlessness characterize people who are attracted to 'professions' which involve either breaking or upholding the law (Lykken, 1982). However, an alternative explanation is that in some cases individuals who are not dissimilar to criminals in certain respects are drawn to a career in law enforcement because it allows them to banish threat to some degree by reinforcing the contrast between criminals and themselves. Such officers may be particularly threatened by those aspects of their role, such as undercover work, that involve developing close relationships with members of the criminal fraternity.

For many police officers, their constructions concerning their work reflect values which are central to their core constructs. For such officers, invalidation of these constructions is likely to be threatening. Consider, for example, the police recruit who joins the force because he or she sees it as primarily engaged in law enforcement but who finds this construction challenged by exposure to the realities of police work, of which it has been estimated that 80 per cent involves duties unrelated to crime (Kroes, 1985). Consider also that police officers often find themselves in situations where their own expectations of their roles appear to contrast with, and be threatened by, those which they perceive as emanating from the public, from such representatives of society as judges and legislators, and even from their superior officers (Bayley & Mendelsohn, 1969; Brieger, 1972; Clark, 1971; Gourley, 1966; Leonard & More, 1971; Manning, 1974; Niederhoffer, 1967; Preiss & Ehrlick, 1966; Westley, 1970; Wilson, 1970). For example, a repertory grid study has indicated differences between officers of different ranks in the value judgements used in construing effective performance as a police officer, and that such differences were greater than those between officers of different gender (Dick & Jancowicz, 2001).

Guilt

Among the qualities which police officers may perceive the public as expecting them to portray are, to quote Vollmer (1947):

> the wisdom of Solomon, the courage of David, the patience of Job and leadership of Moses, the kindness of the Good Samaritan, the strategy of Alexander, the faith of Daniel, the diplomacy of Lincoln, the tolerance of the Carpenter of Nazareth, and finally, an intimate knowledge of every branch of the natural, biological, and social sciences
>   (Vollmer, 1947, quoted in Leonard & More, 1971, p. 28)

These expectations may be internally inconsistent since, as Kunce and Anderson (1988, p. 116) have described, "The policeman's job is unique in that it requires effective use of contrasting personal styles". Those which they identify include combinations of emotional restraint and expressiveness, of empathy and firmness, and of group dependence and independence.

These conflicting demands on police officers are such that they are often likely to find themselves behaving in ways inconsistent with their core roles, or their constructions of their characteristic ways of interacting with others. Kelly (1955) viewed one's core role as "a part one plays as if his life depended upon it" (p. 503) and considered that guilt is experienced when one is aware of being dislodged from one's core role. Guilt is therefore likely to be experienced by the police officer who is faced by situations of role ambiguity and role conflict – for example, between the roles of community servant, as exemplified in the stereotype of the genial British 'Bobby', and of crime fighter; and between the requirement to enforce the law and the procedural constraints imposed on the officer by that same law. These are the types of situation that figure most prominently in descriptions of police stress (Aylward, 1985; Bard & Ellison, 1974; Ellison & Genz, 1983; Kroes, 1985; Lawrence, 1984; Moyer, 1986; Niederhoffer, 1967; Sterling, 1972; Wilson, 1968).

Anxiety

Kelly (1955) equated anxiety with the experience of uncertainty arising from being confronted with events which are beyond the range of convenience of one's construct system. Anxiety is there-fore another 'negative emotion' which is likely to result from the ambiguity of police officers' roles, at least until officers have developed a subsystem of 'professional' constructs which allows them to impose some structure on their work experiences. Such a subsystem is unlikely, however, to be able to subsume all the situations which officers encounter in the course of their duties. As Smith and Gibson (1988) have noted in a repertory grid study of police officers, the situations which they face during their work fall into the helping domain and the enforcement domain, and the elements of one domain may be outside the range of convenience of constructs applied to the other. The officer who customarily employs constructs from an enforcement subsystem but is then confronted primarily by helping situations is likely to experience anxiety. A further anxiety-provoking situation is what Kroes (1985) describes as the culture shock of exposure to sections of society – not only criminals but also members of the legal, judicial, and other professions – whose behaviour and values are markedly different from those with which the officer is familiar.

Confrontation with traumatic events may also be a source of considerable anxiety for police officers if they have no constructs which may be applied to the events concerned. As Sewell (1997) has described, their state may be regarded as one of "constructive bankruptcy". He and his colleagues have provided some support for this model in finding that construing of traumatic events is less well elaborated in people suffering from post-traumatic stress disorder than in those who have been exposed to the same events but have not developed this disorder (Sewell, 1996; Sewell et al., 1996).

Police response to stress

Studies comparing the personalities of police officers with those of civilians (e.g., Aylward, 1985; Gibson, 1982) have not found individuals who join the police force to be a particularly maladjusted group, and indeed some have concluded that the police are "a superior subsample of the population" (Fenster, Wiederman & Locke, 1976). However, there is evidence of differences in personality test scores between recruits and experienced police officers (e.g., Gudjonsson & Adlam, 1983) which are consistent with the observation by Kroes (1985, p. 141) that "it is a rare police officer that does not show some negative personality change as a result of his years of police service". Or, as a police psychologist has put it, commenting on the police culture, "We take healthy people and make them sick" (Meredith, 1984, p. 21). The personality changes which Kroes has noted in police officers include increasing cynicism, withdrawal, and deadening of affect, and he relates them to Selye's (1956) "general adaptation syndrome" in response to stress.

From the personal construct theory perspective, police officers' responses to stress may be conceptualized as strategies which they employ to cope with the invalidating experiences, and negative emotions, with which their work confronts them. Some of these strategies, and their behavioural manifestations, will now be considered.

Hostility

Kelly (1955) viewed hostility as a strategy by which an individual attempts to cope with invalidation of social predictions by tampering with the evidence in order that it may validate one's constructions. Police work, of course, provides opportunities for such tampering to be very literal, and cases of this type are by no means unknown. Hostility in the Kellian sense may also, however, be employed to maintain the police officer's construction of an inimical public when evidence for this construction is somewhat limited. Such hostility may be the basis for some incidents of provocation and violence by the police towards members of the public. Conceivably also, the officer who behaves in a criminal manner but then ensures that he or she is arrested, as is common in the case of officers apprehended for such offences as shoplifting, may in some instances be extorting evidence for the validity of constructions such as that crime does not and should not pay.

Constriction

The individual who is faced with incompatibilities in construing, and consequent anxiety, may adopt the strategy of constriction, drawing in the outer boundaries of the perceptual field to avoid these incompatibilities. Essentially, the person delimits his or her world to those events which their construct system is equipped to predict. This strategy may be considered to be reflected in the isolation and social distance which are often reported in police officers, and which Tifft (1974) has described as serving to reduce cognitive strain and to create beliefs which substantiate the legitimacy of the officer's work and self-image. Its effects have been described by Lefkowitz thus:

> The relevant literature makes it difficult to resist forming an image of a close-knit group of men, sharing a life style and general outlook on the world which includes intense feelings of being misunderstood and misrepresented by outsiders, hence requiring absolute secrecy as well as suspicion towards all such outsiders.
>
> (Lefkowitz, 1975, p. 9)

The principal dimension of the shared police construct system that is likely to be developed by such officers has been described by police psychologists as contrasting "assholes and cops", and as one in which the common enemy is not just criminals but "the community at large" (Meredith, 1984, pp. 22–23).

Tight construing

Constriction of the police officer's social world to others who share similar views, and who are therefore likely to be constant sources of validation, may lead to tightening of the officer's construct system, the predictions derived from it becoming increasingly unvarying. Such tightening may also be used in an attempt to cope with stress since there is evidence that people under stress become more cognitively simple (Miller, 1968), a characteristic which has been considered to reflect tight construing. Indeed, a repertory grid study of members of another occupational group with a level of stress often compared to that in the police force (e.g., Ksionzky & Mehrabian, 1986), air traffic controllers, indicated that tight construing was likely to ameliorate such physical effects of stress as coronary heart disease (Crump, Cooper & Maxwell, 1981).

While rigidity, of the type reflected in tight construing, has been associated with the ability to cope with stress in police officers (Reiser, 1976), and may also be the style best suited to survival in a hierarchical organization such as the constabulary, it is not without its potential drawbacks. To quote from the study of the police by Ellison and Genz (1983, p. 67), "people with rigid personalities suffer less role conflict than those who are more flexible, but rigidity of behaviour is not an asset in jobs where discretion plays an important part". Policing is certainly such a job, the officer often being faced, for example, with decisions concerning whether or not arresting someone who has committed a minor offence is the most productive course of action. There is also evidence, reviewed by Winter (1992), that cognitive simplicity, a characteristic associated with tight construing, is associated with difficulties in forming 'role relationships' with other people, in Kelly's sense of being able to construe their construction processes. Such a limited ability to anticipate the construing of other people might be expected to place a police officer at a particular disadvantage in dealing with the public.

Of some relevance to the questions of whether tight construing characterizes police officers, and of what are the advantages and disadvantages of such features of construing, is a study by Applegate, Coyle, Seibert and Church (1989). They failed to find a significant relationship between length of service in the police force and lack of differentiation in construing, a characteristic which is indicative of a tightly organized construct system. However, they did demonstrate that long service was associated with less abstract construing, speculating that this reflects "the need within an organisation that operates within a potentially dangerous environment to be maximally efficient, especially in regard to duties" (p. 397). However, the concrete construing of some of the officers in their study was also found, as in previous research, not to be conducive to person-centred communication, which takes into account the perspectives of other people.

As well as perhaps not being entirely conducive to effective fulfilment of some aspects of the police officer's role, tight construing may not necessarily be the pattern best suited to the ability to respond appropriately to stress in a police environment. This is an environment noted for the reluctance of its members to seek help from mental health professionals (Fell, Richard & Wallace, 1980; Terry, 1981), even when clearly displaying symptoms of post-traumatic stress disorder (Gersons, 1989). Gersons describes stressed police officers as mostly seeking refuge in denial, and this may be particularly the case in those who construe tightly as suggested by evidence that tight construers tend to obtain high scores on a measure of denial (Catina, Gitzinger & Hoeckh, 1992).

Slot rattling

When police officers do react to stress, their reactions do not necessarily involve complaints of psychological distress but, as Ellison and Genz (1983) describe, may occasionally manifest themselves in criminal behaviour or unnecessary violence towards members of the public, a problem which has been discussed extensively in the literature (e.g., Asch, 1971; Cray, 1972; Danish & Brodsky, 1970; Rhead et al., 1968; Westley, 1970). Such reactions may be considered to reflect the strategy which Kelly (1969) termed slot rattling, in which the person responds to invalidation by reversing their position on a construct, in this case from law enforcer to lawbreaker. Slot rattling may be particularly likely in officers whose construct systems are poorly elaborated in relation to psychological and emotional issues, and are organized tightly, perhaps around a superordinate dimension of police officer versus villain. Since such an individual will have few alternative ways of viewing a situation, any fundamental reconstruction would not be possible for them when under stress. Instead, their only available strategy may be the more superficial, although behaviourally more dramatic, one of reassigning the self to the contrast pole of the officer's principal construct dimension. That violence may also be more likely in such a person is suggested by Chetwynd's (1977) finding that prisoners who have committed violent offences tend to construe tightly, and so perhaps have few options other than violence open to them when in a situation of interpersonal conflict.

In view of these considerations, a repertory grid study of police officers referred for psychological assessment after breaking the law or engaging in violent behaviour tested the hypotheses that their construct systems would be characterized by a dearth of constructs concerned with expression of feelings and by tight structure (Winter, 1993). These officers, compared to those who were referred after displaying signs of stress not involving law-breaking (with the exception of driving offences), were found to use significantly fewer constructs concerning forcefulness and emotions. In Landfield's (1971) classification of construct content, both of these areas are included in a category which he terms "Intensity"; he has also related the use of forcefulness constructs to a concern with self-expressiveness (Landfield, Stern & Fjeld, 1961). It may be, therefore, that the non-offending group in this study, in view of their greater use of constructs concerning intensity of feelings, were more likely to have available to them the option of expressing their feelings directly when under stress. Predicted differences were also observed between the groups in measures of the structure of their personal construct systems, the 'offending' group displaying tighter construing. Furthermore, tight construing in the sample as a whole was related to high scores on a questionnaire measure of extrapunitiveness. In addition, logical consistency in construct relationships, a characteristic which has been associated with superordinate constructs which are not sufficiently permeable to accommodate conflict at more subordinate levels of the construct system, was associated with tendencies to act out hostility, to criticize others, and to admit to guilt feelings. A final finding of this study was that lower scores on various measures of psychological distress were obtained by officers who used more constructs concerning morality. It may be that law enforcement was a less stressful occupation for these officers if they had available to them a greater possibility of viewing their work in terms of morality.

Assessment of the stressed police officer

An assessment of the construct system of the police officer who presents with stress related difficulties, using the repertory grid or other construct assessment techniques, may usefully complement the picture obtained by questionnaire measures of post-traumatic stress disorder and other symptoms. Thus, elicitation of the constructs used by officers may be illuminating in providing an indication of the predicaments and dilemmas with which they are faced, and the pathways of movement open to them.

For example, Bill employed a construct that divided his world into 'policemen' versus 'criminals'. He now found himself in the situation of being prosecuted for criminal activities of exactly the type that his work had largely been involved with controlling. Although he found his behaviour inexplicable, he described a disillusionment with the police force which coincided temporally with his criminal activities. As he said, he joined the force because of "good old-fashioned principles" but found that police work was no longer consistent with these principles since "we're not doing the things we should be doing – going out and arresting people". The invalidation of his construction of a policeman perhaps left him with little option but to construe himself in terms of the contrast pole of his "policeman" versus "criminal" construct, and his arrest may have allowed him to extort some validational evidence for the policeman construction.

With Stephen, a police officer who had been arrested for shoplifting, principal component analysis of his repertory grid indicated that his major dimension of construing contrasted himself, characterized by such positively evaluated construct poles as "steady", "generous", and "daring", with members of a particular criminal fraternity and shoplifters, who were characterized by such negative poles as "think only of themselves" and "talk about others behind their backs". This dimension accounted for 74 per cent of the variance in his grid, indicating a very tightly organized construct system. His police duties in recent years had primarily involved undercover work and the infiltration of the fraternity whose members were rated in the grid. He had been confronted with the conflict of developing a degree of friendship with some of these people, about whom he then had to "talk behind their backs", to the extent that they were arrested and imprisoned. It seemed that his construct system was too tightly organized to allow such inconsistencies to be tolerated, and that the only option for their resolution, reflected in his shoplifting episode, was to slot rattle on his major construct dimension and thereby align himself with his erstwhile companions in crime.

Occasionally, some of a police officer's constructs may pose clear dilemmas because neither pole of a construct presents a desirable option. Such constructs may concern cowardice, for example Roy's construct of "coward" versus "fool" and Terry's construct of "could lose their bottle" versus "unthinking". David, who had been acquitted of assault charges, contrasted "victims" with "assailants", and people who "control things" with those who are "passive, dependent, and controlled". Consider also the dilemma faced by Jim, who was referred for psychological assessment following his superiors' concern that he was not making enough arrests, and who employed the construct "does the job for the bosses" versus "does the job for the people", viewing himself in the latter terms.

In other cases, dilemmas may be revealed by examining the correlations between a police officer's constructs. For example, Joe, who was accused of undue violence toward prisoners, was found to associate the tendency to be violent with truthfulness, practicality, shrewdness, and the abilities to make decisions, to look after oneself, and to say what one thinks. This, the fact that he construed himself as closer to his ideal self than any other person rated in his grid, and his extreme construing of the prisoners involved in the incidents, whom he saw as "stupid", "liberal", "whinging scrotes" (a term of abuse which he said was short for "scrotums"), suggested that he would be unlikely to wish to change his violent behaviour.

As well as examination of general features of the structure and content of the police officer's construct system, specific assessment of the construing of traumatic events may be useful in the officer suffering from post-traumatic stress disorder. For example, the Life Events Repertory Grid (Sewell et al., 1996) can provide an assessment of the extent to which construing of traumatic events has been elaborated, as well as how extremely these events are construed and how differently they are viewed to other events.

Therapy for the stressed police officer

The conceptualization of stress in police officers in personal construct theory terms implies that a therapeutic approach focusing upon reconstruing is likely to be of potential benefit in such cases.

Police officers are frequently highly suspicious of psychotherapists, but I have found them generally to be responsive to the 'credulous' attitude of personal construct psychotherapy, in which the officer's construing is taken at face value and a therapeutic approach is adopted which is not markedly inconsistent with this. Some officers, for example, respond well to the metaphor of therapy as a detective investigation, which may involve the active pursuit of evidence concerning past events, enabling these events to be reconstrued, or experimentation with, and the gathering of evidence for, some new construction. Let us now consider how two police officers were treated by brief personal construct psychotherapy.

Alan presented with phobic anxiety, initially concerning incidents at work but now extending to other situations. Discussion of anxiety-provoking situations led him to appreciate that they involved confrontation and conflict. Previously at work he felt that he was able to handle such situations, at least those involving the public, very effectively by such means as giving trouble-makers "a clip round the ear". Now, however, this course of action was closed off to him because the public "know too much about their rights". All he could do was to engage in hostility, in Kelly's sense of the term, by provoking perceived trouble-makers to such an extent that they attempted violence towards him, at which point he would arrest them. The only alternative was to "turn a blind eye" to miscreants, but he felt unable to do so as he would then see himself as shirking his responsibilities and would experience the guilt arising from feeling dislodged from his core role. His construct concerning being a responsible law-enforcer was so permeable, in Kelly's sense of having a very broad applicability, that even when off duty he felt constantly vigilant and often challenged people whose behaviour seemed in any way unusual and as giving some cause for suspicion. Such challenges were not infrequently received with indignation and occasionally with violence, and Alan's only way of avoiding these situations was not to venture out of the house. In an attempt to reduce the permeability of his constructs concerning responsibility and law enforcement, the technique of time binding was employed, in which a construct is 'bound' to the particular point in time when it developed. It became apparent that the origins of Alan's constructs concerning responsibility and law enforcement, and of his guilt, lay in his childhood, when he was dimly aware that his sister was being sexually abused by his stepfather but failed to intervene. The tracing of the roots of his constructions, and the development of some appreciation of why he had been unable to come to the aid of his sister, appeared to free Alan to apply new constructs to his work situation.

Michael was referred for therapy after beginning to behave in a way which was quite out of character, and which he found inexplicable. This behaviour included neglecting his family commitments and gambling away large sums of money. It became apparent that the character change occurred after an incident at work in which, showing considerable bravery, he arrested an armed man who had committed a murder. To his astonishment, instead of the praise which he was anticipating, he found himself under investigation for undue violence towards the murderer. His response to this major invalidation had effectively been to take the view that if he was going to be criticized he might as well do something for which criticism was deserved, and therefore to slot rattle from his previous self-construction of being a highly responsible family man. Therapy focused initially on identifying the core constructs which had been challenged by the work incident in order to understand why the incident had been so threatening for him. It subsequently involved the examination of ways in which he could attempt to clear his name and correct what he perceived as an injustice.

In Michael's case, as is not uncommon in police officers referred for therapy, symptoms of post-traumatic stress disorder were evident. From the personal construct theory perspective, a central component of therapy for such officers should be the elaboration of construing of the traumatic event, such that the constructions concerned can be integrated with the remainder of the person's construct system (Sewell, 1997). A similar focus can, of course, also be usefully adopted, with a view to preventing the development of post-traumatic stress disorder, in the debriefing of officers following stressful incidents.

Selection of police officers

There is a considerable literature, dating back to the work of Terman and Otis (1917), concerning the use of psychological tests in the selection of police officers and their assignment to particular tasks. However, the predictive validity of many standard measures in relation to measures of task performance has generally been found to be limited (Aylward, 1985; Levy, 1967). The Minnesota

Multiphasic Personality Inventory, although still widely used in the USA in the selection of police applicants (Carpenter & Raza, 1987), has, for example, been described as "practically useless" in this regard (Daley, 1980). Of more value may be an instrument, such as the repertory grid, which allows the assessment of the police officer's personal view of the world; which, having low face validity, is less vulnerable to social desirability response sets; and which was not primarily developed to discriminate psychopathological from normal groups. As we have seen, both the structural and content measures derived from the grid have been found to be of value in assessing the predicament of officers who present psychological difficulties. They may similarly be useful in selecting police officers for such assignments as undercover work and the carrying of firearms, and indeed there have already been some attempts to use the grid in this area (Prentice, 1985). The research findings presented above would indicate that assignment to such tasks, and to other especially stressful duties, may be contra-indicated in cases where assessment reveals particularly tight construing, impermeable superordinate constructs, or a dearth of constructs concerning expression of feelings or morality. As Jancowicz and Walsh (1982) have described, a grid in which the elements are police officers of varying degrees of effectiveness may help to identify the characteristics of effective officers, and be used as a basis for officer selection.

Police training

It follows from the research findings that the training of police officers might usefully include attempts to loosen construing, to increase the permeability of superordinate constructs, and to facilitate construing of events in terms of emotional expression and morality. A further central component of training, not unrelated to some of these other objectives, may be to help officers to construe other people's construction processes, which Kelly saw as crucial to interpersonal relationships. That it might be particularly crucial to a police officer's work may be appreciated by considering the officer who has to negotiate with a hostage taker, to predict the next moves of a serial killer, or to persuade a potential suicide not to jump from a bridge. Construing of the construction processes of others was the focus of an approach developed by Bonarius (1986), which was principally concerned with the development of greater sensitivity by police officers towards the victims of crime. The approach was firmly rooted in Kelly's metaphor of the person as a scientist, who constantly formulates and tests out hypotheses, and it attempted to activate the "scientist" in the individual police officer. The procedure adopted in a pilot study was that, immediately after a victim had reported to a police officer, another officer interviewed the victim about how they had been handled by the first officer. The second officer then gave feedback to the first concerning the victim's experience, and the officers' roles were reversed with the next victim. A psychology student observed, and gave suggestions concerning both types of interview. The interviews, and the information gained from them, were subsequently discussed in team meetings, supervised by a group counsellor, which included the use of role playing to enhance officers' interviewing techniques. Bonarius emphasised that "the study was not primarily directed towards correction of the police attitudes but towards information collection and the development of a more flexible professional approach" (underlining in original). The project was well received and was extended to other police teams. Amongst its effects, according to Bonarius, was that, in contrast to the constriction which has been reported to characterize the police, officers extended their perceptual fields and discovered that the same event may be construed in different ways, some of which may differ markedly from their own constructions.

The involvement of police officers in analysing their own behaviour has also been a component of retraining programmes developed by Toch and his colleagues with the aim of reducing violence by the police (Toch, 1992; Toch & Grant, 1991; Toch, Grant & Galvin, 1975). He points out that particular police officers are involved in situations of violence, and are the subject of complaints, much more than others, in some cases by unwittingly playing a part in the violent "scripts" of members of the public. For example, "Officer Jones, who has been assaulted more frequently than almost any of his fellow officers, sees himself as a practitioner of applied psychology. In dealing with people, he advises and claims the need for patience, flexibility, and diplomacy wherever possible" (Toch, 1992, p. 79). His particular brand of applied psychology was demonstrated in two incidents with a certain individual. In the first of these, having heard of a complaint against this individual, he "got him up against the wall, I drew my service revolver and stuck the barrel of my gun up to the cylinder in his mouth, and I told J. that if he pulled any more capers on my beat, that there would be two witnesses to his murder, he and I, and he'd be dead" (pp. 80–81). In the second incident, Officer Jones decides to arrest the individual in the very dangerous setting of a crowded pool hall. Despite suffering from a fractured arm,

> I knock him through the front of the plate glass window, and I go out after him onto the middle of the street. Finally I get him down and with my hand and my stick, I beat him into a semi-stupor, and at the time, I look up and I see a very, very unhappy crowd of people.
>
> (Toch, 1992, p. 82)

Officer Jones would clearly benefit from developing his applied psychology to include a greater capacity for construing the construction processes of others. As described by Toch et al. (1975), the analysis of situations such as this, and the identification of patterns in officers' violent incidents, may be carried out by officers' peers in an Action Review Panel. Toch et al. (1975) have provided some evidence of a reduction in conflicts between officers and members of the public during the operation of such a panel.

The importance of a focus in police training on understanding the construing of members of the public is suggested by a study by Sexton and Denicolo (1997), which used personal construct assessment techniques to investigate formative incidents in officers' early professional lives. This indicated that interactions with the public were far more important learning experiences than observation of their colleagues in the period just after leaving Training School. Critical incidents during the training period that were recalled by officers were generally not related to development of the skills required of a police officer but instead "almost exclusively charted the development of relationships, the socialisation process and in particular the concerns that existed around successful completion of the course per se" (Sexton & Denicolo, 1997, p. 141). It may perhaps be concluded, as Cornelius (2000) has also suggested in regard to race relations training for police officers, that training focusing on behavioural change and skills acquisition may be of minimal value, and even counter-productive, if not coupled with reconstruing and a greater capacity to see the world through the eyes of others.

Conclusions

Just as in any other individuals, stress in police officers may usefully be conceptualized in terms of experiences of invalidation of construing, and of associated emotions such as threat, guilt, and anxiety. The police officer may use various strategies in order to attempt to cope with, or minimize stress, but these strategies, including hostility, constriction, tightening of construing, and slot rattling, while perhaps achieving their ends to a degree, may not be without some negative consequences.

Assessment techniques derived from personal construct theory may therefore help to elucidate the predicament of the stressed police officer. If the officer requires therapy, a personal construct therapeutic approach may similarly be of value. Since certain features of construing may be regarded as likely to be conducive to the ability to cope effectively with stress, methods for assessment of the construct system might also be usefully incorporated into the selection procedure for police officers, especially for those who are likely to be faced with particularly stressful assignments. Police training programmes could also perhaps be refocused to foster these aspects of construing and, more generally, the ability to take the perspectives of other people.

References

Applegate, J. L., Coyle, K., Seibert, J. H., & Church, S. M. (1989). Interpersonal constructs and communicative ability in a police environment: A preliminary investigation, *International Journal of Personal Construct Psychology*, *2*, 385–399.

Aylward, J. (1985). Psychological testing and police selection, *Journal of Police Science and Administration*, *13*, 201–210.

Asch, S. H. (1971). *Police Authority and the Rights of the Individual*. New York: Arco.

Bard, M., & Ellison, K. (1974). Crisis intervention and investigation of forcible rape, *Police Chief*, *41*, 68–73.

Bayley, D. H., & Mendelsohn, H. (1969). *Minorities and the Police: Confrontation in America*. New York: The Free Press.

Bonarius, H. (1986). Helping the victim of criminal acts: An action approach to police training derived from personal construct psychology. In L. Van Langenhove, J. M. De Waele, & R. Harre (Eds.), *Individual Persons and Their Actions*. Brussels: Vrije Universiteit.

Brieger, S. G. (1972). A profile of the police patrolman: A study of the relationship between the patrolman's self attitudes and his perceived public attitudes, *Dissertation Abstracts International, 32A*, 7103.

Carpenter, B. N., & Raza, S. M. (1987). Personality characteristics of police applicants: Comparisons across subgroups and with other populations, *Journal of Police Science and Administration, 15*, 10–17.

Catina, A., Gitzinger, I., & Hoeckh, H. (1992). Defense mechanisms: An approach from the perspective of personal construct psychology, *International Journal of Personal Construct Psychology, 5*, 249–258.

Chetwynd, J. (1977). The psychological meaning of structural measures derived from grids. In P. Slater (Ed.), *The Measurement of Intrapersonal Space by Grid Technique. Vol. 2. Dimensions of Intrapersonal Space.* London: John Wiley & Sons.

Clark, R. (1971). *Crime in America: Observations on its Nature, Causes, Prevention and Control.* New York: Pocket Books.

Cornelius, N. (2000). Difference, inclusion and exclusion among 'emotional labourers': A search for meanings. In J. M. Fisher & N. Cornelius (Eds.), *Challenging the Boundaries: PCP Perspectives for the New Millennium.* Farnborough: EPCA Publications.

Cray, E. (1972). *The Enemy in the Streets: Police Malpractice in America.* Garden City, NY: Anchor Books.

Crump, J. H., Cooper, C. L., & Maxwell, V. B. (1981). Stress among air traffic controllers, *Journal of Occupational Behaviour, 2*, 293–303.

Daley, R. E. (1980). The relationship of personality variables to suitability for police work, *Dissertation Abstracts International, 41* (4-B), 1553.

Danish, S. J., & Brodsky, S. L. (1970). Training of policemen in emotional control and awareness, *American Psychologist, 25*, 368–369.

Dick, P., & Jancowicz, D. (2001). A social constructionist account of police culture and its influence on the representation and progression of female officers: A repertory grid analysis in a UK police force, *Policing, 24*, 181–199.

Ellison, K. W., & Genz, J. L. (1983). *Stress and the Police Officer.* Springfield, IL: Thomas.

Fell, R. D., Richard, W. C., & Wallace, W. L. (1980). Psychological job stress and the police officer, *Journal of Police Science and Administration, 8*, 139–144.

Fenster, C. A., Wiedermann, C. F., & Locke, B. (1976). Police personality – social science folklore and psychological measurement. In B. D. Salis (Ed.), *Psychology in the Legal Process.* New York: Science Paperbacks.

Gersons, B. P. R. (1989). Patterns of PTSD among police officers following shooting incidents: A two-dimensional model and treatment implications, *Journal of Traumatic Stress, 2*, 247–257.

Gibson, J. (1982). Square pegs in square holes, *Police Review, 90*, 1702–1707.

Gourley, G. D. (1966). *Effective Police Organization and Management, Vol. 7.* Los Angeles: California State College.

Gudjonsson, G. H., & Adlam, K. R. C. (1983). Personality patterns of British police officers, *Personality and Individual Differences, 4,* 507–512.

Jancowicz, A. D., & Walsh, P. (1982). Researching the sergeant's role, *Garda News, 3,* 6–13.

Kelly, G. A. (1955). *The Psychology of Personal Constructs.* New York: Norton. (Reprinted by Routledge, 1991.)

Kelly, G. A. (1969). Personal construct theory and the psychotherapeutic interview. In B. Mayer (Ed.), *Clinical Psychology and Personality: The Selected Papers of George Kelly.* New York: John Wiley & Sons.

Kroes, W. H. (1985). *Society's Victims – The Police: An Analysis of Job Stress in Policing.* Springfield, IL: Charles C. Thomas.

Kroes, W. H., Margolis, B. L., & Hurrell, J. J. (1974). Job stress in policemen, *Journal of Police Science and Administration, 2,* 145–155.

Ksionzky, S., & Mehrabian, A. (1986). Temperament characteristics of successful police dispatchers: Work settings requiring continuous rapid judgements and responses to complex information, *Journal of Police Science and Administration, 14,* 45–48.

Kunce, J. T., & Anderson, W. P. (1988). Assessment of nonpathological personality styles of policemen, *Journal of Clinical Psychology, 44,* 115–122.

Landfield, A. W. (1954). A movement interpretation of threat, *Journal of Abnormal and Social Psychology, 49,* 529–532.

Landfield, A. W. (1971). *Personal Construct Systems in Psychotherapy.* Lincoln, NE: University of Nebraska Press.

Landfield, A. W., Stern, M., & Fjeld, S. (1961). Social conceptual processes and change in students undergoing psychotherapy, *Psychological Reports, 8,* 63–68.

Lawrence, R. A. (1984). Police stress and personality factors: A conceptual model, *Journal of Criminal Justice, 12,* 247–263.

Lefkowitz, J. (1975). Psychological attributes of policemen, *Journal of Social Issues, 31,* 3–26.

Leonard, V. A., & More, H. W. (1971). *Police Organization and Management.* Mineola, NY: The Foundation Press.

Levy, R. J. (1967). Predicting police failures, *Journal of Criminal Law, Criminology, and Police Science, 58,* 265–276.

Lykken, V. T. (1982). Fearlessness: Its carefree charms and deadly risks, *Psychology Today, 16,* 20–28.

McCoy, M. M. (1981). Positive and negative emotion: A personal construct theory interpretation. In H. Bonarius, R. Holland, & S. Rosenberg (Eds.), *Personal Construct Psychology: Recent Advances in Theory and Practice.* London: Macmillan.

Manning, P. (1974). The police: Mandate, strategies, and appearances. In

R. Quinney (Ed.), *Criminal Justice in America: a Critical Understanding*. Boston: Little, Brown and Co.

Meredith, N. (1984). Attacking the roots of police violence, *Psychology Today, 18*, 20–26.

Miller, A. D. (1968). Psychological stress as a determinant of cognitive complexity, *Psychological Reports, 23*, 635–639.

Moyer, I. L. (1986). An exploratory study of role distance as a police response to stress, *Journal of Criminal Justice, 14*, 363–373.

Niederhoffer, A. (1967). *Beyond the Shield*. New York: Doubleday.

Preiss, J. J., & Ehrlick, H. J. (1966). *An Examination of Role Theory: The Case of the State Police*. Lincoln, NE: University of Nebraska Press.

Prentice, T. (1985). Firearms instructors apply new psychology tests, *The Times*, October 1, p. 2.

Reiser, M. (1976). Some organizational stresses on policemen, *Journal of Police Science and Administration, 2*, 158–159.

Reming, G. C. (1988). Personality characteristics of supercops and habitual criminals, *Journal of Police Science and Administration, 16*, 163–167.

Rhead, C., Abrams, A., Trosman, H., & Margolis, P. (1968). The psychological assessment of police candidates, *American Journal of Psychiatry, 124*, 133–138.

Samerow, S. E. (1984). *Inside the Criminal Mind*. New York: Times Books.

Selye, H. (1956). *The Stress of Life*. New York: McGraw-Hill.

Selye, H. (1978). The stress of police work, *Police Stress, 1*, 7–8.

Sewell, K. W. (1996). Constructional risk factors for a post-traumatic stress response after a mass murder, *Journal of Constructivist Psychology, 9*, 97–107.

Sewell, K. W. (1997). Posttraumatic stress: Towards a constructivist model of psychotherapy. In G. J. Neimeyer & R. A. Neimeyer (Eds.), *Advances in Personal Construct Psychology* (Vol. 4). Greenwich, CT: JAI Press.

Sewell, K. W., Cromwell, R. L., Farrell-Higgins, J., Palmer, R., Ohlde, C., & Patterson, T. W. (1996). Hierarchical elaboration in the conceptual structures of Vietnam combat veterans, *Journal of Constructivist Psychology, 9*, 79–96.

Sexton, R., & Denicolo, P. (1997). Formative critical incidents in early professional life: A stimulated recall approach. In P. Denicolo & M. Pope (Eds.), *Sharing Understanding and Practice*. Farnborough: EPCA Publications.

Smith, M., & Gibson, J. (1988). Using repertory grids to investigate racial prejudice, *Applied Psychology: An International Review, 37*, 311–326.

Smith, S. L. (1998). Managing emotional labour. In D. S. Sims, S. Sims, M. Somerville, & P. Jackson (Eds.), *Managing the Future*. Uxbridge: Brunel University Distance Learning MBA Module.

Sterling, J. (1972). *Changes in Role Concepts of Police Officers.* Gaithersburg, MD: International Association of Chiefs of Police.

Terman, L., & Otis, A. (1917). A trial of mental and pedagogical tests in a civil service examination for policemen and firemen, *Journal of Applied Psychology, 1,* 17–29.

Terry, W. C. (1981). Police stress: The empirical evidence, *Journal of Police Science and Administration, 9,* 61–75.

Tifft, L. L. (1974). The 'cop personality' reconsidered, *Journal of Police Science and Administration, 2,* 266–278.

Toch, H. (1992). *Violent Men: An Inquiry into the Psychology of Violence.* Hyattsville, MD: American Psychological Association.

Toch, H., & Grant, J. D. (1991). *Police as Problem Solvers.* New York: Plenum Press.

Toch, H., Grant, J. D., & Galvin, R. T. (1975). *Agents of Change: An Experiment in Police Reform.* Cambridge, MA: Schenkman.

Vollmer, A. (1947). *Police Bureau Survey.* Portland, OR: City of Portland.

Westley, W. A. (1970). *Violence and the Police: A Sociological Study of Law, Custom, and Morality.* Cambridge, MA: MIT Press.

Wilson, J. Q. (1968). *Varieties of Police Behavior.* Cambridge, MC: Harvard University Press.

Wilson, J. Q. (1970). The patrolman's dilemma. In W. H. Hewitt & C. L. Newman (Eds.), *Police-Community Relations: An Anthology and Bibliography.* Mineola, NY: Foundation Press.

Winter, D. A. (1992). *Personal Construct Psychology in Clinical Practice: Theory, Research and Applications.* London: Routledge.

Winter, D. A. (1993). Slot rattling from law enforcement to lawbreaking: A personal construct theory exploration of police stress, *International Journal of Personal Construct Psychology, 6,* 253–267.

Chapter 6

Treating offenders in the community: Assessment and treatment issues and the special challenges of sexual offenders

Anthony Eccles and William Walker

Introduction

This chapter will address the treatment of offenders in the community with a special emphasis illustrating the problems and processes of treatment using the example of sexual offenders. The perspective we will describe is a cognitive-behavioural one, the most effective (Gendreau, Goggin, Cullen & Andrews, 2001) and increasingly common approach to offender treatment in North America. We have worked with offenders in both the prison setting and in the community. While we have been involved with both sexual and non-sexual offenders, the bulk of our involvement concerns the former.

The development of improved risk assessment methodologies in the last ten years has resulted in an increasing focus on the development of programmes to deal with identifiably dangerous offenders (Serin & Preston, 2001). There has also been an increasing awareness of the need to develop programmes that are properly geared to specific treatment needs and criminogenic risk factors (Andrews & Bonta, 1999). Thus, targeting and improving an offender's social skills in an observable way may not have an impact on recidivism if such deficits are not criminogenic for this offender or his offender group. Along with the increasing demands to provide treatment to more clearly defined groups of offenders with programmes efficiently tailored to their offence-related needs, it appears to us that we are witnessing more demand for the development of community-based and other progressive treatment options such as the establishment of more therapeutic communities (e.g., Cullen, Newell & Woodward, 1997). This is in marked contrast to what we observed during most of the 1980s and 1990s when there was a trend toward what Gendreau et al. (2001) refer to as "get tough" strategies for dealing with offenders. Longer sentences and harsher, starker, prison environments may have an appeal to some individuals who perhaps feel that such an approach has a significant deterrent value. While face validity can be seductive, it can also be misleading. Gendreau et al. certainly provide evidence that refutes such a simplistic approach, at least with anything but very low risk offenders, who may indeed be deterred by punitive sanctions. It is the higher risk violent offenders that are much more of a cause for concern and it is to the assessment and treatment of these men that we will now turn.

Working with offenders in the community

Prison-based treatment efforts with offenders are discussed elsewhere in this volume and so we will restrict ourselves here to the delivery of treatment within the community. It has been argued by some that the delivery of treatment in the community has the advantage of being more ecologically valid (Henggeler, Schoenwald, Borduin, Rowland & Cunningham, 1998). In the treatment of aggressive youth, community-based programmes afford the opportunity to work with them in the context of familial and peer influences, thus providing the potential for more meaningful interventions and more robust change. However, community-based programmes have their own particular problems, with poor-attendance, travel and employment conflicts arguably being the most pervasive. Therapeutic communities based within the community (i.e., in a non-penal facility) offer an option that provides for a measure of control that circumvents many of these problems.

Treating offenders in therapeutic communities

In outlining the philosophical roots of forensic applications of therapeutic communities, Roberts (1997) emphasizes the relationship between an individual and the society within which he or she operates. This perspective construes deviant or criminal behaviour as being the product of a breakdown in this relationship, as if the offender voids, or perhaps never even signs the "social contract" with its implicit rules and structures. As such, a therapeutic community is seen as an opportunity for an offender to enter a special community temporarily, within which he or she can have another chance to learn and accept the social values that are requisite for adopting the "social contract" inherent in a smoothly running society. Newell (1996, quoted in Cullen, 1997) describes therapeutic communities as a collaboration between prisoners and staff to form a "community of care and respect which is committed to the development of personal functioning, to address offending and offensive behaviour in order to change". Cullen (1997) also notes that the cumulative effect of the opportunities offered by therapeutic communities is the development of self-esteem, confidence and community responsibility.

The essence of therapeutic communities is their relatively democratic nature. Staff and residents share power and decision making on issues related to the running of the community, from what the meals will be to who will be accepted into the community, and participation is voluntary (e.g., Dolan, 1997). Treatment takes place both informally, in the social milieu of the community, and more formally in groups, such as sex offender groups, substance abuse, and so on. Dolan presents a good description of how a therapeutic community can function in the community (in this case, Henderson Hospital in Surrey, England). The client population there deals primarily with forensic clients with personality disorders. The therapeutic community they provide takes up to about 15 men and 15 women who reside there for about a year. There are no medications and all clients attend voluntarily. Hope and motivation for personal change is instilled through exposure to other individuals who have had similar problems but who have progressed toward strength and stability. Interpersonal interactions and relationships within the therapeutic community are studied and discussed extensively, leading to a better understanding of the roots of their dysfunctional behaviour and its replacement with healthier alternatives. In an analysis of the efficacy of the Henderson Hospital's therapeutic community, Dolan, Wilson and Evans (1992) followed 62 residents for an average of eight months post-discharge. Very significant reductions in symptomatic psychological distress were reported. By quantifying clinical rather than statistical changes of significance, Dolan and her colleagues found that 32 per cent of residents had experienced reliable clinical improvements.

Treating offenders in the community

The promising results of therapeutic communities reported by Dolan and others (e.g., Jones, 1997) notwithstanding, the fact remains that most offenders who are treated outside a prison setting do not have the opportunity to participate in a therapeutic community. In Canada, federal offenders on parole with substance abuse problems have access to programmes such as *Choices* (Lightfoot & Boland, 1993). Other programmes targeting family violence and cognitive skills are also available. A review of their effectiveness is beyond the scope of this chapter. Suffice it to say that evaluations of programme effectiveness have been very encouraging. For example, Robinson (1996) reports that return to custody rates for offenders who take cognitive skills training in the community declined by slightly more than 39 per cent, while the recidivism rate for this group dropped by 66 per cent. Particularly encouraging, was the finding that community-based programmes appeared to reduce the recidivism rate for higher risk offenders, and not simply those of relatively lower risk. Results for offenders taking the *Choices* programme are also promising. In a 12-month follow-up of over 400 parolees who completed the programme and the subsequent maintenance sessions, readmissions to custody dropped by 29 per cent and reconvictions dropped by 56 per cent (Correctional Service of Canada, 1999).

Special considerations when working with offenders in the community

Working in the community requires some special considerations that do not ordinarily arise for those working within an institutional setting, especially if the clinic sees sexual offenders (Eccles & Walker, 1998). We will review some of the more general issues below and address specific issues relating to treatment in later sections. Some of these are specific to sexual offenders but many of the issues relate to non-sexual offenders as well.

Location and security issues for community-based clinics: When establishing a community-based forensic clinic the location of the site is of critical importance, especially where sexual offenders are concerned. Our own efforts to establish a forensic clinic in a suitable location in the community required considerable time and planning. Nonetheless, by applying a set of criteria in our site selection process the endeavour was worthwhile and our forensic clinic has operated successfully for over a decade in this location with not one problem or complaint. The following criteria were used to select our location:

1 The clinic had to be situated in an area without any schools.
2 Any sites in or immediately adjacent to residential areas were ruled out.
3 Only office buildings with no services for survivors of sexual abuse were considered (e.g., counsellors who specialized primarily with abuse victims).
4 The clinic had to be located on or near bus routes to facilitate attendance by offenders lacking their own transportation.

Once these criteria had been met, not an easy task, we made sure that the property manager was fully apprised of the nature of our work to ensure that there were no subsequent complications. The time we took enabled us to find a location where we enjoy strong support and assistance from those running the building as well as from the other tenants, and so it has certainly paid off.

An additional consideration when setting up a forensic clinic in the community is that of security within the office. Our work in the penitentiaries generally occurs in a context of considerable institutional security. However, in the community there are no such precautions and we have found it necessary to be very careful about who we accept into treatment at the clinic. Offenders are carefully screened at the outset to determine to what extent they are suitable. One of the considerations that is made in this regard is whether or not the individual is too violent to be safely treated in such a community setting. There are certainly pressures brought to bear from time to time by referring agencies to take whomever they want to send. However, no clinic can be all things to all people and we believe that it is not good clinical practice to accept into treatment offenders who are too emotionally unstable or volatile to treat in such a setting. In such cases, we will typically refer the individual to a residential treatment programme or for a psychiatric assessment first. In some cases medication can stabilize such individuals. If not, we encourage clinicians to withstand pressures to accept high-risk offenders if this compromises the safety of staff or other offenders in the treatment programme.

In addition to the above, it has been our experience that considerable caution must be exercised with some volatile offenders in the event that they must be provided with negative feedback (e.g., a report that will potentially prevent them from having access to their children). In such cases, we will ensure that other staff are alerted before the offender arrives. If we do not believe that this is sufficient we will arrange for the meeting to be held in a more secure location (e.g., parole office).

Assessment issues in the community: Clinicians in the community are far more apt to be involved in evaluations of offenders for Criminal Court and Family Court proceedings. Unfortunately, there are still some forensic clinicians who misrepresent the profession by providing assessments to the courts indicating that a given client does not fit the "profile" of an offender and therefore is unlikely to have committed the crime. The state of the art is simply not yet sufficiently sophisticated for us to be able to say with any certainty whether any given offender did or did not commit an offence. Phallometric testing is most often used in such flawed analyses. In such cases, the lack of sexual deviance has been argued to indicate that the offender is likely not the culprit. We have seen this, even in cases of alleged familial abuse, despite the fact that most admitting familial offenders will not show any deviant arousal (Barbaree & Marshall, 1989). In general, forensic clinicians have little to offer at this stage of the process and such evaluations are far more germane at the sentencing stage. As a result, we generally discourage referrals for assessments during the trial stage of a criminal case.

Finally, we note here that some clinicians have told us privately that they approach their evaluations differently depending on whether or not the referral is made by the defence or the prosecution. In one such case, the clinician told us he felt "obligated" to identify mitigating circumstances if a defence lawyer made the referral. In our opinion, a truly objective approach to sex offender evaluations will make no such distinction. As a rule of thumb, we recommend that if a forensic clinician finds that she or he is doing considerably more work for either the prosecution or the defence, then they would do well to consider whether or not this is a reflection of a lack of balance in their assessments.

Treatment issues in the community: When he is in the community, an offender must apply the strategies he has identified in the relapse prevention plan he has developed. In the following sections, we discuss considerations about offenders' residence locations, recreational and leisure activities, what jobs to take or avoid, where and when to shop, material possessions to avoid, when and where to have family contact, pornography use, vehicle type, and curfew. Discussion of these issues with offenders can become quite contentious, particularly at the outset, as many offenders regard their probation or parole officers and other formal community supervision personnel as invasive, and see the requirements of supervision as obstacles to their return to a normal life.

In our work with offenders we emphasize that the purpose of community intervention and supervision is to provide support and guidance, helping them to solidify their healthier ways of thinking, rather than imposing limits and controls, though it is often necessary for supervisory or therapeutic personnel to place certain restrictions or prohibitions on an offender's life. We hope that the offender will come to view our efforts as synchronous with his efforts, and will choose to work with community support rather than against it. We want offenders to keep in mind that the ultimate purpose of community involvement is to assist them to lead healthy lives and not victimize anyone else, looking at what is best in the long run for them and for others in their lives.

A comment regarding anti-androgen medications is appropriate here. In our previous discussion of the issues related to location and security for community-based clinics we noted some of the difficulties with emotionally volatile community clients. The presence of persistent and salient sexual fantasies in sexual offenders is an additional impediment to the successful completion of treatment as well as a significant risk consideration for offenders in the community. In such cases, we generally recommend that offenders so afflicted seek a regimen of anti-androgen medications before they start the cognitive-behavioural programme. Otherwise, it is unlikely that they will be able to focus sufficiently on their work for it.

It is important to mention at this juncture that good communication between the releasing institution (Wilson & Eccles, 1998) and the treatment professionals in the community is essential, as is regular contact between therapists and those parole/probation officers supervising the case. There is evidence that such a collaborative effort can reduce sexual recidivism (Wilson, Stewart, Stirpe, Barrett & Cripps, 2000). Furthermore, an emerging and increasingly important adjunct to traditional approaches to community-based sex offender treatment with high-risk offenders is the use of Circles of Support. These initiatives are professionally facilitated volunteer efforts that provide daily support and contact with the offender to meet treatment, social and other needs. This contact, usually with four to five core individuals, is intended to be long-term, and can last up to several years.

Assessment of sexual offenders

Fundamentally, offences occur from the intersection of an offender's desire to engage in inappropriate sexual behaviour and the opportunity to do so. Carrying out the act also requires making decisions that overrule inhibitions stemming from the under-standing that the act is wrong or harmful. Sexual offenders think about committing sex offences before actually doing them (the deviant acts do not spring unbidden from nothing), though it is not always the case that the thinking precedes the opportunity. A potential offender can identify a situation of sexual opportunity (for instance, a woman passed out at a party) and then think further about the specifics of the sexual behaviour.

The point that thoughts precede and are related to behaviours is the foundation of cognitive-behavioural intervention. How and what you think affects what you do. The principle behind cognitive-behavioural treatment for sex offenders is to get the offenders to change their thinking and behaving from criminal thoughts that precede criminal behaviours to more prosocial thoughts that can precede more prosocial behaviours. This treatment is grounded in the constructivist precept that people are active "co-constructors of the personal realities to and from which we respond" (Mahoney, 1991, p. 100), and in the belief that such constructions are open to change (Kelly, 1955). We will now illustrate some of the specific applications of this perspective to the assessment and treatment of offenders in the community using the example of sexual offenders, as these individuals are the ones who tend to be among the most difficult and worrisome for forensic clinicians. However, many of the principles are common to other populations of offenders as well.

The assessment of sexual offenders has been dealt with in other chapters and so our comments here will be brief. In conducting an assessment of a sexual offender, the forensic clinician is interested in: (a) estimating the offender's risk to reoffend; (b) identifying treatment targets; and (c) identifying strategies to manage the offender's risk in the community. An evaluation of a sexual offender will commonly involve clinical interviews, contacts with collaterals, questionnaires and phallometric testing.

Prior to conducting an interview with a client in a community forensic clinic, it is especially important to obtain as much independent information about his offence(s) as possible. Documents from the courts, the police and child welfare agencies are particularly valuable as they generally provide a summary of the victim's account of the offence. The interview proceeds in order to glean as much information as possible to achieve valid results on risk scales and to make determinations about treatment. To this end, the following four domains are reviewed (Andrews, 1995): criminal history; criminal personality; criminal attitudes; and criminal associates. Others include: childhood history (particularly in regard to disrupted homes, anti-social behaviour and school conduct); prior substance abuse; and work performance. Some scales that require the input of dynamic variables for identifying targets to address in treatment, such as the STABLE scale (Hanson & Harris, 2001), provide a semi-structured interview format that can be used as a guide for obtaining information on social influences, intimacy deficits, social isolation, lack of concern for others, sexual self-regulation, attitudes tolerant of sexual assault, cooperation with supervision, and general self-regulation.

Phallometry (also referred to as plethysmography) and viewing time apparati are used to assess the individual's sexual preference and to determine if deviant arousal is an issue for the offender. While this methodology has its limitations (Marshall & Eccles, 1991) a recent comprehensive review indicates that it has established itself as being a very useful tool (Launay, 1999), although it must be used with caution and its limitations kept firmly in mind.

Estimating the risk of recidivism

Following participation in the assessment process, the assessor will write an evaluation of the offender, identifying the individual's targets for treatment (e.g., the specific cognitive distortions to be addressed) as well as recommending the intensity of sex offender treatment required. The guiding principle in this regard should be that higher risk/need individuals should get more treatment. If relevant, the assessment can include recommendations about other treatment that may be required. The assessment should also talk about the individual's risk to commit another offence. A measure widely used for risk assessment, though not originally developed for this purpose, is the Psychopathy Checklist-Revised (the PCL-R, Hare, 1991). However, while we do use this, in assessing sexual offenders, we focus on the STATIC-99 (Hanson & Thornton, 1999) to assess sexual risk and the VRAG or SORAG (Quinsey, Harris, Rice & Cormier, 1998) to estimate violent risk potential. Recently, we have adopted the STABLE (Hanson & Harris, 2001) to determine clinical or dynamic risk. We then present an overall risk appraisal that aggregates these various risk considerations, but which gives more weight to the actuarial instruments that use static predictors of risk.

Treatment of sexual offenders

Once a comprehensive assessment has been completed, an appropriate treatment response needs to be provided. Ideally, the intensity and focus of such treatment will be tailored to fit the needs of the client. From a therapist's perspective, an offender's involvement in both assessment and treatment is regarded as voluntary, as the decision about whether or not to participate rests with the offender. Offenders, on the other hand, often do not initially regard participation in treatment as an opportunity so much as a requirement imposed on them by their parole or probation officer. (We find that this view is much more prevalent in community settings, where there is typically less leverage over offenders. Incarcerated offenders are generally more amenable to treatment, being aware that parole boards are unlikely to release them without it.) As such, community-based treatment services usually have to invest more time at the front-end of treatment to motivate prospective treatment candidates.

A substantial number of offenders accept no responsibility for any sexual wrongdoing, however, even after some participation in regular treatment programmes. In the calculus of what is important to them, avoiding trouble is generally regarded as more important than addressing their problems. On the one hand, admitting to a sexual crime brings with it baggage like "I have committed a terrible crime, I have a sexual problem, I could go to jail, I could lose my family, job, friends, reputation, other offenders in jail will want to beat me up". On the other hand, denying brings benefits like "I might get away with it, I won't have to go to jail, I don't have to think about the possibility that I might have a sexual problem, my family might stick with me, I might keep my job, friends, reputation". It is not surprising, therefore, that many offenders choose to deny responsibility. The men who persistently deny their offences are certainly the hardest to serve. The manner in which these individuals are dealt with varies. Some programmes deny them access to treatment or remove them from treatment if their denial does not change. Our approach has been one that works to encourage them to take responsibility for their offences, and if after some therapeutic effort they do not, to place them into a deniers programme for sexual offenders. For several years now, we have been developing a pilot programme for these men (Walker & Eccles, 2002). We will discuss the provision of treatment for sexual offenders who acknowledge at least some responsibility for their offence(s), who can be accommodated in our sexual offender treatment programme. Although this will be our focus, we will also discuss the differences in the programme we have developed for persistently denying sexual offenders and the ways in which treatment differs for this group.

Group structure

Before the commencement of treatment, the offender should have read and signed a treatment contract and consent form. Such a form should outline at a minimum the staff involved in delivering the treatment, other persons involved in the treatment team (e.g., probation or parole officers), group membership, content of the treatment programme, treatment group rules, limits to confidentiality, and information use and report distribution. Offenders who decline to sign a treatment contract and consent form are not permitted to participate in treatment. However, if the offender provides his informed consent to treatment, he is admitted to the treatment group.

Individuals who have committed sexual offences necessarily have made mistakes in their thinking and have acted on bad decisions. In their individual hierarchies of what is important to them, they have valued sexual gratification over the rights of others, and over their responsibilities to their family and their community. Treatment, typically conducted in a group format, will require the individual to both look at his past and, based on his understanding of his past, redefine who he is (or wants to be) and plan for a better, offence-free future (for himself and others) based on healthier alternatives to who he was. In examining how he came to commit his offence, the offender will discuss and work to understand who he was at the time of his offending and how that person, with his beliefs and values, came to commit his crime(s).

On an intellectual level this process involves the offender recognizing weaknesses to address, mistakes made, and strengths upon which to build. On another level, this process involves having him come to emotionally understand the consequences of his actions – the difference his behaviour has made to his own life, but also the harm caused to his victim(s) and others. In working with clients whose actions have had negative implications for others, it is necessary to imbue the therapy with a sense of social meaning and import. Therapy must not only work to help the individual change how he sees himself in the world, but have him realize that his actions have caused others to revise their constructions of themselves and the world as a result of the crimes against them. For instance, as a result of sexual victimization a son or daughter may question the direction, meaning, or value of their sexuality. Sexual offences are fundamentally selfish crimes that commonly leave in their wake damage to relationships, finances, employment, feelings of betrayal, the theft of childhood or security, and so on.

The provision of this treatment provides many challenges for the therapist. Treatment involves assisting the client to examine the old and generate new ways of thinking. It also involves convincing the client that the new ways of thinking and behaving he is generating can work better than the old ways. Changes made in treatment will not stick if the individual does not apply them. Along with the motivational challenges sex offenders often present, the work of examining one's beliefs, values, and thoughts is foreign to many of these individuals. This newness will enhance the challenge for the therapist.

For treatment to be meaningful during participation and effective afterwards, it requires honesty, understanding, a commitment to change, and the flexible maintenance of change. Cognitive-behavioural treatment programmes for sexual offenders commonly include having the offender do the following:

- Discuss and accept responsibility for his sexual crimes;
- Understand how he has affected his victim(s), understand the importance of not hurting others in the future;

- Understand how and why he committed his sexual crimes (what were important factors, precursors); and
- Plan to live a healthier life and in so doing avoid reoffending in the future.

Our treatment groups generally contain between eight and ten sexual offenders and two group facilitators (ideally one female and one male). We find that this number is optimal; it allows for active discussion, while limiting the extent to which an offender can "hide" by sitting back and letting others do the talking. There are several components to effective sex offender treatment that include the following: (a) cognitive distortions: (i) denial and minimization (ii) attitudes toward women, children and sex (iii) victim empathy; (b) offence analysis; (c) relapse prevention. While these components are generally offered in this order, in practice they are not separate phases that are distinctly independent of one another. That is to say, while the focus of a particular series of sessions may be on, say, victim empathy, we constantly make connections with previous work that has been completed and that which is to come. For example, when completing a component on victim empathy, we might make a reference back to the minimizations employed by an offender as outlined in his disclosure of his offence at the beginning of treatment, stressing how this facilitated the commission of his offences by minimizing the consequences of his behaviour for others. Likewise, we might foreshadow that work which is to come on relapse prevention by stressing the need to reinforce the information that the offenders have learned about victim impact by periodically reviewing their group work or watching quality television shows on the topic. (Most offenders report that unless advised to do otherwise they will studiously avoid doing so because of the discomfort it engenders.) Thus, while the interconnectedness of all the components are stressed throughout to make the rationale for them clearer and to improve retention of the information gleaned, the focus does shift over the course of the programme and each successive element will be discussed in turn below.

Cognitive distortions

Cognitive distortions cannot be neatly broken down into mutually exclusive groups. However, we do find it to be practically useful to approach cognitive distortions by focusing on three major facets: denial and minimization; other cognitive distortions common to rapists and child sexual abusers; and victim empathy. The latter is often identified as a component separate and apart from cognitive distortions. However, to the extent that empathy deficits involve problems of perception, the endorsement of myths as well as a lack of knowledge, we believe that it makes sense to conceptualize it as part of an overall effort to address cognitive distortions.

Denial and minimization: As noted earlier, denial and minimization are targeted early in most sex offender treatment programmes. For example, Barbaree, Peacock, Cortoni, Marshall and Seto (1998) present a staged model of treatment similar to our own. In this programme all offenders who wish to do so enter stage 1 of the programme in which they are encouraged to take full responsibility for their offences. Offenders cannot graduate to stage 2 unless they "pass" stage 1. If they continue to deny or significantly minimize their offence they are removed from the programme and are penalized by a reduction in their level of inmate pay. Offenders who are removed from our treatment programme are placed in a Deniers Programme (discussed later) but having this option available does not diminish our resolve to have offenders overcome their denial and minimization.

Murphy (1990) outlines an approach to changing denial and minimization that he bases on Meichenbaum's (1977) approach to cognitive restructuring. These cognitive restructuring techniques: (a) provide patients with a rationale for the role cognitions have in maintaining sexual abuse; (b) provide corrective information and education to the patient; (c) identify specific distortions, and; (d) assist the client to challenge and explore these distortions.

In providing a rationale to clients, we start by explaining that we all employ cognitive distortions in one way or another, not just sex offenders, albeit in the pursuit of less harmful activities. We might look at such issues as smoking, driving above the speed limit, or breaking the restrictions of a diet, and find that this can greatly facilitate the learning process. For example, in a recent group, one member announced that he was a smoker and would not be quitting because he believed (without any evidence) that smoking protected him from the harmful effects of paint fumes he encounters in his profession as a painter. Not only did this provide an avenue for exploring the role and relationship of minimizations and justifications for this offender, all other group members immediately had a concrete example of the process at work.

Once group members understand this process, we discuss the importance of taking responsibility for their sexual behaviour. This allows us to raise the positive consequences of doing so, especially stressing that it enables them to participate fully in treatment while also providing validation for the victim about her/his experience (although clearly this has more relevance for those offenders who still have some contact with their victims). Many offenders come to find it a relief to be able to talk openly and share their thoughts and experiences in the supportive atmosphere that a group can provide. Research on treatment outcome reveals that group-based approaches to treatment are more effective than individual therapy (Marshall, Anderson & Fernandez, 1999), and we believe that these dynamics are likely to be one of the significant factors contributing to this.

Following the above noted discussion, each group member is asked to prepare a *disclosure* for the group. A good disclosure presents a full account of an individual's history of sexually abusive behaviour (not just the current offence), the frequency of the acts, the specific nature of the abusive acts and how the victim was encouraged not to disclose (e.g., through the use of either overt or subtle threats, intimidation, guilt, etc.). A good disclosure should also provide a description of how the behaviour developed. In many cases, the abusive behaviour begins without the victim necessarily being aware. For example, some child sexual abusers engineer close physical contact (e.g., having a child sit on their knee) before the abuse becomes obvious. Others may have spied on the victim in the bathroom or done things while the victim was asleep. It is also important that the offender provide an account of his thoughts and feelings before, during, and after his offences. Many men are not particularly introspective by nature and find this a difficult thing to do. However, it is crucial that they do not neglect these cognitive and experiential elements of their offending if a complete understanding is to be obtained.

When an offender has completed his disclosure he presents it to the group. It is clinically advantageous to start this process with one or two group members who will do a good job with their disclosures. This makes it easier for the more reticent group members to open up and it provides a model for how they should present their own. After an individual has presented his disclosure, he is asked a series of questions that seek clarification and challenge any minimization of his offences. To this end, the group facilitators may present file information to the group that describes the victim's version. (It is important that it be made clear in the treatment consent form that this may occur.) Challenges are best made in a direct and frank manner that nonetheless maintain the dignity and self-esteem of the offender (Jenkins, 1990). As Beech and Fordham (1997) found in comparing different therapist styles, those that encourage an open expression of feelings and foster group cohesiveness are the most likely to produce gains. We have observed therapists who have been excessively confrontational during this phase of treatment and while a small number of offenders may respond well, it appeared to us that the majority became less inclined to be open and candid as the group progressed. On the other hand, therapists who are confident, warm and supportive but who nonetheless challenge offenders to examine their perceptions and attitudes are those most likely to engender change in their clients. Likewise, other group members must learn appropriate ways of challenging and questioning others, and group facilitators need to be vigilant, especially in the early stages of treatment, for inappropriate verbal and non-verbal behaviour (e.g., finger pointing, excessive voice volume). It is not unusual for an offender to have to present two or perhaps three disclosures before he has come to terms with all the ways in which he has minimized his offending. Box 6.1 presents a number of examples taken from disclosures presented in our groups in the recent past. These examples illustrate the variety of different ways in which the offenders in question minimized their offences and their consequences. Each of these is discussed and dealt with in turn, while stressing throughout how such distortions serve to facilitate their abusive behaviour.

Other cognitive distortions common to rapists and child sexual abusers: There is evidence that the attitudes and perceptions of sexual offenders influence their sexual behaviour (Horley, 2000), although these relationships are complicated and not always consistent (Horley, 1988). There is a body of evidence to suggest that attitudes and hostility toward women play a functional role in the rape of women (e.g., Marshall & Moulden, 2001;Warshaw & Parrot, 1991) and the sexual exploitation of children (e.g., Hartley, 1998). Therefore, we attempt to go beyond addressing the specific rationalizations employed by the offenders in the group that are

Box 6.1 Examples of minimizations used by offenders in an effort to justify and minimize their behaviour.

> ". . . the little lady . . ." An apparent attempt to mask the fact that the assault occurred against a 7-year-old girl.
>
> "I didn't force her to do anything . . ." A comment by an offender insensitive to the fact that his 10-year-old stepdaughter complied because she knew him to be a violent man.
>
> "It was only touching . . ." This comment was made by an offender in his efforts to minimize what he did do by referring to what he did not do (penetration) while employing phrases such as "it was only" or "I just" to downplay what he did do.
>
> "We made love . . ." This distorted remark was made by an elderly man who crept into his 9-year-old niece's bedroom in the middle of the night, told her not to say anything and proceeded with vaginal intercourse. He also used the term "love-sex" to refer to his abuse of her.
>
> "He was abused before so it's nothing new to him . . ." This comment was made in an effort to minimize the impact of an offence on the victim.
>
> "I was just checking to see if they had cleaned themselves properly." This offender attempted to deny his sexual motivation in examining the genitalia of his two young daughters.
>
> "She [a hitchhiker] traveled with me for 600 miles. She knew what she was supposed to give up. It's like a script. She tried to change the rules." This offender demanded sex and then raped a woman in the cab of his truck when she refused.

evident during the disclosure process by following this with discussions about the kinds of cognitive distortions common to many rapists and child sexual abusers. This enables us to tackle the underlying cognitive schemata or belief structures in a more direct manner. For example, we introduce topics for discussion such as children and sexuality. Within this context we explore the meaning of consent and why children cannot consent to sex with adults, the difference between children's physical and cognitive maturation, children's rights, and the responsibility of adults to protect and not exploit vulnerable or sexualized children. Other topics more germane to rapists highlight the right of women to be treated with equality, the role of women in society, how they are portrayed in the media, especially pornography, and how this influences our attitudes and behaviour. Throughout this process the group members are challenged to identify their own stereotypes and attitudes that facilitate acts of abuse against others.

Victim empathy: There is evidence that sexual offenders show empathy deficits for victims of sexual abuse (Fernandez, Marshall, Lightbody & O'Sullivan, 1999; Marshall & Moulden, 2001). Consequently, we endeavour to instill a greater degree of empathy in offenders, particularly for their own victims. Toward this end, we have the offenders engage in a series of exercises. To begin with, they watch and discuss a number of videotapes that highlight the effects of rape and child sexual abuse on the victims. Where case similarities exist, links are made to the offences committed by the group members themselves. They are given some reading material that is designed to provide further information about victim impact issues. Group members are also asked to compile a list of potential effects of sexual abuse on victims. They are asked to consider the immediate effects (e.g., a victim's fear that she might be killed, inability to concentrate in school and dropping grades) as well as the long-term effects (e.g., erosion of self-worth, loss of income potential). They are also asked to keep in mind that those effects can be emotionally-based (e.g., anxiety disorders, suicide) or physical in nature (e.g., sexually transmitted diseases, unwanted pregnancy).

When the above-noted components of the programme have been finished, the group members then engage in exercises in which they discuss the effects of their sexual abuse on their own victim(s) as well as their family and friends. Next they consider the effects of their sexual crimes on the community as a whole (e.g., fear, financial burden, and so on). When discussing their own victims, group members are encouraged to make it personal. In other words, a simple recitation of effects would be regarded as inadequate. Instead, offenders are expected to use their specific knowledge of the victim as well as information gleaned from victim impact statements and the courts. (Allowances must be made in some cases where the victim was a stranger and there is little direct information from the courts; for example if the offender pled guilty obviating the necessity of the victim taking the stand.) In addition, offenders compile mock letters from and to the victim (and we emphasize that these are *not* to be sent). This provides us with an opportunity to assess the degree of awareness and sensitivity each offender has developed in regard to his victim. This is reflected both in the perspective-taking exercise, in which the offender puts himself in the shoes of the victim and writes a letter he believes she/ he would write, and the exercise where he demonstrates how he would address the victim and what he would say. In cases where the offender has actual or potential contact with the victim, this allows us to identify items that would be offensive and generally detrimental to the victim's healing. For example, some offenders have used words and phrases such as "relationship" and "what happened between us" that imply the consent and collaboration of the victim, which would certainly be unhelpful. In cases where there is contact with the victim we also discuss the brief but very valuable section for abusers in the book for survivors, *The Courage To Heal* (Bass & Davis, 1988). There are two pages titled "For abusers: Guidelines for interacting respectfully with survivors" that serve as an excellent basis for offenders in such situations.

Offence analysis

At this stage of the programme, offenders examine their offence history, seeking distal and proximal precipitating factors. The purpose of this exercise is to understand the offence sufficiently that a comprehensive *relapse prevention plan* can be developed in response to the identified risk factors. The term relapse prevention has its roots in the field of addictions (Marlatt, 1982), and was adopted and modified for use with sexual offenders by Marques (1982) and further advanced by Pithers and his colleagues (Pithers, Marques, Gibat & Marlatt, 1983). This model provided a practical framework for working with sexual offenders, although a number of its underlying assumptions were not empirically-based (Ward, Louden, Hudson & Marshall, 1995). Ward and his colleagues have since developed a more empirically based model that emphasizes self-regulation (Ward & Hudson, 2000). There are certainly features it has in common with the traditional model, and while some questions remain to be answered (Eccles & Marshall, 1999) we believe that the reconceptualization as outlined by Tony Ward and Stephen Hudson offers the best model both practically and empirically. In addition, the offenders are asked to consider the role and meaning that sex plays in their lives, and the extent to which they use sex as a coping mechanism for dealing with the stresses they face (Cortoni, 2000).

In conducting an analysis of his sexual offences, an offender provides an account of his experiences that are relevant to these crimes, some of which may go back to his childhood. He is asked to consider three kinds of risk factors functionally related to the development of his sexually abusive behaviour:

1   *Predisposing risk factors*: These are generally chronic, underlying factors that have their roots in early childhood or adolescence. They include anger management problems, anti-social
or other disorders of personality, acquired cognitive schemata
(belief systems), or specific events that compound into other
problems (e.g., sexual abuse).
2   *Precipitating risk factors*: These risk factors are more temporally proximal to the offence. Examples of these acute
factors are the specific emotional state that an offender was
experiencing when he committed his offence, the presence of
alcohol or other drugs, pornography use, and so on. In addition, an offender's perception of his environment and related
cognitive distortions play a functional role as well.
3   *Perpetuating risk factors*: These refer to the events that take
place after an offence has occurred and serve to maintain the
offending behaviour. Examples of these are cognitive distortions that minimize or justify what the offender has just done,
decreased levels of self-efficacy, exacerbation of negative
mood, or, alternately, feelings of elation, excitement and anticipation of the potential for further acts.

We cannot provide a comprehensive illustration of this process
here, but we can provide a brief example of how this is applied.
Consider the following, taken from a case in one of our current
groups.

Predisposing risk factors: Manuel (age 51) lived in Asia until he
was 40 and has resided in Canada for the subsequent 11 years of
his life. As a child, he lived in a small village where there was
little work for his parents. When he was 10 years old they
obtained work in a city several hundred kilometers away.
Although they were able to return home on weekends, during
the week they stayed in the city leaving Manuel with his brother
who was just a few years older. When he was 11 he was followed
by three men who wandered through the village periodically
seeking sexual contact with young boys. While Manuel's
parents were away, each man abused him, separately, for the
next several years. He said that he did not find the contact
aversive, and enjoyed the mutual masturbation, which was as
far as the men went. When he was 16 one of them tried to

perform fellatio on him; he disliked this intently and was able to end the contact with the three men. Manuel was very shy and unassertive. Despite his experiences at the hands of the men, he said that he is heterosexual but did not date in his teens because he was afraid to ask anyone out. When he was 24 his friend attempted to help him by providing him with a 14-year-old prostitute as a birthday present. Not surprisingly, not only did this not solve his problems, it compounded them. He was introduced to brothels, the young prostitutes and the "massage parlours" attached to them. He became fixated on the young girls there because of their youthful bodies, their powerlessness, and the lowered risk of them being infected with a sexually transmitted disease (relative to more sexually experienced adults). For the next 16 years he did not date but went to a "massage parlour" monthly, where he was masturbated by an adult, and saved his money so that he could afford sex with a prostitute once a year. He would have preferred to have had sex with a 12-year-old (the youngest available) but could only afford a 14-year-old. The prevailing climate in the province where he lived was that sexual contact between adults and children was regarded as "no big deal", especially if the child was from a poor family or was paid for sex. At the age of 36 he arranged to start corresponding with a woman from the same country who had emigrated to Canada. She visited when he was 38 and they were married before she left two weeks later. It was another two years before he was granted permission to move to Canada. He says he has been too afraid to visit a prostitute in Canada, although he has returned to the "massage parlours" during two subsequent trips to his former homeland.

Precipitating risk factors: Manuel had trouble adjusting to life in Canada; his extreme lack of social confidence meant that he made no friends here at all. While he had some acquaintances with others who had emigrated into Canada from the same country, he failed to develop any friendships of meaningful depth. As a result, he felt isolated and lonely in a relatively strange country. He and his wife's inability to conceive a child compounded his problems. Doctors told him it was due to his low sperm count and this left him feeling "less than a man", especially when his wife teased him in front of her friends, saying, "he does not know how to make babies". The couple decided to adopt one of his wife's nieces who immigrated to Canada and began to live with them at the age of 9. Because his wife was very busy with her job, Manuel spent more and more time with the young girl. He increasingly began to meet his need for companionship through her. Two years after she arrived she became pubescent. When Manuel saw her in a nightdress similar to the ones worn by the young prostitutes in the brothels he visited he began to sexually fantasize about her. One night, when she was cold, Manuel climbed into bed beside her to keep her warm. He became aroused and began to abuse her.

Perpetuating risk factors: Over the next two years the abuse escalated to intercourse. He knew that what he was doing was wrong, but did not see it as being particularly harmful. In fact, he believed that he was expressing his affection for the girl, and that she would remember the sexual contact with fondness when she was older. He anticipated eagerly the next sexual encounter with her and became increasingly detached from his wife in the process. The abuse was discovered when his niece became pregnant, something he did not expect given what the doctors had told him. While he knew the discovery might lead to some trouble for him, his initial reaction on learning of the pregnancy was joy; he imagined that she would carry the baby to term and that she would raise it along with him and his wife.

An offence analysis such as that summarized above is further refined using a behavioural progression model that emphasizes the potential for the evolution of future offending from an offence-free state: Maintenance (no offending) → Chronic triggers (cognitive schemata, emotional or personality traits) → Build-up phase (negative emotional states worsen, sexual fantasies and offence planning may also be apparent) → Acute triggers (thoughts, feelings or events that serve to advance the problem behaviour from covert thinking to overt action) → Offence → Offence maintenance (cognitive distortions, negative/positive emotions that serve to increase the likelihood of further acts of abuse).

Relapse prevention

This is sometimes called the *self-management* phase of treatment, where offenders develop strategies to better cope and respond to the risk factors identified in their offence analysis. It is essential that these plans are realistically achievable and that they are very specific. For example, it would not be acceptable for Manuel to simply state that he will "make more friends" in an effort to combat his loneliness. He must be clear on what the specific causes of his interpersonal problems are as well, before he can hope to develop a response to them. In the example just given, Manuel has decided that he must (a) improve his English, a significant aggravating factor for his lack of social self-confidence (indeed he has made great strides in school while incarcerated); (b) continue to develop an understanding of how his negative "self talk" undermines his effort to socialize with others, a process he started in group but will need to continue in therapy (with the programme he will attend specifically identified); (c) continue to practice his social skills in the maintenance programmes he will attend in jail and in the community upon release, following a small set of concrete social goals of increasing difficulty and reporting back to the group on his progress (in fact, while initially very difficult, being required to speak in the group for many months has greatly enhanced his skills and confidence – there is also tangible evidence of this transferring to other settings); and (d) he has identified specific (and safe) social activities he will participate in upon his release into the community – for example, he has named a horticultural group in his community, and has specifically noted when and where it meets.

In preparing a plan and improving his ability to cope with the risk factors he has identified, an offender is better prepared to prevent a return to sexual offending. However, a relapse prevention plan must be seen as an evolving strategy that needs to be modified to meet the circumstances and demands an offender faces. Some strategies may not work well and will need to be revised. The relapse prevention plans developed in prison are especially likely to need revision, as there are a number of unknown variables that may not be accounted for while the offender is incarcerated. Thus, it is important that some maintenance programming be provided for offenders both prior to and after their release.

Deniers Programme

It is beyond the scope of this chapter to describe our programme for persistently denying sexual offenders in detail. Nonetheless, we will provide an outline that has much in common with the treatment programme for sexual offenders described above. The goal of the Deniers Programme is to improve these offenders' knowledge of: (a) cognitive distortions; (b) victim impact issues; and (c) relapse prevention.

(a) Cognitive distortions: The offenders are provided with an account of how their thinking affects their behaviour, with a particular emphasis on the role of cognitive distortions and rationalizations that facilitate sexually abusive behaviour. Unfortunately, their denial prevents these offenders from an analysis of their own thinking and how it influenced their offences; however, we do review the kinds of thinking that sexual offenders in general have employed in this regard.

(b) Victim impact issues: Offenders are exposed to many of the same materials presented in the regular treatment programme. If we feel that the group is receptive to it, we will ask the offenders to consider what the effects of their offences have been from the perspective that the offences are *true*. This can produce some significant opposition and, while it works well in some situations, we exercise some caution with this component, as it can serve to alienate an otherwise responsive group if some of the deniers express a lot of hostility toward their victims.

(c) Relapse prevention: While persistently denying offenders do not acknowledge an offence they can analyse, we do have them review mock offence scenarios and perform behavioural analyses of these. This leads then to the development of relapse prevention plans and discussions about strategies typically adopted by rapists and child sexual abusers who successfully complete treatment. In this way, we hope that the men will covertly adopt these strategies even if they do not admit to doing so.

Special risk management concerns in the community with child sexual abusers

When child sexual abusers are released into the community the nature of the environment to which they are being released needs careful consideration. Access to victims is an important risk factor, and while it is impossible to eliminate completely all contact between an offender and children, it is possible to limit and control it. We have summarized the main considerations in this regard as follows:

1. Location of residence
    It is imperative that child sexual abusers be encouraged to live in
    an area where contact with children is minimal. Frequently,
    offenders are released into a relatively new community and thus
    have little knowledge of the different neighbourhoods and little
    time to establish themselves. Even if they are familiar with the
    community, most parolees are short of money and so the
    principal concern for these offenders when looking for accom-
    modation is cost. All too often they end up in low rent apart-
    ment buildings heavily populated with single parents too busy
    trying to make ends meet to provide full time supervision of
    their children. In our experience, this provides challenges to
    offenders, including those who have a genuine commitment to
    remaining offence free. For those with pedophilic tendencies,
    the danger that their resolve will erode is all too real. It is
    essential therefore that those supervising such offenders (and we
    include parole officers and therapists here) be reasonably
    knowledgeable of the high-risk neighbourhoods in their com-
    munities in order that they can direct offenders to the safer
    locales. While this can be challenging at times, it is generally
    possible to direct these offenders to buildings populated prin-
    cipally by seniors, or to areas that do not have a high density of
    children. Of course, there are additional considerations here
    including the location of area schools, parks with playgrounds,
    and so on.
2. Church-related activities
    One of the few opportunities provided to offenders to supervise
    children occurs through church-related activities. There have
    been several cases in which we have been involved when a pastor
    has asked an offender to volunteer in some capacity that gives
    him authority over children. For example, some have been
    asked to drive children to/from a camp or a church outing.
    Others have been asked to provide some form of instruction to
    them. As a result, we now work to ensure that the minister of the
    church be apprised of the offender's history in order to prevent
    such requests from being made. In general, we have found that
    adopting a collaborative approach with the offender is far more
    productive than a supervisor preemptively calling the minister.
    If the offender can be encouraged to tell the minister himself,
    with a subsequent call from the supervisor, the working rela-
    tionship is more likely to remain intact and productive.

3. Shopping

Some time ago, it became apparent to us that a number of offenders who had reoffended had met their victim while shopping. The two principal scenarios were (a) talking with teenagers hanging out at the food court of the local mall; and (b) corner stores frequented by children for small "treats". This experience has led us to prepare for this by making child sex offenders, particularly pedophiles, aware of the risk posed by such situations. We encourage such offenders to do their shopping at the mall while children are in school and to avoid corner stores, especially just after school and on weekends. Building these scenarios into their relapse prevention plans then renders it possible to make the offenders more accountable for their whereabouts.

4. Accessories attractive to children

Pedophiles are well familiar with the acquisition of items that are appealing to children and frequently acquire them with this purpose in mind. Frequently, however, they are obtained without malicious intent but have the potential to be used inappropriately. For example, offenders coming out of custody will sometimes have obtained a game console to help combat the boredom while incarcerated. Nonetheless, children have a high affinity for such game platforms and so it is important that the inherent risk of having these items be clearly understood by the offender. The parole officer, when making a home visit, should also be aware of what to look for in this regard. Other items that offenders have admitted acquiring to deliberately attract children include snowmobiles, fast boats, classic/sports cars, customized trucks, train sets, stuffed toys and pets. There are times when it is not clear whether the item is really necessary (as with a snowmobile or heavily accessorized truck) but at the very least it should raise suspicions and increased supervision. Attendance at events such as a Classic Car Show should be prohibited. In our experience homosexual pedophiles are more likely to employ such tactics although heterosexual pedophiles have employed pets and "hobbies" (e.g., magic) to attract young girls.

5. Employment

Given the financial difficulties many offenders experience upon their release into the community, they are often tempted to take the first job that they can get. Clearly, those jobs that bring them into direct contact with children (e.g., working at a fair) must be prohibited. Other jobs that we include in this category are the seasonal jobs available at campgrounds, marinas and the like. We also note that offenders must be monitored for whom they employ. In our experience, many offenders gain access to children, especially, although not exclusively, teenage boys, by hiring them to work on farms or in other small businesses.

6. Family reunification

Forensic clinicians working in the community will be involved with agencies over and above probation and parole services (e.g., child welfare agencies). Some of the more difficult issues that arise concern the reintegration of an offender with his family and the access he is permitted with his children. Clearly, the clinician will only support such an endeavour in the event that the risk is deemed to be assumable. Generally speaking, such reintegration efforts only occur when the offender's child was not one of his victims. Nonetheless, although the risk may be assumable it will not be negligible and so the conditions under which this risk will be managed need to be carefully spelled out. In our experience, when problems arise it is generally because these conditions were not laid out clearly enough at the outset. These requirements will vary depending on the circumstances (e.g., in some cases unsupervised access may be permitted but not overnight). Furthermore, access and restrictions may be loosened and changed over time as the offender gains credibility. The following provides some examples of the kinds of restrictions that might be considered in such cases:

- All contact with the child must be supervised. The supervisor *must* be in the same room as the offender and the child in question, and not simply in the same residence.
- The supervisor must be an adult, aware of the offender's crimes and be deemed responsible and competent by child welfare authorities.
- Even when supervised, the offender will not engage in prolonged close physical contact with the child (e.g., having the child on his knee, wrestling, tickling, and so on).
- As part of a gradual reintegration plan, we may insist that for a period of time, unsupervised access not include overnight stays.

- The offender will not bathe, toilet or dress the child, nor will he observe these activities conducted by the other parent.
- The offender will not apply any creams or other medications to the child's genital or anal area.
- The offender will not assume the responsibility for any sex education with the child.
- There will be no pornography allowed in the home.
- In cases where an offender is permitted unsupervised access to the child, we may insist that a precondition be that he not be under the influence of drugs or alcohol while he is the caretaker.
- The offender will not sleep in the same bed as the child, even if the other parent is present. If the child has a nightmare and needs to sleep with a parent, the offender will sleep in another room.

Special risk management concerns in the community with rapists

The following presents an overview of some of the general risk management strategies adopted primarily with rapists. These strategies are not necessarily exclusive to rapists, nor is it intended to be an exhaustive list. However, these suggestions are offered to provide a flavour for the kinds of approaches used to safely manage such offenders in the community.

1. Pornography
   In this category we include not just the consumption of pornography but attendance at strip-bars and the use of prostitutes as well. We believe that pornography use contributes to the sexual objectification of women and that this can only serve to facilitate acts of sexual aggression against them. Forms of pornography that depict women in particularly degrading and dehumanizing ways are especially pernicious. Similarly, strip-bars promote a climate within which women are presented as objects for the use of men and do not, in our opinion, contribute in any way to the establishment and maintenance of a sexually healthy lifestyle that sexual offenders would do well to adopt. We note here that the issue is not one of the explicit presentation of sex. Explicit presentations that promote men and women as equal partners may well be a healthy option, or at least an innocuous one. However, the

vast bulk of mainstream pornography simply does not fit this description and so we strongly discourage the use of such materials by offenders.

As technology develops and becomes more readily available, sexual offenders can more easily acquire pornography both while incarcerated and on the street. Both authors have been involved in cases recently where offenders preparing for release were found to have pornography on computer CDs. In one case, it was discovered while the offender's possessions were being prepared to be shipped out of the institution and into the community on the day of his release. Some of this pornography depicted women being bound, gagged, and raped. Most of these discoveries were somewhat serendipitous and we believe that institutions need to be better prepared to screen the files on the computers belonging to offenders. In cases where offenders have been discovered to be using pornography that in any way depicts sexually abusive acts, we make a recommendation that a condition of their release include a prohibition against any Internet access. In one case, where it was deemed that an offender had a legitimate need for his work, he was required to submit his computer for periodic random checks by the Information Technologist for Probation and Parole Services.

2. Anonymous vehicle
    In cases where an offender's vehicle has been integral to the commission of his offence we attempt to minimize this risk as much as possible. The more anonymous the vehicle the more likely an offender is to consider it possible to commit an offence and get away with it. Therefore, in some cases we attempt to have him make his vehicle readily identifiable, especially if it is a non-descript, dark coloured older model vehicle. To do this we have had offenders who are self-employed have the name of their business painted onto the side of their vehicle. In other cases, we have had them install brightly coloured neon wiper blades on their cars.

3. Curfews
    For some rapists a curfew can be a helpful risk management strategy. It is possible to oversell the utility of such a measure; a rapist who has formed the intent to rape will find an opportunity regardless of the time of day. However, our purpose here is to limit the likelihood of providing a rapist

with access to a potential victim at a time when she is perhaps at her most vulnerable. Several offenders have remarked to us that simply walking alone at night can provide them with an anticipatory excitement even if they had not gone out to rape. By limiting unintentional opportunities, there is less likelihood of an offender making a snap decision to taking advantage of them. If an offender does have to go out after nightfall he should be encouraged to wear bright, identifiable clothing and stick to main thoroughfares.

Treatment outcome with sexual offenders

A comprehensive review of the treatment outcome literature is beyond the scope of this chapter. However, the interested reader is referred to Marshall et al. (1999), who provide a review of the treatment outcome literature. The issue of treatment efficacy is a very complicated one. There is no consensus on what defines success. For example, there is disagreement on whether a simple count of recidivism rates for treated and untreated offenders is sufficient and whether the severity of, and time up to, reoffence should be considered if they vary for the two groups. Then there is the problem of comparing studies with varying degrees of methodological rigour, different populations, different approaches to treatment, and different follow-up times. The results of the studies available have led some researchers to suggest that the treatment outcome literature does not support the view that treatment is effective (e.g., Furby, Weinrott & Blackshaw, 1989; Quinsey, Harris, Rice & Lalumière, 1993). However, other studies have presented data that supports the case for the efficacy of treatment (e.g., Hanson & Nicholaichuk, 2000). In a recent review of the treatment outcome literature, Marshall et al. (1999) conclude that on balance it provides strong evidence supporting the efficacy of cognitive-behavioural treatment of sexual offenders. Furthermore, they point out how the resultant drop in rates of recidivism pays off both in terms of reductions in trauma to individuals and in cost savings to the community as well.

Conclusions

In this chapter we have reviewed a community-based application of the cognitive-behavioural treatment of offenders in general and sexual offenders in particular. We have discussed the promising role of therapeutic communities and programmes for offenders on parole in the community. We have illustrated the issues of assessment and treatment with the example of sexual offenders. Denial and minimization, victim empathy, and other attitudes facilitative of sexually abusive behaviour were addressed. Additional foci of the treatment process have been described and illustrated, namely the offence analysis and relapse prevention. We have highlighted some of the issues specific to working with sexual offenders in the community. While we noted the role of phallometric assessment we have eschewed discussing strategies for the behavioural modification of deviant sexual arousal. We agree with Marshall et al. (1999) that there is little evidence for the efficacy of these procedures and we do not often employ them. They are very time consuming and this time can, we believe, be more profitably spent on other aspects of treatment.

There is a sound basis for optimism regarding the efficacy of cognitive-behavioural approaches to treating offenders in the community. And it is this, after all, that keeps most of us motivated to keep going forward with a redoubtable spirit despite the challenges we face working with this difficult population. While we certainly wish the offenders well in their efforts, the bottom line for most of us is to ensure that no more victims fall prey to individuals committing acts of violence and exploitation.

References

Andrews, D. A. (1995). A social learning and cognitive approach to crime and corrections: Core elements of evidence-based correctional practice. In *The Level of Service Inventory (Ontario Revision)*. Hamilton, ON: Ministry of the Solicitor General & Correctional Services, Bell Cairn Centre.

Andrews, D. A., & Bonta, J. (1999). *The psychology of criminal conduct.* Cincinnati, OH: Anderson Publishing.

Barbaree, H. E., & Marshall, W. L. (1989). Erectile responses among heterosexual child molesters, father-daughter incest offenders, and matched non-offenders: Five distinct age preference profiles. *Canadian Journal of Behavioural Science, 21*, 70–82.

Barbaree, H. E., Peacock, E. J., Cortoni, F., Marshall, W. L., & Seto, M. (1998). Ontario penitentiaries' program. In W. L. Marshall, Y. Fernandez, S. M. Hudson, & T. Ward (Eds.), *Sourcebook of treatment programs for sexual offenders* (pp. 59–77). New York: Plenum.

Bass, E., & Davis, L. (1988). *The courage to heal: A guide for women survivors of child sexual abuse.* New York: Harper & Row.

Beech, A., & Fordham, A. S. (1997). Therapeutic climate of sexual offender treatment programs. *Sexual Abuse: A Journal of Research and Treatment, 9,* 219–237.

Correctional Service of Canada (1999). *An outcome evaluation of CSC Substance Abuse Programs: OSAPP, ALTO, and Choices.* Ottawa, ON: T3 Associates.

Cortoni, F. (2000, November). *The role of sexualized coping in sexual aggression.* Paper presented at the 19th Annual Research and Treatment Conference of the Association for the Treatment of Sexual Abusers, San Diego, CA.

Cullen, E. (1997). Can prison be a therapeutic community? The Grendon template. In E. Cullen, L. Jones, & R. Woodward (Eds.), *Therapeutic communities for offenders* (pp. 75–99). New York: John Wiley & Sons.

Cullen, E., Newell, T., & Woodward, R. (1997). Key issues for the future. In E. Cullen, L. Jones, & R. Woodward (Eds.), *Therapeutic communities for offenders* (pp. 252–267). New York: John Wiley & Sons.

Dolan, B. (1997). A community based TC: The Henderson Hospital. In E. Cullen, L. Jones, & R. Woodward (Eds.), *Therapeutic communities for offenders* (pp. 47–74). New York: John Wiley & Sons.

Dolan, B., Wilson, J., & Evans, C. (1992). Therapeutic community treatment for personality disordered adults: Changes in neurotic symptomatology on follow-up. *International Journal of Social Psychology, 38,* 243–250.

Eccles, A., & Marshall, W. L. (1999). Relapse prevention. In W.L. Marshall, D. Anderson, & Y. Fernandez (Eds.), *Cognitive behavioural treatment of sexual offenders.* New York: John Wiley & Sons.

Eccles, A., & Walker, W. (1998). Community based treatment with sexual offenders. In W. L. Marshall, Y. Fernandez, S. M. Hudson, & T. Ward (Eds.), *Sourcebook of treatment programs for sexual offenders* (pp. 93–103). New York: Plenum.

Fernandez, Y. M., Marshall, W. L., Lightbody, S., & O'Sullivan, C. (1999). The Child Molester Empathy Measure. *Sexual Abuse: A Journal of Research and Treatment, 11,* 17–31.

Furby, L., Weinrott, M. R., & Blackshaw, L. (1989). Sex offender recidivism: A review. *Psychological Bulletin, 105,* 3–30.

Gendreau, P., Goggin, C., Cullen, F. T., & Andrews, D. A. (2001). The Effects of Community Sanctions and Incarceration on Recidivism. In L. L. Motiuk & R. C. Serin (Eds.), *Compendium 2000 on effective correctional programming* (pp. 18–21). Ministry of Supply and Services, Ottawa, Canada.

Hanson, R. K., & Harris, A. (2001). *The dynamic supervision project: Stable scoring guide.* Ottawa, ON: Solicitor General of Canada.

Hanson, R. K., & Nicholaichuk, T. (2000). A cautionary note regarding Nicholaichuk et al. (2000). *Sexual Abuse: A Journal of Research and Treatment, 12,* 289–293.

Hanson, R. K., & Thornton, D. (1999). *Static 99: Improving actuarial risk assessments for sex offenders.* Ottawa, ON: Solicitor General of Canada.

Hare, R. D. (1991). *Manual for the Revised Psychopathy Checklist.* Toronto: Multi-Health Systems.

Hartley, C. C. (1998). How incest offenders overcome internal inhibitions through the use of cognitions and cognitive distortions. *Journal of Interpersonal Violence, 13,* 25–39.

Henggeler, S. W., Schoenwald, S. K., Borduin, C. M., Rowland, M. D., & Cunningham, P. B. (1998). *Multisystemic treatment of antisocial behaviour in children and adolescents.* New York: The Guilford Press.

Horley, J. (1988). Cognitions of child sexual abusers. *The Journal of Sex Research, 25,* 542–545.

Horley, J. (2000). Cognitions supportive of child molestation. *Aggression and Violent Behavior, 5,* 551–564.

Jenkins, A. (1990). *Invitations to responsibility.* Adelaide, Australia: Dulwich.

Jones, L. (1997). Developing models for managing treatment integrity and efficacy in a prison based TC: The Max Glatt Centre. In E. Cullen, L. Jones, & R. Woodward (Eds.), *Therapeutic communities for offenders* (pp. 121–157). New York: John Wiley & Sons.

Kelly, G. A. (1955). *The psychology of personal constructs.* New York: Norton.

Launay, G. (1999). The phallometric assessment of sex offenders: An update. *Criminal Behaviour and Mental Health, 9,* 254–274.

Lightfoot, L. O., & Boland, F. (1993). *Choices: A community correctional brief treatment relapse prevention & maintenance program.* Kingston, ON: Correctional Service Canada.

Mahoney, M. J. (1991). *Human change processes.* New York: Basic Books.

Marlatt, G. A. (1982). Relapse prevention: A self-control program for the treatment of addictive behaviours. In R. B. Stuart (Ed.), *Adherence, compliance, and generalization in behavioural medicine* (pp. 329–378). New York: Brunner/Mazel.

Marques, J. K. (1982, March). *Relapse prevention: A self-control model for the treatment of sex offenders.* Paper presented at the 7th Annual Forensic Mental Health Conference, Asilomar, CA.

Marshall, W. L., & Eccles, A. (1991). Issues in clinical practice with sex offenders. *Journal of Interpersonal Violence, 6,* 68–93.

Marshall, W. L., & Moulden, H. (2001). Hostility toward women and victim empathy in rapists. *Sexual Abuse: A Journal of Research and Treatment, 13,* 249–255.

Marshall, W. L., Anderson, D., & Fernandez, Y. (1999). *Cognitive behavioural treatment of sexual offenders*. New York: John Wiley & Sons.

Meichenbaum, D. (1977). *Cognitive-behavior modification: An integrative approach*. New York: Plenum.

Murphy, W. D. (1990). Assessment and modification of cognitive distortions in sex offenders. In W. L. Marshall, D. R. Laws, & H. E. Barbaree (Eds.), *Handbook of sexual assault: Issues, theories, and treatment of the offender* (pp. 331–342). New York: Plenum.

Pithers, W. D., Marques, J. K., Gibat, C. C., & Marlatt, G. A. (1983). Relapse prevention with sexual aggressives: A self-control model of treatment and maintenance of change. In J. G. Greer & I. R. Stuart (Eds.), *The sexual aggressor: Current perspective on treatment* (pp. 214–234). New York: Van Nostrand Reinhold.

Quinsey, V. L., Harris, G. T., Rice, M. E., & Cormier, C. A. (1998). *Violent offenders: Appraising and managing risk*. Washington, DC: American Psychological Association.

Quinsey, V. L., Harris, G. T., Rice, M. E., & Lalumière, M. L. (1993). Assessing treatment efficacy in outcome studies of sex offenders. *Journal of Interpersonal Violence, 8*, 512–523.

Roberts, J. (1997). History of the therapeutic community. In E. Cullen, L. Jones, & R. Woodward (Eds.), *Therapeutic communities for offenders* (pp. 3–22). New York: John Wiley & Sons.

Robinson, D. (1996). Factors influencing the effectiveness of cognitive skills training. *Forum on Corrections Research, 8*, 6–9.

Serin, R. C., & Preston, D. L. (2001). Violent Offender Programming. In L. L. Motiuk & R. C. Serin (Eds.), *Compendium 2000 on effective correctional programming* (pp. 146–157). Ministry of Supply and Services, Ottawa, Canada.

Walker, W., & Eccles, A. (2002). *The treatment of persistently denying sexual offenders*. Manuscript submitted for publication.

Ward, T., & Hudson, S. M. (2000). A self-regulation model of relapse prevention. In D. R. Laws, S. M. Hudson, & T. Ward (Eds.), *Remaking relapse prevention with sex offenders: A sourcebook* (pp. 79–101). Thousand Oaks, CA: Sage.

Ward, T., Louden, K., Hudson, S. M., & Marshall, W. L. (1995). A descriptive model of the offense chain for child molesters. *Journal of Interpersonal Violence, 10*, 452–472.

Warshaw, R., & Parrot, A. (1991). The contribution of sex-role socialization to acquaintance rape. In A. Parrot & L. Bechhofer (Eds.), *Acquaintance rape: The hidden crime* (pp. 73–82). New York: John Wiley & Sons.

Wilson, R. J., & Eccles, A. (1998). Forging a link between institutional and community-based treatment services. *Forum on Corrections Research, 10*, 39–41.

Wilson, R. J., Stewart, L., Stirpe, T., Barrett, M., & Cripps, J. E. (2000). Community-based sex offender management: Combining parole supervision and treatment to reduce recidivism. *Canadian Journal of Criminology*, *42*, 177–188.

Chapter 7

Psychological treatment of offenders in institutions

James Horley and Jody Bennett

Individuals who are charged and convicted of crimes generally enter the criminal justice system with a disposition involving probation. Contrary to common assumptions, the majority of adjudicated criminal offenders do not receive a custodial prison sentence. In addition, only a very small minority of individuals charged with a criminal offence are detained for any length of time in forensic psychiatric facilities after being found not criminally responsible for their actions, which, of course, means that they are not criminal offenders although they may well be dangerous individuals who require institutional confinement and treatment.

Incarceration of offenders can serve to control reoffending or recidivism temporarily through incapacitation. Supervision, too, can limit recidivism. Incarceration and supervision are intended as deterrence by punishment. Previous examination of the psychological literature regarding criminal conduct indicates that punishment without rehabilitation does not reduce reoffence rates (Andrews, Zinger, Hoge, Bonta, Gendreau & Cullen, 1990). In the United States, approximately two-thirds of offenders released from state prisons are rearrested within three years (Henning & Frueh, 1996), and only a small percentage have been provided with any form of therapy. Psychological change through some form of treatment appears necessary to reduce criminal reoffence. Appropriate psychological treatment of offenders in institutions has the potential to assist offenders and to reduce the number of victims of crime. This chapter will examine the use of psychological treatment within forensic institutions. Types of treatment, treatment efficacy, and special issues regarding treatment of offenders will be considered.

Types and efficacy of treatment

The history of psychological treatment of offenders in institutions is relatively brief. Prison-based psychological services in the United States appear to date from the early to mid-twentieth century, in Canada from the mid-twentieth century, and other countries in the West from similar times (Bartol & Bartol, 1999). Institutionalized treatment, almost needless to say, is influenced by the dominant political policies and beliefs of the time. The concept of offender rehabilitation was accepted in the 1960s but was questioned during the 1970s, especially in the United States (see Martinson, 1974), resulting in a return to harsher sentencing and punishment. Currently, there is more of an interest in determining what type of rehabilitation is effective rather than assuming that meaningful rehabilitation is impossible. The thrust of government initiative, however, tends to concentrate on law enforcement through institutional means rather than more constructive and preventative measures (Petersilia, 1995), and this has translated into larger numbers of incarcerated offenders in countries like the United States (Milan, Chin & Nguyen, 1999). The rehabilitation of offenders can be undermined by sentencing reforms (Andrews et al., 1990), although clearly certain individuals require lengthy confinement due to valid public safety concerns.

The psychological treatment of offenders within corrections and forensic hospitals varies greatly. The ultimate goal of treatment is seen frequently as a reduction in recidivism, but reducing threat, or the severity of future reoffence, and psychological/emotional improvement in the confined individuals are also possible goals. The overall efficiency of a treatment programme can be defined by its ability to reduce recidivism, a rather easily quantified outcome.

The ability of psychological intervention to rehabilitate offenders has been and to a certain extent continues to be debated despite data that support the ability of at least certain treatments to reduce recidivism rates (Gendreau, 1996). Broad statements about the effectiveness of all psychological treatments with offenders cannot be taken at face value because certain treatments (e.g., those described as cognitive-behavioural) have been found to be more effective than others (e.g., those classified as psychodynamic). It is also important to bear in mind that offenders do not represent a homogenous group, and certain distinguishing variables (e.g., type of offence) are undoubtedly important in rehabilitation outcome.

Discovering which variables may predict future criminal activity is an important area of research. Certain research has indicated that risk of recidivism can be predicted (e.g., Quinsey, Harris, Rice & Cormier, 1998), however inexact the science. There will always be variables beyond the control of correctional investigators at the time of assessment. For example, an offender could have a drastic change in personal circumstances that is unpredictable but influences that individual's risk for criminal behaviour. Also, effective treatment, whether in the institution or community, should lower risk (Studer & Reddon, 1998). Even if it is assumed that the predicted risk level is fairly accurate at the time of assessment, the longevity of predicted accuracy is questionable.

With psychological treatment of offenders, it is the community-based programmes that have shown the most substantial treatment effects (see Eccles & Walker, Chapter 6, this volume; Gendreau & Andrews, 1990). This outcome is understandable for a number of reasons, such as the nontherapeutic nature of correctional settings (see Horley, Chapter 3, this volume). Treatment of offenders within the institution can be effective, however, because there are a variety of other relevant factors. Appropriate treatment (e.g., clearly prosocial) has been found to be more effective than inappropriate treatment regardless of setting (Andrews et al., 1990). Though the institution is not necessarily the ideal place for psychological change, it does represent an opportunity to assist offenders to make important changes that can have a positive impact on their futures and the futures of others. Prison offers an opportunity to provide treatment to a considerable number of offenders. A recent study in the United States on psychotherapeutic services in one correctional institution indicated that approximately 20 per cent of male inmates received group psychotherapy (Morgan, Winterowd & Ferrell, 1999), although it was not reported why the majority of the prison population were not receiving treatment at the time of the study. In Britain and Germany, as well, psychological rehabilitation has remained available to only the minority of offenders (Roberts, 1997). With limited funding available to corrections, the priority appears to remain with punitive, security measures.

Forms of therapy

Within the institution, therapy can involve either group or individual counselling. Each approach to therapy offers certain advantages and disadvantages. Some of these pros and cons require consideration.

Group therapy is a broad term that encompasses a variety of treatment types. There are general aspects of group therapy that exist fairly independent of the type of group treatment that is provided. Group therapy in prison can offer offenders the opportunity to discuss their shared difficulties in a constructive manner that allows for positive feedback (Morgan, Winterowd & Fuqua, 1999). Essentially, individuals are able to discuss relevant issues under the guidance of therapists or facilitators. Group therapy, however, can also include confrontational approaches where a 'hot-seat' is used to pressure clients to accept features of their pasts, especially crimes. The concerns of such groups include breaching the defences and rationalizations that offenders can use to protect themselves from anxiety or threat that their harmful behaviour can produce. Group work offers an obvious financial efficiency as more individuals can receive treatment than with individual therapy (Wilson, 1990).

Although it is important to examine the efficacy of the specific type of treatment provided by the group, general statements about its effectiveness can be made. Morgan, Winterowd and Fuqua (1999) noted that a variety of different group treatment programmes have been found to be effective with offenders; in particular, groups that aim to increase interpersonal effectiveness and also allow offenders to examine their own thoughts are useful. Other research indicates that there are very specific factors that are important for effective correctional group therapy. Logically, if there are certain psychological factors that are relevant to committing crime, sometimes referred to as criminogenic needs or factors (e.g., Andrews & Bonta, 1998), treatment that targets those factors should be more effective than treatment that does not. How idiosyncratic those factors are will likely influence the ability of therapy to target them effectively.

Group therapy may well be the approach of choice in correctional institutions because of demand and limited resources, but individual therapy is also employed effectively (Morgan, Winterowd & Ferrell, 1999). Unfortunately, there are often limited numbers of qualified therapeutic staff to deal with offender clients so that individual therapy cannot be offered. When individual therapy is available, it can afford a degree of privacy in a setting where unsecured personal information can literally mean death.

Individual treatment with offenders can also provide an offender client with the personalized assistance and structured programme planning that may be unavailable in a large group format. Groups consisting of 20 to 30 men can be found in some institutional settings, and such a large group, meeting perhaps only once a week, would hardly allow an individual time to speak, however briefly.

Efficacy and type of therapy

A variety of different psychological treatments are used within institutions. Examples of some of these treatments include anger management, cognitive restructuring, substance abuse, and relapse prevention (Morgan, Winterowd & Ferrell, 1999). Even programmes addressing domestic violence are offered in institutions, with one Canadian programme finding a decrease in impulsivity and an increase in nurturance among batterers who participated in their 'Relating without violence' programme (Wolfus & Bierman, 1996). These offerings, unfortunately, are presented frequently in a 'one-size-fits-all' manner (e.g., where all assaultive or homicidal individuals are encouraged to participate in anger management because they must have 'anger issues'). Sexual offenders can have access to the aforementioned treatment formats, but often very specific therapeutic options are available for them. For details about some of the programmes and treatments designed for sexual offenders, see Marshall (1999) and numerous other writers (e.g., Eccles & Walker, Chapter 6; Horley, Chapter 3; Houston, 1998; Laws, 1989).

The theoretical underpinnings and goals of each group or individual-based treatment may vary according to the therapists or facilitators. For example, interpersonal group therapy can be based on psychodynamic, client-centered, or various behavioural orientations. With incarcerated offenders, meta-analysis has revealed that psychodynamic and client-centered therapies are not effective, while cognitive-behavioural therapies appear more successful (Andrews et al., 1990). Psychodynamic and client-centered therapies do not appear to allow therapists to target specific behaviours and thought patterns. Upsetting childhood experiences, as a single example, do not appear to be related to criminal behaviour (Andrews et al., 1990). In the case of sexual offenders, while some reviewers find little solid research on which to draw any specific conclusions (e.g., Furby, Weinrott & Blackshaw, 1989), some research (e.g., Rice, Quinsey & Harris, 1991) showed little effectiveness for behavioural programmes, especially employing aversion therapy.

There are numerous factors that can influence the efficacy of a treatment programme in a correctional institution. It is important to note that treatment efficacy can be demonstrated by both recidivism measures as well as pre- and post-treatment measures. Although the ultimate goal of therapy may be the reduction of recidivism, reoffence rates are not always the measures used to determine the impact of the treatment. A variety of tools have been used to assess the effect of a treatment programme. Examples include repertory grids (Houston & Adshead, 1993) and the Minnesota Multiphasic Personality Inventory, or MMPI (Valliant, Hawkins & Pottier, 1998), although the validity of the MMPI as an assessment tool for prediction and measurement has been questioned (Andrews & Bonta, 1998). As a preliminary measure to predict the influence of a treatment programme or as ongoing assessment of how the programme is affecting the participants, different assessments can be very important. If the main goal is to reduce re-offending, however, recidivism reduction should be incorporated into the programme in some manner. For the purposes of research, long-term recidivism data require a much longer duration of the research project. The critical measure of a psychological treatment programme may not come from recidivism data. Programmes may produce some positive changes but not influence recidivism. In conjunction with recidivism data, effective assessment techniques may assist researchers in further under-standing the psychological aspects of criminal conduct which is, in turn, important for programme improvement.

Certain aspects relevant to variations in recidivism have been identified. The main sources of variation are the characteristics of the offender(s) prior to treatment, the correctional workers' char-acteristics, the content and process of the planned and delivered services, and individual changes within the offender, both personal and circumstantial (Andrews et al., 1990). The characteristics that an individual offender brings to treatment, and even the char-acteristics of the correctional workers, may be difficult to alter, but the content and process by which treatment is provided can be controlled and does have the ability to influence personal changes for offenders.

When considering recidivism, the type of reoffence is significant. Index recidivism refers to whether reoffenders commit the same type of offence that they were previously incarcerated for. For example, a treatment programme for men with convictions for family violence may be considered successful if the participants are living in violence-free homes, even if there were subsequent arrests and convictions for property offences. When dealing with crimes that likely have a different psychological basis, the effectiveness of the programme may be more specific to that offence. The basis of family violence may involve power and control whereas theft could have a different basis entirely.

With respect to therapeutic interventions with offenders, one of the important factors that has been noted is type of treatment. Type of treatment has been found to be the strongest correlate to effect size of the treatment (Andrews et al., 1990). Much current research indicates that cognitive-behavioural therapies tend to be the most effective with offender populations. Some research has shown cognitive-behavioural therapy can significantly affect attitudes, self-esteem, and aggression of offenders (Valliant et al., 1998). Cognitive-behavioural therapies with offenders tend to focus on factors perceived to influence criminal behaviour. For example, cognitive distortions may be the treatment target. The focus on cognitive distortions assumes that effective treatment requires inmates to be taught to identify and to alter criminogenic thought patterns (Henning & Frueh, 1996) or, expressed alternatively, the structure and nature of personal construct systems that support antisocial versus prosocial behaviour require examination and change. Pithers (1994) found that highly-specialized programming with sex offenders did influence distortions related to justification of sexual violence. It is those changeable factors related to criminal behaviour that should provide the ability to change criminal behaviour. Therefore, the focus of cognitive-behavioural therapy on the specific thought patterns that relate to criminal behaviour is very important. Again, however, rather that focusing on the belief content, therapists operating from personal construct theory (PCT) would have serious therapists look beyond at underlying values or core constructs (Horley, 1991, 2000; Winter, 1992). Given that each offender brings very different life experiences and circumstances into treatment, it is important to have the ability to assess how to go about rehabilitation effectively. The risk of recidivism, criminogenic need, responsivity of the offender, and professional discretion are four main areas that can assist in selection of effective rehabilitation programming (Andrews, Bonta, & Hoge, 1990), as these factors are relevant to determining the type, focus, and level of rehabilitative programming.

Risk, need, and responsivity have been identified by meta-analyses as the main sources of variation affecting recidivism (Andrews et al., 1990). With respect to risk, it is the risk of reoffending that needs to be determined. The risk principle assumes that further criminal behaviour can be predicted (Andrews & Bonta, 1998). For those with higher risk, more intense treatment is recommended, as high risk individuals respond better to more intensive treatment than low risk individuals (Andrews, Bonta & Hoge, 1990). To effectively utilize the risk principle, consistent and accurate assessment of individuals' risk of further criminal behaviour is required. A number of studies have had results that supported the risk principle (Andrews, Bonta & Hoge, 1990).

The second relevant factor to consider relates to the focus of the rehabilitative efforts. It is important to be able to look at the specific and changeable factors that relate to an individual's criminal behaviour. Service itself should be designed to meet the criminogenic needs of the offender (Andrews, Bonta & Hoge, 1990). As would be expected with any treatment, the focus of the treatment has to be relevant to the specific problem or difficulty. Criminogenic needs are not exclusive of risk assessment factors. Changes in criminogenic needs are associated with changes in recidivism and, therefore, should be related to risk assessment. One assessment tool that has been developed is the Level of Supervision Inventory-Revised (LSI-R). A number of studies have indicated that changes on LSI-R scores are related to changes in recidivism (see Andrews & Bonta, 1998), although it should be noted that the LSI-R, and most risk prediction devices for that matter, have limitations in terms of offender types. The LSI-R, for example, was not designed for use with sexual offenders.

For rehabilitative efforts to focus on altering criminogenic need factors, facilitators need to know what their specific targets include. We have only a relatively vague notion of the nature of these factors at this point in time. Criminogenic need factors are proposed to include antisocial/procriminal attitudes and association with others that share antisocial views, as well as other dynamic variables related to criminal behaviour (Andrews & Bonta, 1998).

In addition to the level and focus of the treatment, the individual features of the criminal behaviour are also relevant. The responsivity of an offender is based on the learning style and capabilities of the offender as well as the circumstance of the criminal offence itself (Andrews, Bonta & Hoge, 1990). By focusing on the specific needs and factors of criminal behaviour for the offender, it seems more likely that effective treatment can be provided. While the most efficacious therapies may involve social learning and cognitive-behavioural principles (Andrews & Bonta, 1998), this may not be true for all offenders, and personal variables that could influence the effectiveness of treatment should be considered. Given the group nature of most institutional rehabilitation efforts, it is expected that the group would have to be at least relatively homogeneous on certain variables to be effective for the majority of individuals. Certain areas of concern with the effectiveness of programmes include mentally disordered offenders and ethnic minorities (Milan et al., 1999). Aside from assessing risk, need, and responsivity, professionals involved with psychological treatment of offenders should exercise their judgement. Professional discretion can be utilized to override the other principles of assessment in cases where the individual may have other specific needs that influence the effectiveness of treatment.

Based on meta-analysis, a variety of factors with a positive impact on recidivism have been identified. Programmes that were intensive tended to have a positive effect (Gendreau, 1996), as well as treatment that was behavioural, often using cognitive or modelling aspects (Gendreau, 1996). More specifically, programmes should focus on values, attitudes, and beliefs – or personal constructs, especially core construction (Horley, 1991) – that support prosocial behaviours (Gendreau & Andrews, 1990). The effective programmes were also designed to encourage the learning of prosocial skills (Gendreau, 1996). Part of a cognitive-behavioural treatment programme may involve altering self-statements that justify or minimize aggressive behaviour (McGrath, Hoke & Vojtisek, 1998).

Another influential factor in effective correctional treatment is the quality of treatment staff. Trained, supervised therapists who interact in constructive and sensitive ways have been found to influence treatment efficacy (Gendreau, 1996). This finding indicates the importance of having appropriate staff that are monitored. In addition to this, facilitators have to support openly, and to demonstrate, prosocial attitudes (Andrews, Bonta & Hoge, 1990). The difficulty of finding properly trained staff to administer prison-based therapy in the United Kingdom has been noted by Cullen (1997).

In addition to research data, therapists themselves often have ideas about what is important in group psychotherapy. A survey of 162 correctional mental health providers indicated the following goals, topics, or areas of improvement were perceived as important: recognizing the connection to other inmates' difficulties; acquiring more realistic beliefs; assisting others with advice; managing stress; personal growth; conflict resolution; teaching new behaviours through practice; as well as preparing for life in the community (Morgan, Winterowd & Ferrell, 1999). Many of the aspects identified involve assisting inmates to learn healthy and positive ways of interacting with others while developing themselves personally. Existential factors have been identified by male inmates as important factors in group psychotherapy (Morgan, Ferrell & Winterowd, 1999). This indicates the development of meaning and purpose may also be important topics. All of these factors may be important in their own ways but not necessarily relevant to further criminal behaviour.

In describing group cognitive-behavioural therapy, there is no specific structure that defines its process. In spite of indications that cognitive-behavioural therapy constitutes 'best practice', there is a noticeable lack of structured programmes available for correctional psychologists (Morgan, Winterowd & Ferrell, 1999). While cognitive-behavioural programmes may assist individuals to alter behaviour and beliefs, the specific process is often not defined. In order to better evaluate efficiency, it would be beneficial if the programmes within correctional facilities were better defined. Henning and Frueh (1996) provide an example of an institutional programme based on cognitive self-change that reduced offender recidivism. The initial eight week orientation stage of the programme taught offenders the theory behind the programme, recognition of the most common cognitive distortions that are related to criminal activity, and techniques required for self-monitoring. The first part of the programme was essentially a learning component, not focused on changing behaviours or thoughts. Following the initial stage, treatment groups of five to ten participants met between three and five times per week. During the sessions, participants presented reports to the group on their prior antisocial behaviour. The report included both an objective description as well as the thoughts and feelings that occurred prior to, during, and after the event. The group used these reports to identify the cognitive distortions that may have led to the antisocial response. The further identification of emotions and thoughts that went with the incident was sometimes aided by role plays. The reports and following discussion were used to help each offender identify their criminogenic thought patterns or needs, after which the group discussed intervention strategies to help prevent future antisocial activity. Examples of prevention strategies included cognitive strategies (e.g., challenging personal cognitions) or behavioural strategies (e.g., avoiding high-risk situations). Behavioural aspects of treatment gave the participants the opportunity to apply what they had learned.

Participants also completed homework assignments and kept daily journals. In this study, the length of treatment was dependent on the time left in the participants' sentences. The results indicated that significantly more of the offenders not in the treatment programme had re-offended than those in the treatment programme. The group of offenders in this study had convictions for a variety of different offences. The risk of recidivism was substantially increased in those participants with prior convictions for property offences. Since recidivism was the only measure used to determine success of the study it is possible that those individuals were not as positively influenced by this treatment programme. Though not without weaknesses, this study was relatively well structured with both a learning and affective component. In order to change thought patterns, clients must be able to identify thoughts that concur with criminal behaviour. This type of programme requires serious commitment on the part of each offender client. After release from prison with each progressive year, the rate of reoffending increases (Henning & Frueh, 1996). This indicates the need for ongoing programming in the community to reinforce the initial treatment. Andrews et al. (1990) also identified the likely need for followup in the community to maximize the efficacy of treatment.

Horley (1999) employed similar ideas in a multi-modal therapy programme for sexual offenders based explicitly on PCT. The thrust of all components of this programme, both individual and group, was on identifying and changing patterns of construing. The various forms of therapy from this programme, such as fixed-role therapy (FRT) (Kelly, 1955) and relapse prevention (Laws, 1989), can and have been offered to a range of offenders (see Horley, in press-a). We (Horley, Holliston & Bennett, 2000) have operated community-based therapy groups for physically and emotionally violent males, and, within institutions, we have provided therapies, such as FRT, for offenders to change their construal of themselves and others. Fixed-role approaches, described in detail elsewhere (e.g., Winter, 1992), as well as other dramaturgical approaches, are particularly appropriate for offender clients, even so-called psychopaths, who understand and regularly practice confidence games or role-playing. They very quickly acquire new characters or roles, at least when fixed-role sketches are presented in a manner "emphasizing creativity" (Kelly, 1955, p. 381). Despite some distinct disadvantages of fixed-role approaches (Horley, in press-a), especially presented in non-therapeutic settings like prisons (Horley, in press-b), such techniques can prove useful. The following case example might illustrate the use of FRT with incarcerated offenders.

'Dan', a man in his mid-20s with a long history of assault and drug convictions, approached a psychologist, reportedly for the first time in his life, because he was "tired of the life [he] lived on the street". He listed his occupation as a construction worker, but he had made a living for over ten years as a drug dealer. His father, also a convicted drug dealer, and his friends were, Dan claimed, the main reason why he was unable to straighten out his life and stop the revolving door of drug sales, drug use, violence, and incarceration. He feared killing someone and spending the rest of his life behind bars. Despite relatively little formal education, Dan was articulate, introspective, very "street-smart", and took to the idea of "trying on a new personality" via FRT. He provided much needed detail with a long autobiographical sketch and role construct rep grid. His personal constructs included a number of prison constructs (e.g., "solid versus rat") and several psychological constructs (e.g., "clever versus dumb"). He received the resulting fixed-role sketch as a challenge to his intellectual and social skills. The sketch, far from a "solid citizen", allowed him his "habits" (e.g., beer drinking, marijuana smoking), but provided him with a new set of constructs through which to examine himself and those around him. Replacement of prison constructs with nonsubcultural ways of construing others was a primary in writing Dan's new role. Although limited by the setting (i.e., a maximum-secure prison), Dan tried out his new identity and, with some revision of the original character, managed over the course of three months (two-hour long sessions weekly) to adopt the more pro-social 'Doug' rather comfortably. The long-term success of this young repeat offender has yet to be established, but he does appear to have broken the revolving door of prison and release with three years without criminal convictions.

Another approach to psychological treatment in institutions involves therapeutic communities. The therapeutic community is based broadly on the belief that criminal behaviour is the result of a breakdown in the relationship between the individual and society, where deviant behaviour is seen as a failure of primary social-ization (Roberts, 1997). Given the view that a failure in socializa-tion is related to criminal behaviour, it should be changeable by altering values, attitudes, and beliefs. The ideal of the therapeutic community focuses on providing social, ethical, and moral values to the offender (Roberts, 1997). Within a therapeutic community, cognitive-behavioural programmes can be utilized. In a prison environment, the therapeutic community may be a small unit that has an independent culture but is set within a larger prison (Jones, 1997). In this sense, a therapeutic community is more intensive because it establishes an all-encompassing living unit unlike tradi-tional rehabilitation efforts in prisons. Because of its structure, however, a therapeutic community can also be very expensive to operate (Roberts, 1997). With this type of programming, recidivism rates have been linked to the amount of time spent in treatment and the reason for leaving treatment (Jones, 1997). The process of change in The Max Glatt Centre, a UK prison-based therapeutic community, was thought to be brought about by confronting core criminogenic beliefs about the self and others that caused the individual to experience cognitive dissonance, and negatively effecting the individual's self esteem (Jones, 1997). It is through this process that the individual is given the opportunity to change and seek more positive strategies and to alter their beliefs (Jones, 1997). Facilitators of this programme recommended at least 12 months of treatment in the programme. The focus of therapeutic communities tends to be on personality disordered offenders and substance abuse. The therapeutic community represents an interesting model and variation for psychological treatment of offenders. It is unclear, however, whether this type of environment influences recidivism rates more than other approaches within the prison setting.

Special issues

The treatment of offenders within a prison setting has obvious differences from the treatment of offenders in the community. The prison environment is governed by the rules and constraints of security in a very hierarchical paramilitary culture, and, as such, it is a unique setting (Morgan, Ferrell & Winterowd, 1999). Much of the work of therapists operating in such a setting will be short-term interventions, such as crisis intervention and stress debriefing (Mobley, 1999). Long-term programming, especially in some maximum-secure institutions, can be the exception rather than the rule.

Participation in prison-based treatment is often not truly voluntary, a consideration that can influence the effectiveness of programmes. It is important to ensure the motivation and commitment of all inmates through pre-group interviews but particularly those inmates that are not considered voluntary participants (Morgan, Winterowd & Ferrell, 1999). Having coerced participants also presents some ethical concern when doing research. It is interesting to note that some research has indicated a notable lack of ongoing research in prisons. Morgan, Winterowd and Ferrell (1999) found that 80 per cent of US correctional workers who responded to their survey indicated that no research was being done at their institutions despite the use of therapy programmes for inmates. To further the knowledge about the psychological aspects of criminal behaviour, it is very important to investigate and to disseminate the findings of such investigation.

Psychological treatment in institutions can also be hindered by prison administrators. Often administrators have little or no training in areas related to treatment of criminal behaviour – indeed, many are guards or security personnel who have risen through the ranks – and they have no experience in helping professions (Gendreau, 1996). It is important to have the support of administration to effectively do research and provide effective treatment to inmates. When treatment staff and other institutional staff deliver a consistent message, it can provide a better environment for rehabilitation (Glick, 2000). The prison environment itself may limit the effectiveness of treatment. Inmates may not feel comfortable discussing personal issues in front of other inmates out of fear that it may be used against them outside the therapeutic group. To a certain extent this difficulty is addressed by therapeutic communities, as they tend to be somewhat independent of the main prison, but always the security and/or punitive concerns of the larger institution take priority.

One issue that may influence the effectiveness of rehabilitation programming is addiction. It has been reported that men who abuse alcohol or drugs, especially in the commission of an offence are more difficult to treat (Lothstein, 2001). The abuse of substances may hinder the ability of therapy to assist effectively an offender, and it is likely beneficial to have offenders with addictions receive treatment prior to or concurrent with other therapy (Milan et al., 1999). This issue certainly raises the question of the importance of multi-modal programming in corrections (see Horley, Chapter 3).

An issue that does not receive a lot of attention in research is the potential variability of the psychology of criminal behaviour between genders. The majority of the research focuses on male offenders but we should not assume that the same holds true for female offenders. Comparisons of treatment efficacy between genders might prove valuable.

Reflections, concerns, and conclusions

While much remains unknown about reducing criminal behaviour, theory and research have provided a framework for what is beneficial when treating incarcerated offenders. The notion that treatment of offenders is completely ineffective is disputed by available research. To the extent that treatment providers, and on a larger scale the criminal justice system, have the resources to provide rehabilitative measures to offenders, they should be provided. Those offenders who have an interest in changing antisocial ways have a better chance of success with psychological treatment than without.

While there appears to be mounting evidence that cognitive-behavioural intervention strategies do work with offenders, both within institutions and in the community, we need to determine more precisely exactly what types of these interventions are effective with what types of offender clients. One focus of therapy should be values, attitudes, and beliefs. We would suggest a PCT-based programme that is multifaceted in order to address the wide range of problems that any single offender client might present in the institution. While there do not seem to be many programmes based specifically on PCT, and almost no direct data to support efficacy, we believe that the indirect evidence points in the direction of further efforts at establishing such programmes for offenders.

PCT-based programmes might be particularly helpful with offenders viewed as primary psychopaths (Hare, 1970) or antisocial personality disordered (American Psychiatric Association, 1994). Antisocial personality disorder is a common diagnostic label in corrections – applied or applicable to as many as four out of five incarcerated offenders (Correctional Services Canada, 1990) – and current clinical thinking regards these offenders as difficult if not impossible to treat (Houston, 1998). As much as some offenders, especially manipulative and seemingly uncaring ones, may present a challenge to forensic clinicians, it appears premature to conclude that nothing can be done to produce movement in psychotherapy. We should not dismiss as incorrigible many offenders without first trying different approaches, such as FRT, that may capitalize on their personal skills and thus prove successful.

Institutions present a special challenge to clinicians hoping to assist offenders in altering offensive patterns of behaviour. First and foremost, they are not very therapeutic settings. One possible exception includes programmes based on therapeutic community principles, but even these programmes must exist within a larger, brutal environment that is a prison. Months of therapeutic progress with individuals in treatment programmes can be erased quickly by intentional or unintentional comments or acts in a correctional setting. As one client, who was serving a lengthy penitentiary sentence for a series of armed bank robberies, so eloquently expressed, prisons are full of vultures, including both guards and inmates, who prey on any sign of weakness, and intensive psychotherapy makes you weak, or at least appear weak. Creation of a setting where freedom can be restricted without the brutalizing effects of typical contemporary correctional institutions should become a major social priority in many countries. Indeed, Milan et al. (1999) have argued that "the creation of a more humane prison environment may prove to be one of the most significant components of corrections professionals' efforts to ensure that prisoners are not harmed by the prison experience" (p. 581). Until such time that we can claim honestly to have caring prison environments, the best that most forensic clinicians can hope for is a microcosm that at least does not punish those who attempt to address personal demons via therapy. We should all remain aware of the reality that, eventually, most incarcerated offenders will leave the institution. Do we really believe that the use of coercive power will eliminate their antisocial beliefs and offensive behaviours? If not, we need to adopt practices that invite offenders to participate in a relationship and experience that, given a real desire to change, has a good chance of helping them address their goals.

References

American Psychiatric Association (1994). *Diagnostic and statistical manual* (4th ed.). Washington, DC: American Psychiatric Association.

Andrews, D. A. & Bonta, J. (1998). *The psychology of criminal conduct.* Cincinnati, OH: Anderson Publishing Co.

Andrews, D. A., Bonta, J., & Hoge, R. D. (1990). Classification for effective rehabilitation: Rediscovering psychology. *Criminal Justice and Behavior, 17*, 19–52.

Andrews, D. A., Zinger, I., Hoge, R., Bonta, J., Gendreau, P., & Cullen, F. T. (1990). Does correctional treatment work? A clinically relevant and psychologically informed meta-analysis. *Criminology, 28*, 369–404.

Bartol, C. R., & Bartol, A. M. (1999). History of forensic psychology. In A. K. Hess & I. Weiner (Eds.), *The handbook of forensic psychology* (pp. 3–23). New York: John Wiley & Sons.

Correctional Services Canada (1990). *Forum on corrections research.* Ottawa: Supply and Services Canada.

Cullen, E. (1997). Can a prison be a therapeutic community? The Grendon template. In E. Cullen, L. Jones, & R. Woodward (Eds.), *Therapeutic communities for offenders* (pp. 75–99). Chichester: John Wiley & Sons.

Furby, L., Weinrott, M., & Blackshaw, L. (1989). Sex offender recidivism: A review. *Psychological Bulletin, 105*, 3–30.

Gendreau, P. (1996). Offender rehabilitation: What we know what needs to be done. *Criminal Justice and Behavior, 23*, 144–161.

Gendreau, P., & Andrews, D. A. (1990). Tertiary prevention: What the meta-analyses of the offender treatment literature tell us about what works. *Canadian Journal of Criminology, 32*, 173–184.

Glick, H. L. (2000). Sober and socially responsible: Treating federal offenders. *Federal Probation, 64*, 19–23.

Hare, R. D. (1970). *Psychopathy: Theory and research.* New York: John Wiley & Sons.

Henning, K., & Frueh, C. (1996). Cognitive-behavioral treatment of incarcerated offenders. *Criminal Justice and Behavior, 23*, 523–541.

Horley, J. (1991). Values and beliefs as personal constructs. *International Journal of Personal Construct Psychology, 4*, 1–14.

Horley, J. (1999, July). *A PCT-based treatment programme for sex offenders*. Paper presented at the 13th International Congress on Personal Construct Psychology, Berlin, Germany.

Horley, J. (2000). Cognitions supportive of child molestation. *Aggression and Violent Behavior: A Review Journal, 5*, 551–564.

Horley, J. (in press-a). Fixed-role therapy with multiple paraphilias. *Clinical Case Studies*.

Horley, J. (in press-b). Forensic personal construct psychology: Assessing and treating offenders. In F. Fransella (Ed.), *Personal construct psychology: A handbook*. Chichester: John Wiley & Sons.

Horley, J., Holliston, M., & Bennett, J. (2000, April). *Implementing and evaluating a programme for abusive males: The Camrose 'Changing Ways' Programme*. Paper presented at the First Annual Conference of the International Association of Forensic Mental Health Services, Vancouver.

Houston, J. (1998). *Making sense with offenders: Personal constructs, therapy and change*. Chichester: John Wiley & Sons.

Houston, J., & Adshead, G. (1993). The use of repertory grids to assess change: Application to a sex offenders group. *Issues in Criminological and Legal Psychology, 19*, 43–51.

Jones, L. (1997). Developing models for managing treatment integrity and efficacy in a prison-based TC: The Max Glatt Centre. In E. Cullen, L. Jones, & R. Woodward (Eds.), *Therapeutic communities for offenders* (pp. 121–157). Chichester: John Wiley & Sons.

Kelly, G. A. (1955). *The psychology of personal constructs* (2 vols.). New York: Norton.

Laws, D. R. (Ed.). (1989). *Relapse prevention with sex offenders*. New York: Guilford Press.

Lothstein, L. (2001). Treatment of non-incarcerated sexually compulsive/addictive offenders in an integrated, multimodal, and psychodynamic group therapy model. *International Journal of Group Psychotherapy, 51*, 553–570.

McGrath, R., Hoke, S., & Vojtisek, J. (1998). Cognitive-behavioral treatment of sex offenders: A treatment comparison and long-term follow up study. *Criminal Justice and Behavior, 25*, 203–223.

Marshall, W. L. (1999). Diagnosing and treating sexual offenders. In A. K. Hess & I. B. Weiner (Eds.), *The handbook of forensic psychology* (pp. 640–760). New York: John Wiley & Sons.

Martinson, R. (1974). What works? Questions and answers about prison reform. *The Public Interest, 35*, 22–54.

Milan, M. A., Chin, C. E., & Nguyen, Q. X. (1999). Practicing psychology in correctional settings: Assessment, treatment, and substance abuse programs. In A. K. Hess & I. Weiner (Eds.), *The handbook of forensic psychology* (pp. 580–602). New York: John Wiley & Sons.

Mobley, M. J. (1999). Psychotherapy with criminal offenders. In A. K. Hess & I. Weiner (Eds.), *The handbook of forensic psychology* (pp. 603–639). New York: John Wiley & Sons.

Morgan, R., Ferrell, S., & Winterowd, C. (1999). Therapist perceptions of important therapeutic factors in psychotherapy groups for male inmates in state correctional facilities. *Small Group Research, 30,* 712–729.

Morgan, R., Winterowd, C., & Ferrell, S. (1999). A national survey of group psychotherapy services in correctional facilities. *Professional Psychology: Research and Practice, 30,* 600–606.

Morgan, R., Winterowd, C., & Fuqua, D. (1999). The efficacy of an integrated theoretical approach to group psychotherapy for male inmates. *Journal of Contemporary Psychology, 29,* 203–222.

Petersilia, J. (1995). A crime control rationale for reinvesting in community corrections. *Spectrum, 68,* 16–27.

Pithers, W. (1994). Process evaluation of a group therapy component designed to enhance sex offenders' empathy for sexual abuse survivors. *Behavioral Research and Therapy, 32,* 565–570.

Quinsey, V. L., Harris, G. T., Rice, M. E., & Cormier, C. A. (1998). *Violent offenders: Appraising and managing risk.* Washington: American Psychological Association.

Rice, M. E., Quinsey, V. L., & Harris, G. T. (1991). Sexual recidivism among child molesters released from a maximum security psychiatric institution. *Journal of Consulting and Clinical Psychology, 59,* 381–386.

Roberts, J. (1997). History of the therapeutic community. In E. Cullen, L. Jones, & R. Woodward (Eds.), *Therapeutic communities for offenders* (pp. 3–22). Chichester: John Wiley & Sons.

Studer, L. & Reddon, J. (1998). Treatment may change risk prediction for sexual offenders. *Sexual Abuse: A Journal of Research and Treatment, 10,* 175–181.

Valliant, P., Hawkins, T., & Pottier, D. (1998). Comparison of psychopathic and general offenders in cognitive behavioral therapy. *Psychological Reports, 82,* 753–754.

Wilson, M. (1990). Psychotherapy with depressed incarcerated felons: A comparative evaluation of treatments. *Psychological Reports, 67,* 1027–1041.

Winter, D. A. (1992). *Personal construct psychology in clinical practice: Theory, research and applications.* London: Routledge.

Wolfus, B., & Bierman, R. (1996). An evaluation of a group treatment program for incarcerated male batterers. *International Journal of Offender Therapy and Comparative Criminology, 40,* 318–333.

Name index

Subject index